SLAVERY ABOLISHED BY
GREAT BRITAIN
1834

THE GREAT
ABOLITION
SHAM

THE GREAT ABOLITION SHAM

The True Story of the End of the British Slave Trade

MICHAEL JORDAN

SUTTON PUBLISHING

Sutton Publishing Limited
Phoenix Mill · Thrupp · Stroud
Gloucestershire · GL5 2BU

First published 2005

British Library Cataloguing in Publication Data
A catalogue for this book is available from the British Library.

ISBN 0-7509-3490-5

Endpaper illustrations, front and back: the emancipation medallion of 1834, showing on the
reverse sober politicians and on the obverse liberated slaves dancing joyfully. (*Courtesy of
Bristol Museums and Art Galleries*)

Typeset in 10/14pt Photina MT.
Typesetting and origination by
Sutton Publishing Limited.
Printed and bound in England by
J.H. Haynes & Co. Ltd, Sparkford.

CONTENTS

INTRODUCTION

'It is clear then, that some men are by nature free, and others are slaves, and that for these latter slavery is both expedient and right.'

Aristotle, 384–322 BCE

'I am far from having any particular esteem for the Negroes but I think myself obliged to consider them as Men. I am certainly obliged to use my best endeavours to prevent their being treated as beasts by our unchristian countrymen who deny them the privileges of human nature.'

Granville Sharp, 1776

'Africa! Africa! Your sufferings have been the theme that has arrested and engages my heart.'

William Wilberforce, House of Commons, 2 April 1792

'Wilberforce was either a fanatic or a hypocrite.'

William IV, 1830–7

Unless we have been sufficiently resolute to dip our noses into scholarly reading, our impressions of African slavery are likely to have been honed and coloured by the Hollywood film industry and by a raft of popular fiction titles. The most celebrated of these has surely been Margaret Mitchell's epic *Gone with the Wind*. Published in 1936, it earned the Pulitzer Prize and shortly thereafter became the subject of a blockbuster film with Clark Gable and Vivien Leigh. Perhaps in recognition that Mitchell had opened up a lucrative genre, the early postwar decades saw a plethora of novels taking up the subject of slavery. Penned by writers among whom Kyle Onstott and Lance Horner are most notable, these books do not necessarily pay huge attention to authenticity but paint lurid scenes relishing 'the inhuman, shameful deeds burned into the history of the American South'. Dark brush-strokes depict the venomous servitude imposed upon black charges by white masters. These blend with titillating splashes of colour, wherein a person of the one engages in servitude of a more agreeable nature to relieve tedium in the wives and daughters of the other.

Perhaps coincidentally, perhaps not, most of these fictional views emerged in the wake of a serious and groundbreaking exploration of the slave system by West Indian writer Eric Williams. Published in 1944, some have said a little ahead of its time, his *Capitalism and Slavery* refuted many traditional ideas about Afro-Caribbeans in the British colonies and the trade that fuelled their presence. Williams's work opened up a large hole in conventional opinion. In arguing his case he also awoke a hornets' nest of scholarly wrangling that, far from having gone away or been properly quieted, has if anything become even more lively. It is not slavery per se that has become the main focus of debate among modern pundits, rather the tardy nature of its abolition. Interest, at times verging on paranoia, has arisen over why doing away with such a blot, which in our self-analytical and socially correct world we regard as being beyond redemption, took such an extraordinary length of time to secure.

In publications with a focus less specifically on events than individuals, men like William Wilberforce, the Yorkshire political firebrand whose name has become indelibly linked with abolition, are delivered up as modern-day Joshuas. The iniquitous and the profane first tremble, then fall helpless before their trumpetings, or so we are asked to believe. Hagiographies published in the last year or two credit Wilberforce as the 'hero of the faith' and 'hero for humanity'. In a popular 1984 publication he earned the title, a shade ambitiously perhaps, of 'The Man who Freed the Slaves'.

Among contemporary eighteenth-century commentators, one notable is the Scottish philosopher Adam Smith, who delivered a series of Glasgow lectures on economics and their moralities in the 1770s. Subsequently those talks became compiled into a volume, *The Wealth of Nations*, published in 1776. Smith gives us the simple, uncluttered truth that slavery loses out every time against the recruitment of hired labour and can never succeed in the face of a free market. There is significance in that his prediction came a little more than a decade before the first abolition movement was founded in England.

In recent decades some writers on slavery have taken to agonising over the minutiae, to the extent that they appear to have put aside the fact that cause and effect can be, and often are, quite simple. They have focused on issues that, if not irrelevant, are no more than fine-tuning and did not affect the outcome in any measurable way. A point to which we seem largely oblivious is that there was no single logic at work driving the process. What persuaded politicians to reverse decades of anti-abolitionism was not necessarily that which attracted the largely unenfranchised public to get up and cry foul. Its mood of moral indignation and the growing clamour for change put an additional pressure on government, true, but in itself this was never sufficient to sway the insular voting habits of the Houses of Commons and Lords. It has been said that under the law of the conservation of moral outrage, if hackle-raising does not attach to one thing it will attach to another. Politicians, irrespective of time and place, are a hardened bunch. They recognise that public sentiment is largely whimsical and is only ever worth taking seriously if the rancour threatens to spill over into violence and insurrection. The mood against slavery in the English shires showed no signs of such progress during the late eighteenth and early nineteenth centuries.

An investigation of the British parliamentary debates that took place on the subject of slavery between the initial Commons debate on 9 May 1788 and the final act of emancipation in 1833, linked with the correspondence of abolitionists and the records of their various activities, brings a number of facts clearly to the fore. The main thrust, the key to the whole process of abolition, was the ending of the slave trade, not, as some authors have maintained recently, the subsequent move towards emancipation. It was the abolition of the trade that took up the greater amount of parliamentary time and spanned more than thirty years, against the ten in which debate took place leading up to emancipation. There can never have been much doubt in the minds of people who understood the logistics that getting rid of the trade would set the seal on the ultimate demise of slavery. History was on their side because slavery as an institution had never been self-sustaining. In antiquity the organisation of Rome and its slave-based constitution broke down once the supply of raw material dried up. So it would have been, in any event, with Afro-Caribbean slavery and the slave-plantation owners knew this full well. Once the abolition of the trade had become a certainty, they made desperate efforts to boost their stocks, realising that the door was about to be shut. This was a damage-limitation exercise, not a solution. Very few, if any, of the plantations had ever become self-sufficient in maintaining a breeding stock, not helped by the fact that vastly more male than female slaves had been imported during the history of Afro-Caribbean slavery.

The abolitionists understood these realities, yet they were not necessarily united. Popular history suggests a wholesome commitment to emancipation but as early as 1 June 1788 one finds an amendment to the Proceedings of the London Committee for the Abolition of the Slave Trade wherein the words 'evil of slavery' have been scratched out of the Minutes and replaced by 'evil of the slave trade'. Pragmatists like Thomas Clarkson, who genuinely found the institution of slavery repugnant, knew that dreams of emancipation depended first on closing down the traffic in slaves. For public consumption an objective of abolishing only the trade was aired because to suggest differently risked a stampede of parliamentary members into the anti-abolitionist lobby and the House of Lords manning its Luddite barricades. Yet other prominent abolitionists, most notably

William Wilberforce, were of a different mind. In denying that their aim was emancipation many were probably holding true to personal convictions that the eventual liberation of slaves was undesirable.

The first petitions pressing for emancipation had been put on the Commons table by Wilberforce in March 1788 on behalf of the Society of Friends, and the first Commons debate was tabled on 15 May 1823 to air the matter of slave emancipation. A clearly irate Foreign Secretary, George Canning, delivered a stinging criticism of Fowell Buxton, now the chief spokesman for the abolitionist MPs, for doing so. Canning fumed that 'in all former discussions, in all former votes against the slave trade, it surely cannot be forgotten that the ulterior purpose of emancipation was studiously disclaimed'.

It also becomes clear that the key players in the abolition debate were not necessarily those who later rose to prominence in popular tradition. Of the four names most often paraded, Pitt, Wilberforce, Clarkson and Fowell Buxton, the authority of the last two was most significant. William Pitt tended to fly with the popular parliamentary mood, but the most inaccurately characterised figure is William Wilberforce. It cannot be denied that he raised the issue of slavery many times in the Commons and attended a number of meetings of the London Committee for the Abolition of the Slave Trade, but far from being the magical orator behind the abolition success, he comes across too frequently as a puffed-up and rather self-righteous bore. His parliamentary speeches are more notable for their length and rhetorical prose rather than sound research and substance. Behind the niceties of correct parliamentary protocol, irritation was abroad over his tendency to sermonise at fellow MPs on the immorality of slavery. Whatever contributed to the thirty years' delay in securing the abolition of the trade, Wilberforce bears a measure of responsibility. He was quick with his own piety and importance, yet at the same time largely reluctant to acknowledge the labours of those who made his job possible, most notably the tireless Thomas Clarkson. After the abolition of the trade, the champion of emancipation was never Wilberforce but Buxton, in many ways a better-informed and more compelling orator.

This is the story of the abolition as it really was, not as popular history has painted it.

NOTE ON TERMINOLOGY

In recent decades the term 'Negro' has become offensive in the ears of some people. My decision to use it occasionally relies on the yardstick of whether or not it was employed in the historical context. If I encountered the term during the research into a contemporary source, then I have faithfully retained it since to do otherwise would constitute a distortion of history and a dilution of the authenticity for which I have consistently striven. It is not intended to cause distress.

Chapter 1

ORIGINS

In the year 1441, on an unconfirmed date, a Portuguese sea-trader, Antam Goncalvez, picked up a consignment of blubber and sea-lion skins from traders on the West African coast. More or less as an afterthought he also collected a less conventional cargo of livestock, which took the shape of a handful of locals that Goncalvez considered would provide a novel present for his master, Prince Henry.

I hazard a guess that the word 'slavery' takes most of us down a limited number of paths. It may conjure up the spectacle of gladiators facing an untidy demise in the Roman arena, but it probably draws us just as easily towards a more recent phenomenon, that of the slave-owning plantations in the American southern states and the British West Indies. These two examples are familiar and they are also useful at the beginning of a search for definitive answers about slavery and its abolition because they negate any popular sentiment that the institution of human bondage has been an isolated aberration. The Roman and American examples, separated as they are by considerable spans of time and place, blend into a much larger design. The buying, selling and exploitation of human chattels has been an integral part of the fabric of society since history began and probably for some time before that. Slavery and the trade that serves it has not only affected personal lives and communities but has also provided the bedrock of major economic systems around the globe over the course of some 10,000 years. Without recourse to enslavement of one individual by another, many of the great civilisations might never have achieved their greatness.

Within an enormous timescale, slavery has been a poor respecter of race, colour or creed. It has been condoned by virtually every major belief system, with the notable exception of Buddhism, which sees no reason to extend human misery beyond that already endured in treading the mystical wheel of life. Islam has condoned enslavement. Throughout the period of Muslim expansionism from the mid-seventh century one of the prime motives for conquest lay in the acquisition of manpower in the form of slaves to underpin the machinery of empire. In the Middle Ages, the Ottomans were fundamentally reliant on Turkish forced labour in their military successes. Christians have rarely experienced qualms about taking others into bondage either. They have felt justified in ensnaring non-Christians, relying on the moral argument that pagans and others need educating in the ways of Christ and, in the meanwhile, are thoroughly deserving of a life of bondage. Adam, so goes the reasoning, guaranteed humanity a prospect of subservient misery at the Fall. Thus in the past Christians saw no impediment to enslaving Muslims, Jews, idolaters and even other Christians. The suggestion from some quarters that early Christianity was a religion of slaves has to be viewed with a measure of scepticism. Jesus Christ may have had a place in mind for the humble and meek but the ecclesiastical establishment did not always see things in the same way and slavery has been tolerated and exploited by the Catholic Church from the outset, more often than not behind a welter of earnest cant. Protestantism can claim precious little moral high ground either, since it has been culpable of some of the more bizarre dual standards. One of the most intriguing twists to be unravelled in the ensuing chapters lies in the fact that the Protestants provided the bedrock of colonial slave ownership both in America and the British West Indies and were responsible for some of the most outrageous conduct against black Africans. Yet it was also from among Anglican dissenters on both sides of the Atlantic that a groundswell of public opinion was to be fostered in favour of abolition. Nor should we be under any illusion that slavery has gone away. It is alive and well in various parts of the world and, if one is to believe recent reports of African, Arab and East European children being imported into the United Kingdom for forcible servitude, remains a constant presence close to home. This book, however, is specifically an investigation of the enslavement of black Africans in the Americas until the mid-nineteenth century and the circumstances under which their bondage was eventually terminated.

The critical feature of the abolition process lay with the control and eventual elimination of the seaborne slave trade, starting in 1807, not, as some authors will claim, the emancipation of American and British-owned slaves, which followed during the thirty years after 1833. Emancipation may have settled in popular sentiment as the great landmark achievement and the trade may present less-familiar ground, but pragmatic minds at the time surely realised that slavery would inevitably wither away if you first cut off the supply of raw material feeding it. The business that stocked the plantations, largely controlled and dominated by British maritime power, involved a three-cornered route across the Atlantic between Europe, Africa and the Americas, the so-called 'Atlantic Triangle'. It was to this traffic that Goncalvez and his human cargo provided an almost insignificant prelude in transporting the first African slaves to the West.

Insignificant because in the four centuries that followed, prior to the final emancipation of slaves in America in January 1863, some 15 million black Africans were forcibly seized and expatriated to the West.

The battle for abolition is one that many authors claim was fought as a two-horse contest. This popular view envisages battle lines drawn up between those who came to see slavery as contrary to the laws of Nature and, therefore, to the laws of God – the abolitionists – and others for whom the prospect of abandoning slavery added up to ruin as well as a threat to life and limb – the plantation owners. Paradoxically those condoning slavery also regarded it as an institution permitted by the laws of God and Nature, which made the contest even more immovable. It is hard for a modern reader to understand, far less empathise with, the fact that from the foundation of the first British abolition society in 1787 more than fifty years passed before the black people of the British West Indies were finally released from bondage. During half a century decent and concerned citizens, men of honourable character and sound breeding all, failed to reach any decisive conclusion. Those entrusted with responsibility to guard the hallowed institutions of the nation argued and procrastinated over the rights and wrongs of ending something that, as we look back, seems a particularly unattractive stain on the British character. After all, this was not a battle fought in ancient Rome or Babylon: the field was Britain, only a few generations removed from ours. The hostility took place in an era of genteel society, of William Pitt and the Duke of Wellington, of Stephenson's 'Rocket' and Isambard Kingdom Brunel, who designed engineering feats that remain in service to this day.

In the 180 years since abolition, perhaps to cover our shame and put our past conduct in the best light, we have tended to create a mythology about the British institution of slavery. What better explanation than to assert that, in the end, we 'did the decent thing' against the vested interests of a few callous sugar-cane and cotton planters? Wanting acceptable solutions we have created heroes whose conduct did not actually merit the accolade and we have missed, or sidestepped, some simple truths about the whys and wherefores. Fact and fiction will be sorted out in the following chapters but it seems to me, after trawling through the daunting stack of literature and records, that the most convincing answers are actually to be found in the views of people living at the time. Not least among our difficulties in understanding the anomalies of slavery is that we have lost touch with the way of thinking of bygone generations. Late eighteenth- and early nineteenth-century Britain may be only a skip back in time but its mentality was vastly different from that of today. In getting to grips with why so much agonising took place, and to make any sense of a procrastination that may seem to us both incomprehensible and obscene, we also need to share the mindset of the people living at the time when the abolition debate was taking place.

Nowhere is our way of thinking more at odds than in the way we apply and react to hypocrisy. It is as much in evidence today as it was 200 years ago, but with some essential distinctions. The modern media circus, something that the Georgians did not have, gives us ready access to sham in all its juiciest forms. We delight in ferreting it out, calling it sleaze or spin, blazoning its lurid details in newspaper headlines and then ruffling our feathers in moral indignation. By comparison with the modern passion for soul-searching we were a thick-skinned lot in past centuries. The Georgians just shrugged and accepted hypocrisy as a fact of life, and this did not change even when abolition and emancipation came about. Generations of English aristocracy owed the 'good life' to the sweat of slaves, knew it and privately cared little. Lord bishops of the Church delivered pulpit rhetoric about pastoral care and thought nothing of being the owners of slaves. To the bitter end the Bishop of Exeter hung on to his 655 slaves and received just short of £13,000 in compensation when forced to free them in 1833. Men who had grown fat on the proceeds of slave-worked plantations far from home bleated with seemingly clear conscience about the obscenities of the trade. Missionaries voyaged to the Caribbean bringing Christianity and the love of Jesus to the savage but stood complacently aside when his God-fearing overseer brutalised him with the lash and the shackle.

There is no single answer to what lay at the root of such a lengthy stand-off between abolitionists and anti-abolitionists. A number of quite diverse factors jostled for effect. We fought over the deeply entrenched principle in English law that a man has inalienable right to his property and we held a genuine fear of what would happen if a million slaves were to be freed. We fretted about the possibility that old rivals like the French and the Dutch would take over what we had abandoned. On a more altruistic level the age saw a resurgence of 'practical Christianity' and the desire to do good by our fellow man. Yet behind all these considerations lay a matter of simple, raw economics. It was this, not the impact of urgent petitioners or Christian do-gooders that eventually persuaded the hard-nosed men of parliament to cancel out centuries of tradition. When changing times and industrial advances proved slavery to be uneconomic, slavery had to go. The catalyst would be reform of government and a new breed of parliamentarians. But in the meantime some of the ingredients of delay were matters of history and deeply cherished traditions, which leads neatly back to those widely separated popular examples.

We need constantly to keep in mind that slavery was not a phenomenon rising and falling in isolation. Enslavement of one man by another is an intrinsic part of the fabric of society. It has a social and economic context, built up over thousands of years. Before we go much further into exploring more-immediate cause and effect we need to take a dip into history and the attitudes of societies that have given us most of the foundations of our culture.

The classical empires of Greece and Rome were by no means the first civilisations to maintain slaves. Some of the earliest historical records of such practice come from the Ancient Near East and the empires of the Assyrians and Babylonians. Both employed captives taken during military campaigns as slave labour, and warfare was often undertaken for the purpose of acquiring such booty. Slaves were identified in the streets of Babylon by a distinctive hairstyle called the *apputtum* and its unauthorised shaving-away could find an offending barber losing his hand. More-severe punishment was reserved for the man who had ordered the application of the razor, and included impalement in his own doorway. Slaves of Mesopotamian owners could, however, also obtain official freedom, their *apputtum* legally removed in a ceremony known as 'clearing the forehead', and the children of freed slaves were generally allowed to remain free.[1] In reality there was not a great deal of lifestyle choice, since there were only two effective social classes. The elite, who made up about 5 per cent of the population, controlled and owned virtually everything, and the peasantry, who largely comprised the rest, owned nothing. Although not always slaves in the legal sense, they sweated their lives away in the interests of society's cream, without rights, identity and destiny, either in this world or the next.[2]

For the Classical Empire-builders of Europe, slavery was also quite acceptable. It worked in their favour and that is the way things stayed until slavery eventually helped bring the Roman economy to its knees. The Athenian philosopher Plato, born in 427 BCE, did not know this, of course, and thought that the institution was a necessary component of the perfect state. He pictured two groups, iron and bronze, gold and silver pulling against one another. The latter, by nature rich in their souls, attempt to draw iron and bronze back to virtue and their original constitution, including slavery. The core of Plato's particular vision is the premise that the body and soul of mankind run on parallel tracks but yet end their respective journeys at different termini.[3]

In the eye of the Greek philosopher Aristotle, born a little less than fifty years after Plato, slavery is predestined for certain individuals and such a condition is expedient and right. 'From the hour of their birth, some are marked out for subjection, others for rule.' Aristotle's view is that those members of society having, at best, the use of their bodies to offer are by nature slaves. In this he delivers the commonly held homily that slaves are to be viewed in the same light as domesticated livestock. As he puts it, 'the use made by tame animals and slaves is not very different, for both minister to the needs of life with their bodies. Nature would like to distinguish between the bodies of freemen and slaves, making the one strong for servile labour, the other upright.'[4]

In ancient Rome, slavery had been an integral part of the fabric of society since the foundation of the Republic in 510 BCE and the later Empire undoubtedly rose and fell as an organisation built on slave labour. Eventually more than half the population of the city of Rome consisted of slaves. Josephus, ever one for painting choice cameos, observes in his *Antiquities*, completed in about 66 CE and tracing history from the creation of the world, that so many Jewish slaves had descended on Rome by 4 BCE, sent on by Pompey after quelling Hasmonean insurrection in Judaea, that as many as 8,000 once turned out as the welcoming party when an official deputation arrived in the city from Jerusalem. In such statistics lay the root cause of many subsequent problems for Rome. Slaves not only worked the land in the Italian provinces, they were responsible for seeing to virtually all the practical business in town and countryside. This left the Roman upper crust to a life of pleasure and occasional government duties. Sons of Roman fathers studied arts and literature and discussed serious matters at the baths, but were hopelessly unqualified to keep the economy turning. They were not merely unwilling to get their hands dirty and engage in the undignified job of production, but bore no experience to fill the void when the supply of slaves started to peter out. At the dawn of the Christian era, particularly in the provinces, there were few manual labourers to work the estates. In the Italian countryside one result of more-or-less protracted military service had been the depletion of most of the old rural population, carried away either to the heavenly fields of Elysium or to more mundane parts of empire. Empty farmland thus fell into the hands of a few lucky entrepreneurs and the only solution to the staffing problem was to bring in an immigrant population of enslaved prisoners of war. These captives became a source of cheap labour, against which what was left of the rural free peasantry that had been allowed to stay put or had trudged home from the battlefield could not compete.

The supply was not inexhaustible, however, and the influx of slaves began to dry up. This reduction in the available labour force began sometime towards the turn of the third century, when the wars of conquest, the primary source of fresh slave muscle, were over. The last such campaign had been conducted against the Germanic lands early in the second century by the emperor Trajan. For the average member of the Roman elite faced with this unanticipated situation, everything from civil engineering to home maintenance was by then a complete mystery. The daily bread was collected and served up by one slave, having been baked and sold by another slave, with flour grown, harvested and milled by yet more slaves. By the fourth century, when the make-or-break need to modernise came, it was all too late. While other nations were starting out on the road towards industrialisation, Rome found itself locked into a lifestyle that was rapidly becoming not merely anachronistic but highly vulnerable.

Nor did the problems rest solely in practicalities of everyday life. In the early days of the Republic, Rome had experienced more-serious disruptive problems with slaves in the shape of no less than three Italy-based revolts in less than fifty years. Unrest was particularly prevalent in the provincial countryside, where a larger number of slaves was required to keep the produce rolling in and where they tended to be treated more harshly than in Rome itself. Records seem to suggest that slaves put to work on Roman-owned farms were, at first, treated fairly kindly. But as estates grew in size and affluence, the more-personal relationship that had existed between master and slave began to break down. Increasingly slaves were treated much as cattle. Cato the Elder, who wrote the first history of Rome, described the management of his own farm slaves strictly in terms of minimal clothing and feed, regulated according to the season. The treatment was not intentionally unkind, since it was no different from that which he would afford to his sheep and cattle, though his horses would probably have experienced higher standards.[5] In Italy the last major slave insurrection, led on this occasion by gladiators and known popularly as the war of Spartacus, came in 73 BCE. It brought devastation to large areas and was put down only after two bloody years involving massive loss of life, by the Senate's henchman, Marcus Licinius Crassus.

The enforced conscription of slaves into the military was to backfire severely on Imperial Rome. Towards the end of the glory days, the home-bred Roman legionary had become virtually an extinct species, replaced by mercenaries and foreign recruits, many of them extracted from conquered territories. When the legions found their position increasingly untenable in the face of Gothic aggression they started to retreat on all fronts. The Visigoth general Alaric seized his chance in 410 CE and successfully laid siege to Rome. That particular end-game was helped along when droves of well-armed and well-trained slaves recognised that the opportunity had arrived to get the better of their Roman persecutors and possibly go home free. They absconded en masse to join Alaric's forces ranged around the city. This, of course, was not quite the finish of the Roman Empire in the west, which continued to crumble steadily until the last emperor, Romulus Augustulus, was deposed by the German king in 476 CE. Nor did Alaric's triumph mark the end of slave uprisings. In 417 CE the Roman army was obliged to crush a serious revolt in northern Gaul. But a few years earlier, in 406 CE, as Rome faced a fresh barbarian assault, the situation had become so fraught in the western provinces that the emperor Honorius advised all governors, or *provinciales*, to take up arms in their own defence and to tempt any slaves who cared to join them with the prospect of freedom. Some of the promised change in status clearly materialised. In 1806 a statue was unearthed on London's Ludgate Hill dedicated to a woman named Claudia Martina. According to the inscription a freed slave, Anencletus, who had served the provincial authority as a soldier, erected it in memory of his wife.[6]

Slavery amounted to a norm throughout much of Europe during this period of history. There is also unequivocal evidence that slave trading was established in various parts of the continent well before the Roman Conquest. The Greek geographer Strabo, who collected information from earlier writers in history, lists preconquest British exports as including grain, cattle, gold, silver, iron, hides, slaves and hunting dogs.[7] When the Romans arrived in Britain, they effectively treated much of the agricultural workforce as slaves, but they were not averse to including elements of the British aristocracy, and enslavement of members of Boudicca's family was arguably one of the factors that led the Icenian queen to mount her ill-fated revolt against the occupying forces in 60 CE.

The first-century writer Tacitus describes how the German tribes kept slaves. When their marauding war-parties plundered the Low Countries and rowed across to Britain, much of the Celtic population that had not had advance notice, and thus had not managed to escape to Wales or Brittany, found itself enjoying little more than slave status. But here the distinctions between master and servant were often blurred. The relationship seems to have been more akin to a business arrangement. 'Master cannot be recognised from slave by any flummery (without distinction and without cosseting and pampering for the better born) in their respective bringing up: they live in the company of the same cattle and on the same mud floor till years separate the free-born and character claims her own.' Tacitus concedes that slavery in the rest of northern Europe was not organised on the lines familiar to citizens of the Roman Empire. 'Slaves are not organised in our fashion: that is by an exact definition of services throughout a household. Each freeman remains master of his own house and home: the master requires from the slave as from a tenant a certain quantity of grain or cattle or clothing. The slave so far is subservient; but the rest – the services of the household – is discharged by the master's wife or children. To beat a slave and coerce him with hard labour and imprisonment is rare.'[8]

Overall, trading in slaves was probably the most extensive business activity across Europe by the dawn of the Middle Ages and, irrespective of time and place, however badly or well treated, a slave was personal property. He or she, adult or child, was part of a man's estate and was valued as his collateral security. The principle of a slave being a chattel amounting to personal equity was time-honoured. Under the Babylonian Code of Hammurabi an able-bodied male was valued at 20 shekels, although among rank-and-file dealers this was considered inflationary and most were traded for less. In the second millennium BCE slave trading amounted to serious business for Arab shippers, who are thought to have cleared stock from Africa and shipped it to the Gulf. The slaves were then sold on to caravaneers in what is now Bahrain, who drove their cargoes into Babylonia. Some 2,000 years on, in Celtic Ireland, female slaves actually became recognised as units of currency, identified as the *cumal*, roughly worth six heifers or three milch cows on the open exchange.[9] The slave was bought and sold, put to constructive use and maintained throughout the term of indenture as a negotiable asset along with four-legged farm stock and other chattels. It was this view of the slave being part of a man's undeniable property that raised one of the biggest obstacles to nineteenth-century emancipation and bled the British taxpayer of millions of pounds in compensation to deprived plantation owners.

Slavery covered the whole spectrum of society in antiquity and was by no means limited to the pagan cultures. The Old Testament Hebrews were slave owners. They thought nothing especially untoward of owning human property and, as far as they were concerned, owning slaves did not incur divine punishment. The Book of Genesis contains numerous references to bondage. The Patriarch Abraham fathered Isaac through an Egyptian slave-woman named Hagar, earning the rebuke of his wife Sarah. 'And God said unto Abraham, Let it not be grievous in thy sight because of the lad, and because of thy bondwoman; in all that Sarah hath said unto thee, hearken unto her voice; for in Isaac shall thy seed be called.'[10] More often than not, Hebrews enslaved other Hebrews as opposed to gentiles, and the arrangement could even be a voluntary one. 'Yet now our flesh is as the flesh of our children, our children as their children; and lo we bring into bondage our sons and our daughters to be servants, and some of our daughters are brought into bondage already.'[11] Josephus provides details about Jewish slave regulations. 'A Hebrew sold to another Hebrew shall serve him for six years; in the seventh let him go free (and his wife if he has one). But if having had children by a slave woman at the house of the master who bought him, he, out of love and affection for his own, desires to continue to serve him, then on the coming of the year of the jubilee – which returns every 50 years – let him be liberated, taking his children and wife, also free, along with him.'[12] A Hebrew slave could also purchase his way out of bondage by paying off the cost to his master. All of this undoubtedly influenced the way that slaves were treated. According to another Jewish author, Philo, who lived from about 20 BCE to 50 CE, the masters of slaves 'ought to be gentle to them even though they had a thousand times over given their masters absolute power and authority over them. He is a hireling who is called a slave and he is also a man, having a most sublime relationship with you, inasmuch as he is of the same nation as yourself;

and perhaps he is even of the same tribe and the same borough as yourself, and is now reduced to this condition through want.'[13]

It has to be said that not all of the Jewish sects supported the institution of slavery. Philo reports that the eccentric Essenes looked upon the possession of servants or slaves to be 'absolutely and wholly contrary to nature, for nature has created all men free, but the injustice and covetousness of some men who prefer inequality, that cause of all evil, having subdued some, has given to the more powerful authority over those who are weaker'.[14] Seventeen hundred years later the Scottish philosopher Adam Smith was to remark on the same undesirable facet of human nature as being one of the driving causes of enslavement. 'The pride of man makes him love to domineer. Wherever the law allows it and the nature of the work can afford it, therefore, he will generally prefer the service of slaves to that of freemen.'[15]

From the outset the attitude of the Christian establishment towards slavery was either ambivalent or wholly indifferent. Plato's notions of the dual nature of body and soul found their way into early Christian doctrine and it helps explain some of the attitudes of the Church towards slavery. If the soul is immortal and separate, the life of the body is of comparatively little importance. What does enslavement and physical cruelty matter in this world if a spiritual paradise of freedom and joy beckons in the next? When challenged on morals of Afro-Caribbean slavery the Church generally defended its position by trotting out Biblical texts indicating that approval came from above. If God was relaxed about the Children of Israel dealing in slaves then it stood to reason that he was not going to be worried about the eighteenth-century merchants of Bristol and Liverpool engaging in similar business. The Church took care to sidestep sensitive details, including the distinction that slaves in Biblical society were expected to serve for a maximum of seven years, not for life, were generally treated well and rarely experienced beating or shackling. The early Christian Church largely recruited its converts from the middle classes, for whom slaves and slavery did not hold too much interest. Churchmen may have complained occasionally about the morality of bondage among their secular neighbours, but did not do so very loudly. Love of fellow man was not the safest of reasons for fledgling-Church leaders to support unpopular measures when Christianity was still regarded as an illegal operation, tolerated by the authorities so long as it caused no trouble. History would have revealed objection to slavery to be gross double-talk, since the Church was not averse to purchasing slaves, although, as we have established, it frequently justified its action as a means of bringing godliness to the heathen.

The redoubtable seventh-century historian Bede relates how, at some time before investiture as pontiff, Pope Gregory I visited a Roman slave market and was intrigued by the 'fair complexions, fine cut features and beautiful hair' of boys put up for sale. Bede's story goes that having been informed that these youths were ignorant heathens from Britain, Gregory vowed to have missionaries sent to convert the English people to Christ.[16] Evidence from a separate source suggests that Gregory wrote to one of his agents, a man named Candidus, travelling in Gaul in the autumn of 595 CE, urging him to buy English pagan adolescents 'in order that they may be dedicated to God and make progress in monasteries'.[17] The shrewd view must be that Gregory's interest lay more in obtaining a supply of robust monastic labourers than in bringing the word of Christ to dispossessed English adolescents. Lesser members of the Church establishment seem to have taken a similar line to Gregory, namely that freedom of the body was of minor interest beside liberation of the soul, and most of those released from bondage only escaped as far as monastic confines. According to Bede's accounts, in about 680 CE a certain Bishop Wilfrid was granted a large parcel of land at Selsey, where he built a monastery. Since all the local inhabitants had also been generously gifted to him, he undertook to baptise 250 slaves and grant them their freedom, presumably to work his lands. On the other side of the Channel, at Elnone on the Franco-Belgian border, another monk named Amandus is reputed to have collected up English slaves and paid for their release. Having baptised them, he gave them a form of education and sent them to different churches as missionaries, the advantage to Amandus being their ability to converse freely in the Germanic language of the people among whom he worked.

Bede also described the quaint affair of a young Northumbrian nobleman called Imma. Wounded in a battle against the Mercians near the River Trent, he was captured and, claiming to be an innocent peasant, was nursed back to health under the care of one of the Mercian leaders. His kinsman, meanwhile, started offering Masses for the repose of his soul, thinking that he had been killed. On recovering a degree of fitness Imma was obliged to reveal his identity, which earned him a spell in chains and eventual sale into slavery. After his purchase in a London market, however, Imma's new Frisian owner found that his shackles continually fell loose. In some despair, and presumably after reprimanding his blacksmith more than once, the Frisian permitted Imma his freedom with the provision that he obtained a suitable sum of ransom money and brought it back. It was only when Imma returned to Northumberland that he discovered his chains had become miraculously unlocked coincidental with Masses being offered on his behalf. Bede's account is a jolly little story but it serves to confirm the fact that the Christian Anglo-Saxons saw nothing untoward about selling captives from neighbouring Christian kingdoms as slaves.[18]

The most devout of prelates eventually came to support the slavery system and from the sixth century onwards, as the Byzantine era unfolded, the Church openly paraded its slaves for what they were. John Chrysostom, one of the more notorious fourth-century dispensers of fire and brimstone, would thunder from his pulpit that the unpleasantness of being a slave was all part of divine retribution for Adam's sin and this was the way things were going to stay. He might therefore have been interested to hear Abraham Lincoln deliver his emancipation speech in 1862. The American Civil War, Lincoln lamented, was God's punishment for the long toleration of slavery. In the end Chrysostom might have felt partly vindicated, however, since emancipation promptly gave way to a hundred years of white racism in America. Admittedly not every Christian leader in the early Church saw the institution in quite such clear-cut terms. St Augustine seems to have had nagging worries about the principle of enslavement, although generally he fell in line with Chrysostom that it was a necessary evil resulting from the Fall. He also believed that its abolition would undermine the social order.

Augustine's worry about instability was another of the time-honoured arguments that the British anti-abolitionists paraded throughout the protracted debates of the eighteenth and nineteenth centuries. Freeing slaves would result in insurrection and the massacre of every white man, woman and child in the West Indies. Plato had actually delivered an uncanny prediction on this score. In the *Republic* he posed the question of 'what would happen suppose some god should catch up a man who has fifty or more slaves and waft him with his wife and children away from the city and set him down with his other possessions and his slaves in a solitude where no free man could come to his rescue. What and how great would be his fear lest he and his wife and his children be destroyed by the slaves?' Plato took the argument a step further. 'But suppose that god established round him numerous neighbours who would not tolerate the claim of one man to be the master of another, but would inflict the utmost penalties on any such person on whom they could lay their hands. His plight becomes still more desperate.'[19] Plato was not far from the truth: the prospect of emancipation did lead to some extremely bloody uprisings, first in the French slave colony of St Domingue in 1791, and then in British-owned Jamaican plantations.

After the departure of the Romans, conversion to Christianity in Europe progressed unevenly, and we cannot readily measure its slave systems according to whether they were operated by Christians or non-Christians. The whole slave industry became something of a mishmash. It also became, probably, the most widespread business activity of the early medieval world.[20] From the eighth century through to the thirteenth, various Saxon and Viking warlords became involved in the trade, as did many other petty rulers across Europe. All filled their coffers with money earned from the sale of captured human booty, especially to the Islamic world, and in many ways this made good economic sense. In an era of

Muslim expansionism, western Europe watched a steady flow of gold draining out of Christian reserves, and the sale of slaves played no small part in balancing the books. The Christian Saxons looked eastwards and capitalised on an insatiable Islamic demand for heathen Slavs; purchased by Jewish traders they were sold on to Muslim clients. A charter issued by the Holy Roman Emperor, Louis the Pious, had already given royal assent to Jews dealing in slaves, provided that their merchandise was bought and sold outside the limits of empire. But the arrangement was open to abuse and this caused considerable irritation to some in the Church establishment. In about 825 CE Agobard, Bishop of Lyons, let loose a scathing criticism of the Jewish entrepreneurs. Agobard was piqued not because the Jews were dealing in slaves who, after all, were largely heathens that deserved no better. His irritation was over the reluctance of Jewish traders to hand over any enslaved men and women who had decided, while trudging the roads through Christian territories, that there was potential benefit in becoming Christian. Agobard went so far as to accuse the traders, on occasions, of underhandedness in selling Christians to Muslims.[21]

On their part the Vikings carried on a no-less-lucrative trade with the Islamic markets in Spain, making generous profits out of selling furs, amber and slaves to Muslim buyers. They also traded directly with the ruling caliphate in Baghdad. In later medieval centuries, when the Muslim threat became serious and crusades were de rigueur, Islamic captives in Christian-held parts of Spain regularly had the offer of freedom dangled before them in return for agreeing to convert. Christian Iberian slave owners were less than happy with the arrangement and, determined to nip their potential loss of labour in the bud, responded by denying rights of baptism to Muslims. This particular tactic was developed to the extent that in 1206 Pope Innocent III was driven to fire off some severe reprimands to the clergy at the cathedral in Barcelona who had allegedly colluded with the slave owners. Matters became sufficiently vexatious that Innocent's nephew, Pope Gregory IX, issued a bull to the effect that while it was right that slaves should be encouraged to embrace Christianity, Jesus's compassion for the underdog need not be read as approval for their liberation.[22]

In England, long after the arrival of the Normans, slavery by whatever name one chooses was never properly abandoned. It was replaced by serfdom, different in name but not much else. Characteristic of the manorial economic system, this gave the medieval serf or villein his own home, his plot of land and his meagre livestock in addition to some customary rights, courtesy of the lord of a landed estate, but he was not exactly free in the accepted sense of the word. He was bound to the soil he tilled just as securely as a black slave was shackled to the plantation system by his master, and he paid his lord in both services and cash in exchange for what little entitlement he had. After the abortive Peasants' Revolt of

1381 some peasants did gain title to their smallholdings, and serfdom began to decline during the late Middle Ages in western Europe.

Whether one can say that attitudes towards the principle of slavery changed much is questionable. The Western world might seem to have moved forward since the Classical era, but as late as Elizabethan times the institution was not only condoned in high places but positively encouraged. Enslavement was still considered by many Christians to have been ordained by God as punishment for the Fall in the Garden of Eden, the so-called 'original sin': we transgressed, and permanent servitude was heaped onto some of us by way of punishment. Aristotle thought nothing of equating slaves with animals, and Shakespearean England was apparently little more enlightened. In *The Tempest*, Shakespeare has Prospero deliver some revealing sentiments about Caliban: 'I pitied thee, took pains to make thee speak, taught thee each hour one thing or other: when thou didst not, savage, know thine own meaning but wouldst gabble like a thing most brutish, I endowed thy purposes with words that made them known.' In his choice of words to summon Caliban from his festering hovel, Shakespeare also lets fly another common notion. 'Thou poisonous slave, got by the devil himself upon thy wicked dam, come forth!'[23] Shakespeare consciously blends the two, the sins of the mother and the animal nature of the slave, into a seamless whole. Nor were the English alone in their sentiments. It comes as a pithy discovery that as late as the sixteenth century, the Catholic ecclesiastical authority in Spain was still pondering over whether Negro slaves could possess souls or were just God's animal creations in human form. It was not until Protestants started to question the more conservative views of the Church on slavery that a breeze of change began to blow and this, as I have noted, was not without its anomalies.

In eastern Europe human bondage continued until comparatively modern times and, if anything, was strengthened. Adam Smith, writing in the mid-eighteenth century, describes how slavery was still rife in Russia, Poland, Hungary, Bohemia, Moravia and other parts of Germany. In England what amounted to slave labour may have lessened, but working and living conditions for the lower classes remained appallingly bad, whether in town or country. In the newly industrialised workplaces of the early nineteenth century, people became resigned to working well-nigh inhumanly long hours in return for subsistence wages. This was one of the factors that determined a degree of working-class opposition to the emancipation of West Indian slaves. A petition of cotton workers put before the Commons in 1818 complained about fourteen- or fifteen-hour work shifts with only forty minutes of relief for meals. Why should anyone be concerned about the plight of black Africans many thousands of miles away when, in the Lancashire cotton mills, adults and children alike were forced into a different kind of slavery merely to stay alive?

Until as late as the parliamentary reform of 1832 the resilience of a conservative landowning rump affected any attempt to alter the social balance in Britain. The overwhelming majority of the population were employed in agriculture, had no voting franchise and little more education. Most could neither read nor write and the average annual wage for 1½ million agricultural workers was £31 a year. Most farmers brought in about £120. Shopkeepers earned a little more. There existed a comparatively small middle class, perhaps amounting to ¼ million people, who might earn as much as £1,000, but their influence was still largely insignificant. Against the general backdrop of grinding poverty a small minority of the old ruling classes still controlled more-or-less everything and at the top of the social pile the great lords took their vast collective income from land rents. It has been calculated that at the turn of the nineteenth century the Duke of Newcastle was earning in excess of £120,000 a year (just under £5 million in today's money).[24] The existence of this small elite, wielding disproportionate power over the political system, the land and the lower orders, was therefore of immense importance not only in the history of Western civilisation but also in the continuation of slavery. Until the reforms took place, depriving the old nobility of much of their power base, the majority of them stood firm with the plantation owners. Indeed many of them *were* plantation owners and were acutely aware of what was at stake and the risks that accompanied any change in the system.

In the debate about the future of slavery that took place in Britain between 1787 and 1833 (and a similar story is to be told in what became the United States), three groups of interest were set to vie with each other: government, abolitionists and plantation owners. To these must be added the voice of the largely unenfranchised British public. The interests of the slaves themselves, of course, didn't count. Or did they? Towards the end of the eighteenth century, statistics were a major cause for alarm among those with interests in the West Indies. It has been calculated that in 1745 about 877,000 people lived in the British Caribbean islands, of whom about 750,000, or 85 per cent, were slaves; or, to put it another way, the white plantation owners were then outnumbered by roughly six to one, and these numbers were set to increase. The sugar planters genuinely feared that they and their families would be massacred if the slave population sensed a change in the wind. It must have been very obvious that any large-scale uprising would overwhelm the limited forces of law and order stationed in the British West Indies. The planters also envisaged their personal financial security disappearing overnight along with the exodus of liberated labour, if there was no provision for compensation.

But perhaps the strongest factor in the anti-abolitionist armoury was that which we have just established. Slavery had been a normal and accepted part of the British way of life since before anyone could remember. The planters had, after all, received the full support of the British government since the reign of Queen Anne in their reliance on slave labour. We see the procrastination as something disgraceful, but norms always change with time and what is acceptable one year is outlawed the next. A test of our sentiments today would be a ruling placed on us that we no longer drive motor cars. The argument of the anti-road campaigners has been that the automobile pollutes the atmosphere and is therefore anti-social, so henceforth we must rely wholly on public transport and Shanks's pony. In comparative terms the prospect of abandonment of slavery was as unwholesome to the English plantation owners, the shipowners and the merchants as this would be to us.

Chapter 2

THE THREE-CORNERED TRADE

From fairly modest beginnings shortly after the dawn of the European Renaissance in the mid-fifteenth century the slave trade between Africa and the Americas built to its peak at the end of the eighteenth century. It was set to involve a number of European powers, most notably the British, French, Dutch, Spanish and, at the outset, the Portuguese. It is this period of rather more than 300 years that sets the scene and outlines the circumstances that led not only to the rise of the American and European abolition movements but also much of the resistance they encountered from anti-abolitionists.

Goncalvez did not launch the slave trade. Technically the credit goes to another Portuguese, the Receiver of Customs in Lagos, called Lançarote, who obtained permission to visit the African west coast in 1444 in order to 'obtain vendable slaves'.[1] Two hundred and thirty were sold in Lagos on 8 August of that year. How was it, therefore, that Portugal, a small nation perched like a blister on the Spanish rump and with little influence in the rest of the world, became the entrepreneur in a form of business not only intrinsic to the expansion of Europe but also destined to persist for more than three centuries? In the fifteenth century, Spain and Portugal led the world into a new Christian age of exploration and discovery. Initially Portuguese excursions abroad were encouraged by the Catholic Church, which anticipated an effective new means of imposing the Christian ideology in foreign parts. Charity was not foremost among the Church's motives. A papal bull, issued in 1455, gave the country a virtual blank cheque to 'reduce to servitude all infidel peoples'. Issued by Callistus III, an austere and rigidly pious pontiff whose abiding preoccupation was waging holy war against the Turks, the bull allowed the Portuguese an early edge in European exploration, but her larger and more powerful Spanish neighbour immediately registered a protest about this monopoly, demanding an even-handed settlement. It was left to one of Callistus's more licentious successors, Alexander VI, to issue a second bull in 1493, curbing the original generosity to Portugal and drawing a line of demarcation a hundred leagues west of the Azores. This edict gave Spain authority to explore to the west of the line and Portugal to the east. Unwittingly it was destined to create a market, one that involved human traffic, wherein Portugal became the first purveyor, Spain the first consumer.

In the short term the deal struck by Alexander VI swung the balance of opportunity too much in favour of the Spanish and further negotiation the following year resulted in the Treaty of Tordesillas, earning Portugal a sop in the form of rights to colonise Brazil. The arrangements left Portugal and Spain thumbing their noses at one another, while some countries outside the Iberian peninsula chose to turn a deaf ear on papal jurisdiction. In England, notwithstanding recent treaties with Spain, a disgruntled Henry VII responded in 1497 by sponsoring the Italian-born explorer John Cabot to investigate the potential of the North American coastline. In the meantime the Spanish conquistadores wasted no time in exploiting their advantage and headed for the Americas, where they anticipated the prospect of first-come-first-served military gain. Perhaps more to the point they caught the scent of gold, although initially their quest for El Dorado was disappointing since none of the places they touched yielded measurable quantities of mineral riches. It was not until 1518 that their fortunes were to improve when a Spanish ship made the first landing on Mexican soil near modern Veracruz.

Historians are reasonably clear that Spanish voyages of discovery were prompted by avarice and dreams of world domination, but it is less evident what stimulated Portugal's enthusiasm. Perhaps it was simply that the Portuguese had little else to do and they chose to explore the world out of curiosity. In the mid-fifteenth century our view of Earth beyond the confines of Europe and the Near East was dominated by ignorance and superstition. Half the world had yet to be discovered and the 'dark continent' of Africa was aptly named. We guessed that beyond the known horizons lay untold riches, but with terrors to match. Probably neither Africa nor America meant much more to Europeans than the surface of Mars does to us. Columbus may have visited America on four different occasions but in hindsight he had no better idea of where he had been than at the start. It was not until Ferdinand Magellan circumnavigated the globe between 1519 and 1522 that traditionalists reluctantly agreed that the Earth was round. It was also finally accepted that the Atlantic was a separate ocean from the Pacific. Hitherto, natives of America, the land named after the 'Chief Pilot' of Spain, Amerigo Vespucci, who made several voyages there between 1497 and 1504, were thought to be inhabitants of the Indian subcontinent, hence 'Red Indians' and anyone who argued otherwise was considered not to be in touch with reality.

The general consensus of opinion, however, is that Portuguese adventurers set out in their small and rather vulnerable ships across uncharted seas largely in pursuit of trade. The rise and fall of Afro-American slavery is firmly rooted in considerations of economics, political and financial, and only secondarily has the issue been touched by sentiments concerning humanitarianism and race. The Portuguese possessed no clear source of domestic revenue and their interest lay not in their larger Iberian neighbour's preoccupation with blood-letting but in profitable trading. From the outset, under Portugal's mandate to 'look east', the African continent posed an irresistible lure. Portuguese adventurers believed correctly that there were rich pickings to be had by sailing south and east from the Straits of Gibraltar and, like the Spanish, they had also scented gold.

In 1439 Portugal claimed the islands of the Azores in the Atlantic, from which many of the expeditions departed. Her explorers journeyed down what must have seemed the never-ending coastline of that vast and distinctive bulge of the West African mainland before turning east into the Gulf of Guinea, the aptly named 'Ivory' and 'Gold' Coasts. The Catholic Church looked on at this meritorious spirit of enterprise and adventure with approval, relishing a first-rate opportunity to bring Christianity to the beastly savages who had been discovered to live in sizeable numbers beside those uncharted shores. Other, more-worldly strategists, concerned about the ever-present threat of Islamic expansion, anticipated the prospect of obtaining new allies among the natives.

Whatever may have been the initial reasons for exploration, Portuguese sailors and traders were set to dominate the African scene for nearly a hundred years, doing so with the full and essential blessing of the Catholic Church. Within four decades they had built a chain of fortified trading stations on the Gold Coast, most notably São Jorge de Mina, or 'El Mina', a heavily defended outpost lying about 200km from modern Accra at the western tip of the Bight of Benin. By that time Portuguese explorations were also reaching far beyond northern Africa, and nearly 1,000km to the south they were the first Europeans to establish colonies in what is now Angola. On the other side of the continent they also developed commercial interests along the coasts of Mozambique. Through their burgeoning commercial stations they would obtain gold, timber, spices and slaves in exchange for cheap brass and copper trinkets, cheap cotton goods and ironware. The latter commodity, tragically for Africa as it turned out, included firearms.

The history of the slave trade is one that takes place contemporaneously on three continents, with Africa providing the source, Europeans acting as the commercial driving force and America coming to stimulate the demand, though not immediately. The account of slave-taking in West Africa follows a confusing chain of twists and turns. Long before Europeans arrived, Africa had been comfortable with slavery, and local kingdoms fought other local kingdoms on a regular basis to obtain slaves for domestic use. We may fondly imagine that obtaining slaves for European buyers on the West African coast was a one-sided arrangement, but once the demand arose, Africans were happy to oblige and without their cooperation the trade would have been much less successful. Muslim Arab incursions from the north had provided extensive experience of being on the receiving end of bondage and displacement to the Near East via a murderous trek across the Sahara desert, so the more entrepreneurial tribes had little problem with reversing roles as and when opportunity presented itself.

The potential for new business came when the sails of Portuguese ships first appeared over the horizon. Goncalvez may not knowingly have set out on a slaving trip but it marked the first occasion on which Europeans obtained a human cargo from Africa and took it away for the purposes of exploitation. Voyagers in his wake discovered a vast untapped resource of manpower that could be purchased on much the same basis as domestic livestock. At first the trade in human chattels was directed into the European home market in small numbers. The massive expansion in response to the needs of the New World did not come immediately. For their part West African barons awoke to new potential in an old cash crop. Merchants living on the coast soon discovered that rich pickings were to be had by setting themselves up as middlemen between the European traders and the powerful tribes inland in the West African forests. The Ashantis and Dahomeys found that rounding up their neighbours for the Europeans, who were soon demonstrating a lucrative appetite, amounted to a superior enterprise because of the shop window of goods on offer by way of payment. Ethnic rivalries and local blood-letting gained added piquancy if the winner was also able to earn rewards not necessarily available to neighbours. Guns undoubtedly fell into this category. Not only did their possession gain considerable respect from the people down the way, it also made the process of rounding up marketable goods a great deal faster and more economical. In this way some African rulers became extremely affluent at the expense of others, and at the same time enhanced still further their personal prestige and control of labour. What made the arrival of the Portuguese different was not the emergence of slave-taking, since this had been going on for centuries. Nor was it the export of Africans in bondage to foreign masters, since the Muslim kingdoms of the Near East were creaking with such people. The distinction lay in that trade in human beings as chattels developed on an unprecedented commercial scale and became associated with a level of violence and brutality that was also unmatched.

In the Americas, however, initial reliance amounting to a prelude to African slavery was placed on indigenous American Indians or 'Amerindians'. On returning from his first voyage to the New World, Christopher Columbus had informed the Spanish monarchs, Ferdinand and Isabella, that a good supply of slave labour was waiting to be plucked from the West Indies. On his second homecoming in 1447 Columbus disembarked 300 survivors onto the Lisbon quayside to be transported on for sale in the newly constructed slave market of Seville. These were the luckier ones from among an original complement of 500 that he had stowed aboard his ships, the rest having been reduced to corpses en route and flung into the sea. Like West Africans, Amerindians were thus initially transported back for enforced servitude in Europe but the practice was short-lived and it was in the Americas that their chief exploitation was to take place.

The supply of Indians, however, was strictly limited. The New World of the first settlers was never a continent bursting with people and the sparsity increased after the first Spanish immigrants to the Americas, the army of conquistadores, had helped to kill off a high proportion of inhabitants by gifting them typhus, smallpox, pleurisy and other such microbial aliens. Under the quaintly named heading of 'Columbian exchange', Europe received only syphilis, supposedly brought back by Columbus's crew and passed on to the unwitting dockside community of Barcelona in 1493. Amerindians who escaped the ravages of ship-borne epidemics were then further depleted by force of arms. Neither the Spanish nor the English were particularly squeamish about blood-letting among the local populations, but the violence was more acute in Spanish-controlled parts of the New World. After the turn of 1519, when the Spanish forces directed their attentions to Mexico, having first overrun Cuba, they engaged in a two-year period of mindless butchery, managing to reduce the Aztec Empire to dust along with most of its subjects, under the command of Hernando Cortez.

The Spanish had gone to Central and South America primarily in search of precious metals and stones. Having eventually discovered these in abundance in their new territories, they set about turning much of the Amerindian population into an enslaved workforce to mine gold and silver. In effect the use of Amerindians went on for as long as they were available. Some were captured and traded by Europeans. War-parties of the stronger tribes also raided their neighbours and carried off prisoners partly for their own use, partly to be sold on to Spanish buyers. Exploitation by Europeans, however, was a comparatively short-lived business that dwindled away for two reasons. The conditions in the mines proved no less murderous and many of the remaining able-bodied that had escaped initial slaughter at the hands of the military enjoyed only a short reprieve. They died in such prodigious numbers through ill treatment and mining accidents that the precious metal industry threatened to grind to a halt. Furthermore the temperament of the indigenous adult male did not lend itself to enslavement. A brisk local market had developed in women and children but the men were seen fairly quickly as a risk and proved unpopular for prospective buyers. Demographic statistics and physical abuse, therefore, largely combined to dictate the future course of events. With the demand to fill the coffers at home soaring, the Spanish colonialists found themselves saddled with a labour problem largely of their own making. They faced limited options, since Europeans were generally not able to endure the conditions in the mines any more than the Amerindians. In order to redress the balance and avert a staffing crisis that threatened supply to his nation's treasury, Ferdinand of Spain issued a decree in 1510 to purchase 250 Negroes from Portuguese traders operating out of the African west coast and have the consignment shipped to the Americas.

It is probably fair to say that Ferdinand's instruction launched three centuries of the transatlantic slave trade. Some West Africans had already arrived in the Americas from Portuguese Guinea a few years earlier in 1502, but in reality the first few decades of black African slavery saw most shipments through the Guinea outposts destined for work in Europe. After Ferdinand's decree, however, all eyes turned towards the apparently inexhaustible potential of Africa to solve the labour problems of the American colonies. By 1513 the Spanish government, although not directly involved in slave shipment, was issuing licences to traders in Negroes, making itself handsome profits in the process, and within a little more than ten years slave importation to the Americas represented a flourishing industry.

Among modern authors, controversy has long prevailed over the root cause of reliance on black Africans and not all agree that it was purely a matter of demographic shortfalls. Arguments have been aired, some of which I find less than convincing, that reasons also lay in the ambivalent view of what exactly Africans and Indians *were* in the order of things. When Goncalvez had sailed home to the Portuguese port of Lagos back in 1441 with his gift for Prince Henry the Navigator, the human element of his manifesto was viewed with jaw-dropping astonishment, since few people had actually seen a black man before. Indeed the sight prompted instant heated discussion on whether the cargo constituted members of the human race or some lesser creatures. In the centuries that followed, this vexing question about the precise identity of Africans would not only determine much of their treatment by white slave-traders and plantation owners but also influence British and European public opinion.

Nearly a hundred years after Goncalvez's voyage, the debate about the biological origins of non-European aboriginals was in full swing, but by this time distinctions were surfacing. It stimulated the beginnings of a form of discrimination that would play its own part in shaping the nature of enslavement in the New World since it involved critical comparison of the indigenous populations in America and Africa. When commenting on Amerindians in the Spanish American colonies in 1537, Pope Paul III felt sufficiently confident of having received God's word on the human species to proclaim that 'all Indians [meaning Amerindians] are truly men, not only capable of understanding the Catholic faith, but . . . exceedingly desirous to receive it'.[2] He went so far as to instruct that the sacraments should be withheld from any colonist who disregarded the principle. At first, however, people on the ground were not entirely confident that the pope had got things right and Paul III felt himself under sufficient popular pressure to revoke the penalty the following year.[3] On the other hand the sixteenth-century view of black Africans and their place in the order of things was somewhat different. The possibility of their receiving the Eucharist was not even on the table for discussion, since it was not considered possible that they could be made aware of its significance or value.

The American author David Brion Davis, writing the Pulitzer-prizewinning book *The Problems of Slavery in Western Culture* in 1966, appeared to contend that a sentimental distinction between native American Indians and West Africans contributed, in part, to the fact that by 1510 the Spanish had largely abandoned the local purchase of the one in favour of importing the other. Davis asserts that the European conscience was more troubled by the plight of the Indian, who in the early centuries of colonisation was seen in a vaguely mystical light, the noble savage in an Arcadian landscape from which Eden had never actually departed. He was as free from avarice as he was from clothes and tiresome conventions. On the other hand the black African was made available to the white man through the business activities of fellow Africans who demonstrated a thorough aptitude for thuggery and kidnap and certainly could not claim innocence or spiritual nobility. These distinctions took substance in the European mind and led to stereotyping: the proud Indian defender of freedom, and the humble African born for slavery. Davis suggests that this led to an aversion against taking Indians into slavery.[4] This particular argument seems ill considered since among the major Indian tribes, the Cherokee, Choctaw, Creek, Chickasaw and Seminole all kept slaves running into thousands, and when they were moved to the Indian territory west of the Mississippi in the 1830s and '40s they took their slaving customs with them. Indians were not infrequently hired to track and catch runaway African slaves, although the attitude of the tribes to bondage was somewhat different from that of the European colonists. Slaves of Indian masters were regularly permitted to carry weapons, own a horse and possess other personal property. The Seminole adopted a particularly sympathetic view of fugitive Africans and occasionally took them in as 'property' to protect them from other slave-catchers. Nevertheless the vague idea that developed among romantics that the Indian was a defender of freedom amounts to wishful thinking.[5]

Trendier, modern anthropologists have even described the arrival of Europeans in America as 'a meeting of cultures'. It was nothing of the sort, unless 'cultural exchange' can be interpreted as a euphemism for slaughter and degradation.

True, there was a genuine difference in temperament between Indians and Africans. Once enslaved, the African was no more trustworthy but, unlike the Indian, would work all day under a hot sun, providing that the lash was kept dangling somewhere in his range of vision. As a French West Indian proverb ran, 'To look askance at an Indian is to beat him; to beat him is to kill him; to beat a Negro is to nourish him.'[6] In practical reality, however, the European colonial slave-owner is unlikely to have given much thought to such niceties. Any character distinctions based on ethics are largely 'pie-in-the-sky' since the American Indian was no more or less averse to intertribal raiding and slave-taking than his African counterpart. Nor, it seems to me, is there any substantive evidence that stereotypical images grew in the European mind, since the two ethnic groups were exploited and mistreated to an equal degree, though not perhaps in the same way.

Davis, nonetheless, continues to argue the case for a moral distinction in our view of African against Indian slaves, pointing out that Europeans invaded the territory of America by force of arms, while in the African scenario we kept our presence to a series of shoreline trading posts. This explanation seems equally lacking in conviction. European Christians tended to regard aboriginals of whatever colour and ethnic background as deserving of servitude, whether their territory was invaded or not, on the grounds that they were pagans and not brothers in Christ. Closer to the truth about the preference for Africans, as Davis concedes elsewhere, is the fact that selective slave-taking in the lands where you lived carried considerably more risk than if the source was many thousands of miles away across an ocean. African war-parties were unlikely to sail the Atlantic in rescue missions, whereas Indian tribes might well feel inclined to take an opportunistic poke at the white man on their doorstep for having carried off sons and daughters into bondage.

There is greater truth in the idea that the 'prepackaged' African presented a more convenient purchase to the European trading system. This was so even before he left the Guinea coast. He was already shackled and partly broken-in by the tribes, largely the Ashantis and Dahomeys who dominated the business in West Africa. By the time he had endured his shipboard spell through the infamous Atlantic middle passage, if indeed he was fortunate enough to survive it, debilitation and intimidation had served to complete the process of making him docile and manageable. Enslavement of the American Indian, on the other hand, involved a process that was often messy and always a risk to the health and safety of Europeans. When faced with work down a mine or on a plantation, the Indian was rarely keen for compliance and constantly sought the opportunity to break loose and flee to the woods and home. Such a way of escape was not readily available to the West African, newly arrived on shores thousands of miles distant from his own. But as for the notion that the white man felt any moral obligation to treat the American Indian differently, history proves this to be a risky assumption.

The nub of why Africans became the preferred choice of slave-owners in the Americas, however, probably rests in the oft-voiced and concise Spanish view that, even if local labour had remained available, one African was worth four Indians.[7] The reasons for Africans becoming the prime source of slave labour over American Indians can be summed up fairly simply. The American Indian, by and large, tended to be aggressive and a poor worker. The African might be resentful of his lot but was willing to work hard provided that he was kept suitably close to the threat of physical violence. Indian labour came to be in seriously short supply, could only be taken with risk and, once captured, demonstrated an abysmal attitude to work. The supply of Africans, on the other hand, was inexhaustible and soon became not only well organised but also an extremely lucrative business for those who engaged in the slave trade.

Irrespective of the finer points of ethnicity, the demand for slave labour in the American colonies arose, first and foremost, as a product of the spirit of enterprise that had gripped its immigrant pioneers. It is not always made clear in the investigation of slavery that had it not been for the imperial expansion of Europe into the New World the African trade would never have developed. The peculiar conditions of the one determined the demand for the other and the two have always been inextricably linked. In short, slavery became a necessity of colonial business operations. Europeans saw the promise of unlimited profit in a vast country that possessed potential in all but manpower; but the kind of labour needed and the conditions under which it would operate did not generally suit Europeans.

In the seventeenth century a not-dissimilar story was to unfold when European colonisers opened their tobacco plantations in the Chesapeake, the Atlantic coast region bordering on Maryland and Virginia. As the wider spread of settlers arrived on the American mainland, Amerindians would also find themselves toiling on agricultural plantations in Virginia and the Carolinas. But here, too, they were regarded as poor, unreliable workers and their employment was rarely popular with the settlers.[8] The era of their enslavement may have been limited but this is not to say that it disappeared completely and sometimes it persisted in a small and localised sense. As recently as 1741, Jamaican legislation was enacted to curb the importation of Amerindian slaves and to make it an offence not to release any that had been taken illegally. Only in parts of Canada, however, employing Pawnee brought in from remote parts of the territory by tribal war-parties, did Indian slavery operate with a degree of success, although never in integration with that of Africans.

Once the use of local workers proved untenable the immediate recourse was to summon labour from home in the form of indentured Europeans or 'poor whites' as they came to be known. These were often people either seeking a way out of poverty or considered by the home authorities to be troublemakers. The exercise was not particularly satisfactory, as the immigrant labour force, destitute, felonious or otherwise, was frequently unwilling to endure sweated toil for very long. The conditions under which they worked were virtually indistinguishable from those of slave labour and they also earned the tag of 'white slaves'. Their loss of liberty was for a limited duration, however, and therefore they tended to head smartly for the first available ship home, once their seven-year term of indenture was over. In the first half of the seventeenth century the plantations on the Caribbean islands were also being developed apace, but work on them proved no more attractive for impoverished Europeans, once the harsh realities began to sink in of having signed indenture papers in order to buy a passage to the new colonial lands of opportunity. Once again, large-scale reliance came to be placed on forcibly recruiting the black African to the slave-owning plantations rather than the indigenous American.

The Portuguese may have been the pioneers but the breakdown of their alliance with Spain opened up opportunities to other nations keen for a slice of the African cake, and almost immediately the Dutch took an interest, ending the Portuguese monopoly. They possessed a substantial fleet of merchant ships and in the fifteenth century had developed good contacts on the West African coast. They also exercised virtually no colonial interest in the Americas and so were ideally placed to become slave-suppliers. The Dutch, however, were unable to control the situation for very long and, as time passed, power ebbed and flowed between various nations, with trading companies coming and going.

Although Britain was finally to dominate the slave trade through her superior maritime capacity and colonial acquisitions, she represented a late entry to the market place. Up to the mid-sixteenth century, English ships visiting the Guinea coast did not deal to any measurable extent in slaves nor did they sail on to the Americas. The traffic remained with the Portuguese, the Dutch and, as comparatively late arrivals themselves, the French. England's insertion into the chronicle of Afro-American slavery came, albeit in a somewhat unorthodox fashion, in the autumn of 1562, through the enterprise of the buccaneering adventurer John Hawkins.

Caring little for Portuguese monopoly and the legality of the 1493 papal bull, Hawkins masterminded a raiding exercise in which he first attempted to hijack slaves from Cape Verde, the spit of land that pokes out like a nipple as the westernmost point of Africa, in modern Senegal. When these tactics proved unproductive he supplied mercenaries to a local African chief, who employed them to attack a neighbour, providing Hawkins with captives by way of compensation. For the rest of his cargo he negotiated with less-than-scrupulous Portuguese dealers. Having transported the Africans across the Atlantic and sold them to Spanish colonists in the West Indies, Hawkins returned to England with a cargo of gold, silver, pearls and sugar. He was then foolish enough to carry part of this valuable freight on to Seville for sale, where it was promptly confiscated by the Spanish authorities. Queen Elizabeth I, no lover of Spain, was less than amused and by way of answer extended her royal patronage to Hawkins. Two years later, to facilitate another, more-successful trip, she lent him one of her own merchant ships and an escort of armed cruisers. Hawkins eventually made a third excursion between 1567 and 1569 in company with Sir Francis Drake, but by that time the Spanish had the measure of his activities and engaged his flotilla in a vicious battle off San Juan de Ulloa in Hispaniola. The incident led to a further souring of Anglo-Spanish relations and the curtailing of Hawkins's commercial activities.[9] Ultimately England's interest in plundering Spanish settlements in the Caribbean led to twenty years of war with Spain between 1585 and 1604 and the accumulation of prize money amounting to anything from £100,000 to £200,000 a year. The English Crown did not overtly support these hit-and-run tactics in the Caribbean, but discreet financial investments in such enterprises were not hard to come by.

English involvement in the trade stayed at an entry level until the establishment of the first of her Caribbean colonies when the Virginia Company expanded into Bermuda in 1612. The island was rapidly carved up into tobacco plantations on which the owners began experimental use of indentured labour. This was but the start of a process of land acquisition and when the Virginia Company went into the receivership of the English Crown in 1624, covetous English eyes settled on the Caribbean islands of the Lesser Antilles as places for permanent settlement. These specks of land were made attractive because the Spanish, who still dominated the region, had not been able to exploit them for precious metals and therefore omitted to defend them. The island of St Kitts effectively became English real estate in the same year, followed by Barbados in 1627, Nevis in 1628 and Montserrat and Antigua in 1632. By 1640 English entrepreneurs had begun to dominate the Caribbean, and colonial authority was further cemented in 1656 when, under the authority of Oliver Cromwell, Jamaica was removed from Spanish control.

It was the demands of the Caribbean islands of the West Indies that determined the extent of British involvement in the slave trade because the mainstay business at the American end of the triangle was no longer to be extraction of minerals, but an insatiable demand for another commodity virtually unknown in Europe before the Middle Ages. By the turn of the eighteenth century, to all intents and purposes, the islands had become an extension of the British Empire, occupying a very special place in the economic prosperity of the nation, and it was the growth of British sugar plantations, more than any other factor, which fuelled involvement in the slave trade, raising the statistics of displaced lives from thousands to millions. Incidentally, the use of the terms 'English' and 'British' may seem confusing and is often loosely applied. James I of England, also James VI of Scotland, coined the terms 'Great Britain' and 'British' so as to bring home to his disparate subjects that a constitutional change had taken place in 1603 with the Union of Crowns and the formation of a multiple kingdom. The name 'Great Britain' had no substance in history but became gradually accepted to represent the peoples of the three kingdoms, England, Scotland and Ireland, plus the principality of Wales.[10]

Cultivation of sugar cane had begun in the Mediterranean basin sometime around the mid-fourteenth century. After this, small-scale plantation schemes, little more than pilot projects using forced African labour, were established in some of the islands off the West African coast, including Madeira, the Canaries and the Portuguese possession of São Tomé. On the other side of the Atlantic the Portuguese had discovered that the Brazils also offered suitable climatic conditions and there they experimented with the first major growing and harvesting of sugar in the Americas. English attention, however, was focusing on the West Indies.

For a time the Caribbean islands had produced limited amounts of another cash crop. Mid-seventeenth-century Barbadians saw the first slave-operated plantation cultivating and exporting cotton, but interest among the islands' new landowners was of short duration. The extensive demand for labour on cotton plantations came at a later date and centred on the American mainland, chiefly after the 1793 introduction of Eli Whitney's cotton gin, which facilitated the separation of cotton lint and seeds and made cotton cultivation commercially viable. From the outset the West Indies offered ideal conditions for sugar planting and growing. The crop was comparatively straightforward to maintain, and more or less limitless demand for the refined product in Europe offered the potential for vast profits. There was but one obstacle. Sugar cane cultivation and harvesting were physically demanding and required very large amounts of labour under tropical conditions. The planters were reliant, therefore, on securing a resilient labour force capable of handling long hours of energy-sapping toil beneath a hot sun. Amerindian labour, largely unavailable because the Lesser Antilles possessed only small indigenous populations, was already proving problematic, since the Callinago, or 'Caribs', were resistant to being worked by the immigrants. Thus, as a first recourse, European labourers were enticed to come and provide their services on the Caribbean sugar plantations.

The English government was at pains to promote the West Indies as a favoured destination for moneyed classes and paupers alike. From about 1628 onward, English entrepreneurs, lured by the prospect of quick-fix profits tinged with romance and excitement, were settling the Caribbean apace and the economic importance of the islands to the home country began to outstrip that of mainland North America. By 1660 the population of émigrés reached 47,000, by which time, as the historian A.E. Smith put it succinctly, the American colonies as a whole had become 'a haven for the godly, a refuge for the oppressed, a challenge to the adventurous and the last resort of scoundrels'.[11] At first the policy worked reasonably well. Shipping out British indentured labourers underpinned a healthy colonial dependence on 'Mother England' and also provided an excuse to get rid of nuisances to society. Uprooting to the Americas, however, either to purchase plantation acres or, for those less desirable or well heeled, to take up the indentured service, was leaving Britain dangerously underpopulated. The theory of mercantilism, in vogue with the economists of the time and which we shall come to in more detail later, included an argument that the potential for commercial and agricultural expansion lay in having the largest-possible workforce. This point of view was as much relevant at home, however, as it was in the colonies. Some kind of anti-emigration policy therefore demanded urgent attention. Britain needed to keep its brawn at home, yet the burgeoning American plantations also continued to demand supplies of manpower. To redress the balance, and not without an eye to commercial gain, Charles II sponsored the foundation, in 1660, of the Company of Royal Adventurers of England for carrying on a Trade to Africa.

The business transacted between the three essential points of commercial exchange, England, Africa and America, became known as the Atlantic Triangle; but how did it operate? We could effectively dip in at any of the points on the triangle but it seems logical to begin at the English ports. Here the ships destined for the West African coast were loaded with goods to barter with local dealers, mainly cloths, pots and pans, trinkets and, of course, firearms. The ships' masters also carried cash for the hiring of mercenaries, sometimes necessary to the effective capture of more slaves. Formerly the Dutch had supplied textiles to Africa, and from 1677 their patterns were copied in England. We began to export home-produced woollen goods. These, however, were hardly going to be popular purchases in tropical climates and English merchants probably re-exported far more of the products arriving from the East India possessions, including lighter-weight textiles as well as the cowrie shells that frequently served as currency in West Africa.

On arrival at the trading stations off the Guinea coast, the ships exchanged their cargoes for slaves, gold, spices, hides and wax. Except for slaves these items represented a comparatively minor contribution to the English economy. Even the gold supplied to the Royal Mint by the Royal African Company, successor to the Company of Royal Adventurers, and cast into elephant-headed 'guineas' amounted to only about 7 per cent of the total metal turned into coinage. What mattered in commercial terms was the shipment of human cargo destined for the American colonies. Those 'passengers' that survived the middle passage across the Atlantic were sold to the plantation owners in return for consignments of coffee, tobacco, cotton fibre, and most notably, sugar, destined to be carried on the third leg of the triangle to England for manufacture.

The 1660 sponsorship of the Company of Royal Adventurers of England was not the first occasion on which royal dispensations had been granted for African trading. In 1618 James I issued a charter to 'Sir Robert Rich and other citizens of London' authorising them to raise joint stock for the purpose of trading to Africa, and in 1651 Charles I granted this original company exclusive charter rights, exclusions, prohibitions and penalties. Such early commercial ventures in Africa were not without drawbacks. From the outset, independent traders, so-called 'interlopers', broke into the business, running clandestine operations off the Guinea coast and, in addition, the company-leased ships suffered frequent mauling from opportunist Dutch and Danish raiders that seized vessels and cargoes.

The founders of the Royal African Company, as the Company of Royal Adventurers came to be known, responded in 1661 by establishing on James Island in the Gambia the first of a series of fortified English trading posts that would eventually stretch down almost the length of the west coast. With a desire to give the company more-effective legal status Charles II provided it with a stronger 'exclusive' charter the following year. This extended monopoly rights for 1,000 years and, although it specifically authorised the company to supply Guinea gold to the English treasury (hence the name of the gold coin), its charter terms also encompassed slave marketing. Since the company's foundation was coincidental with the beginnings of serious settlement in colonial British America, its owners not surprisingly came under pressure to meet demand for human cargoes. Although their main business remained in the bullion market, supplying enough gold dust to mint between 30,000 and 50,000 guineas at a time, they also undertook a yearly supply of 3,000 slaves to the West Indies and when, in 1663, the enterprise was rechartered, it was with the incorporation of slave trading. At first African slaves were marketed at anything from £14 to £22 a head, but within ten years demand was so great that the supply had soared by 200 per cent and the average price had fallen by a third.

The Dutch did not take this intrusion lying down. They were already smarting from a conflict that had boiled over between 1652 and 1654 when the English took them on in the Caribbean, mauling the colonial settlements of the Dutch West India Company. A catalogue of West African skirmishes led to a second Anglo-Dutch war, declared in 1665, when the Dutch admiral de Ruyter was sent to the Gold Coast with a squadron of thirteen warships. He succeeded in seizing ships and goods owned by the Royal African Company and in capturing most of the stations that the English then controlled, including a vital fortified base at Cormantine. With a loss of assets calculated at upwards of £200,000 (just under £8 million in today's value) the company was looking financial disaster squarely in the face and it all but ceased to trade after 1665. It was replaced by a new administration in 1672 and this later organisation, formed only after the fresh raising of joint stock, was also granted its charter by Charles II. Although still dealing substantially in gold, it was set up with greater emphasis on trading in slaves and it raised the supply level to 6,500 a year in order to meet the burgeoning needs of the West Indian and Virginian sugar and tobacco planters. Its foundation contributed to the start of a third round of hostilities with Holland, after which Dutch involvement in West African slavery declined sharply, although they retained a dominant slice of interest in the gold trade.

Experiencing similar problems to its predecessors, the latest Royal African Company found its business regularly undermined by the activity of 'interlopers', including French privateers eager to join what was fast becoming a maritime trade free-for-all. The Royal African Company shareholders controlled a fleet of some seventy merchant ships but against this, records collected between 1679 and 1682 indicate that not less than thirty-two privately run English-registered vessels were also obtaining slaves from the Guinea coast and shipping them to the West Indies. The 'interlopers' were operating with a motley assortment of vessels – privateers, ex-navy ships of the line, cargo boats owned by Quakers, even colliers. They sailed from several major ports outside London, including Bristol and subsequently Liverpool, and from small, provincial harbours around the English coastline, such as Topsham, at the head of the Exe estuary near Exeter and Lyme Regis in Dorset.

During the Anglo-French war that erupted in 1689, in which some of the hostilities took place in African waters, about a quarter of the English company's authorised ships were seized, thus adding to its woes. The company was also weakened politically by the overthrow of James II and his replacement by Mary and William of Orange in the so-called 'Glorious Revolution' of 1688. This negation of Catholic supremacy brought about the framing of the Bill of Rights, curtailing the royal prerogative and ensuring that the monarch ruled according to the law. The legality of the Royal African Company's monopolistic trading position was immediately placed in some doubt and this spurred the energies of the interlopers. By the 1690s the company had been rendered virtually insolvent and in 1697 its monopoly was officially revoked by parliament, which laid trading doors open for the next thirteen years. The company presented a case for relief but critics had argued successfully that freeing up the West African business would encourage the discovery of new trading outlets, which would in turn stimulate the market. The government took the same view, though, by way of compensation, a levy was then imposed on the flurry of independent slave traders. A levy of 10 per cent was charged on the value of outgoing cargoes to West Africa and passed back to the Royal African Company to defray charges on the fortified factories it owned, deemed by the government to be essential for the ongoing defence and preservation of the trade. The duty earned the freelancers the nickname of 'Ten Percenters'.[12]

According to the contemporary political commentator Charles Davenant, the freeing-up of the trade, not surprisingly, brought howls of condemnation from both sides. The Royal African Company regularly subjected the independent operators to verbal attack, accusing them of non-existent accounting methods and a plethora of other unacceptable practices. These included the random seizure and theft of natives, ivory and other goods that happened to fall conveniently within reach. It was reported that the interlopers were not averse to walking away without making payment for goods taken or to offering the redemption of captives 'of distinguishing character', in other words those that might be worth ransom, at an exorbitant exchange rate of three to one. The independents responded with their own list of complaints. The Royal African Company, they suggested, obstructed the sale of English manufactured goods, prevented more seamen and ships being gainfully employed, advanced the interests of other nations by their limited enterprise, fixed prices and further hindered discovery of new sources of trade. Such was the pressure on the company that in 1707 the shareholders addressed a new petition, this time to Queen Anne, that she might represent their case for relief to parliament. The petition was referred to the Commissioners for Trade and Plantations but was again set aside as being unrealistic.[13]

Relaxation of the Royal African Company's monopoly undoubtedly brought an increase in the number of natives shipped, although the figures were immediately a subject of dispute. In 1708 independent traders claimed to be transporting some 25,000 adults a year to the West Indies. However, based on their known earnings from the sale of manufactured goods to Africa, averaging a maximum of £34,000 over several years, and the likely cost of purchasing slaves in the order of £8 per head at the cheapest, Davenant calculated that the true figure of freelance turnover was nearer 4,235 and the remaining 20,675 represented a fiction, unless the cargoes had 'dropped from the clouds'. Nonetheless the ensuing commercial rat race resulted in progressively worsening conditions as more captives were packed into each vessel in order that operators might remain competitive. Some estimates have suggested that the Ten Percenters were shipping three-quarters of the slaves imported into the Anglo-American colonies by 1708, yet the fact that the ships' masters kept scant records of business activities makes this impossible to verify. It also means that unpalatable details of disease, overcrowding, inhumane treatment and mortality rates during the middle passage were also kept largely hidden.[14]

It was, therefore, the peculiarly labour-intensive needs and massive cash potential in the cultivation of sugar, tobacco and, at a later date, cotton in the Americas that fuelled three centuries of demand for African slaves. For England the richest prize that they produced was sugar. As Adam Smith was to comment, 'The profits of sugar plantation in any of our West Indian colonies are generally much greater than those of any other cultivation that is known either in Europe or America.' And so it was, although the cultivation of tobacco came a close second. It is interesting to draw comparison with the profitability of corn, the staple crop of the early Quaker farmers in Pennsylvania. Adam Smith also made the observation that 'planting of sugar and tobacco can afford the expense of slave cultivation. The raising of corn, it seems, in the present times, cannot.'[15] Corn cultivation was less demanding of heavy manual labour but also yielded far slimmer profit margins. For this reason it appears that the Quakers had no problem in eventually liberating their slaves on the American mainland, since the numbers they employed were too small to make an appreciable difference to assets or management. The very limited interest in slave labour for corn farming provides one of the first clues that economics lay at the heart of the abolition issue when it eventually arose. In the mid-seventeenth century, however, mercantile arguments had reached a consensus that commercial success in growing and harvesting sugar cane, tobacco and cotton lay with the use of slave labour in one form or another, supported by monopolisation and the introduction of selective import tariffs. It was to be the dismissal of mercantile arguments that had held sway through much of the Tudor period and beyond, a change for which Adam Smith may claim a degree of credit, that would also bring a shift of sentiment about the value of slavery in the economic system of the European empire-builders and, ultimately, lead to its demise.

Chapter 3

BRITISH RESISTANCE

Thus far we have followed an outline of how and why internationally the Afro-Caribbean slave trade developed, but none of this yet begins to explain British resistance to its abolition. A wide range of conflicting factors came into play and made the institution hard to dispose of both politically and, until arguments swung in another direction, economically. Authors who claim that the decisive outcome in the first half of the nineteenth century is to be explained by a single overriding consideration, be it religious, ethical or economic, perhaps miss the point that many elements all bore upon and affected each other. A tangle of circumstances both encouraged and hampered the progress of the slavery debate.

To begin with, it is not always made clear that there existed a direct and fundamental correlation between the attitudes of the people in Britain towards slavery and their deep-rooted sense of being 'British'. This sense of national 'character' was also firmly embedded in the psyche of the expatriate colonists, though the authorities at home took a somewhat different view of their position. The essence of 'Britishness' had been distilled from an assortment of elements that, it was believed, set Britain aside from the other imperial powers in Europe. Being British included pride in being a member of the largest empire to have stepped onto the world stage since that of the Romans and, unwittingly, we emulated the Romans a little too closely. Slavery underpinned the British Empire but also risked becoming its Achilles' Heel.

The slavery debate that unfolded, generally tedious, occasionally passionate and frequently acrimonious, was as much steered by a sense of national identity and imperial pride, by strategic considerations and issues of economic security, as by any humanitarian or ethical arguments. Of one aspect we can be fairly sure, however. Throughout the seventeenth and eighteenth centuries the British Empire and British mercantile trade overseas distilled the ethos of 'Rule Britannia'. These institutions made the nation 'great' in the world and provided her wealth. They were also the inseparable, if at times uneasy, bedfellows of slavery and slave-taking. In simple terms it was all a matter of guarantees. The

British imperial status quo owed its security to an immense and much-vaunted naval force. The money that greased the wheels of both empire and its enforcement was secured by an international trade system known as mercantilism, the smooth running of which was then ensured by imposition of selective trade tariffs. These in turn created monopolies and at the hub of the entire trade network, underpinning all, was assembled a massive force of slave labour in the West Indies.

Although the elements of imperialism, military strength and mercantile trade were all deeply interwoven, they can be considered one by one. England was never a particularly aggressive empire-builder, and when she did acquire her overseas possessions it was to be chiefly for strategic and economic reasons. From the time of Henry VII, England toyed, though was not necessarily busy, with this objective. The Tudors and Elizabethans had been fairly non-committal about adopting a policy of takeover comparable to that of the Spanish, although it is true that explorers such as John Cabot and Walter Raleigh had been given dispensation by their monarchs to 'conquer and possess' lands not in Christian hands as they saw fit.[1] Henry VIII and his daughter Elizabeth, having rid themselves of papal rule, certainly demonstrated no particular keenness for expansion. In the sixteenth and as late as the seventeenth century, therefore, the term 'empire' did not mean a great deal to the man in the street and scarcely more to the Crown. It is fair to say that Henry VIII savoured and promoted the imperial tag, having broken trust with Rome, but more to broadcast the independence of England from other states and, in particular, from papal interference in her sovereign affairs. Even when the Union of Crowns, bringing England and Scotland together under one monarch, came about in 1603 under James I (a partnership distinct from the full Act of Union that took place in 1707) it still did not trigger an overt wish to proclaim imperial control over hitherto foreign territories and the trade routes that linked them. One suggestion to explain the reluctance of England to make proprietorial claims when it came to early transatlantic policy lies in the comparative paucity of riches among the peoples whom the English encountered in North America compared with the Spanish experience in Central and South America.[2] England, therefore, tended to be more interested in settlement and commerce and less in outright ownership. The meaning of the terms colonisation and plantation quickly became synonymous, amounting to the exploitation of natural resources wherever settlement took place.

Colonisation had begun in Ireland and Scotland in the first half of the seventeenth century and this provided a degree of experience before spreading to more-distant parts. Roughly at the beginning of the seventeenth century, some of the London merchant houses started to look seriously at the business potential of America and, to a lesser extent, Asia. This interest had been stimulated initially by the writings of Richard Hakluyt, born in around 1553. He argued for the establishment of an English colony in Virginia and his most significant work, *The Principal Navigations, Voyages, Traffics and Discoveries of the English Nation*, published between 1598 and 1600, became widely respected. Investment in new companies with eyes on overseas potential thus kick-started a process of expansion. The focus was chiefly on America and for this, essentially, there were two other reasons aside from Hakluyt's enthusiasm. Protestantism aspired to thumb its nose at Catholic Spain, already far too well represented in the Americas for anyone's good other than that of Catholic Spain. There was also the more altruistic wish to 'bring the true religion to the native'. Enlightenment about the Christian faith was preferable to the horror of less-fortunate fellow men being left to rot in the dark embrace of heathen idols. How we actually exported God to foreign parts did not really matter so long as we did so, and this ambition to proselytise and save the savage soul would play its minor part in the slavery debate, albeit perversely and with a distinct whiff of hypocrisy.

Settlement in Asia was to be a more reluctant affair, held in check to no small extent by the arguments of commentators such as Thomas Bowdler in the 1630s that all excursions to the Orient resulted in high loss of life and were therefore undesirable.[3] British colonial interest in the East remained limited for a long time after the Portuguese navigator Vasco da Gama sailed around the hazardous Cape of Good Hope in 1498 and discovered a sea-route to the subcontinent of India. There had been half-hearted attempts to expand trading contact with the East Indies (a name which, at the time, encompassed the whole of South East Asia and India) from about the 1580s but the East India Company was not incorporated until 1600 and then only came in response to worries about commercial rivalry from the Dutch. During the ensuing decades the East India Company developed a commercial traffic to and from the Orient and, in doing so, it gradually assumed quasi-governmental powers in India and points of landfall further into Asia. During the seventeenth century the East India Company took control of three settlements – Bombay, Madras and Calcutta – and, over the course of time, these grew into the major British bases in India. But it was not until the nineteenth century that conquest in the subcontinent changed the British position there to any great extent. By 1815, Britain, still operating through the East India Company, had taken control of more or less all of eastern India, most of the peninsula and a large part of the Ganges valley.[4] Slave trading and slavery had become major components of the economy of the Indian Ocean countries, but here Britain adopted a somewhat hypocritical lack of interest when it came to abolition. She was not responsible for slave trading or enslavement in this region of the world, since Indian and Arab entrepreneurs carried on both. She could therefore reap the benefits of the slave system while claiming to be detached.

The lands of opportunity westward across the Atlantic were, at any rate in theory, more attractive and less dangerous than those in the Orient. So English settlement beyond the shores of the British Isles saw its debut in Virginia and Bermuda, following much the same practice that had evolved in Ulster. This did not always work, of course, because the early colonists discovered that their American landfalls were rife with virulent diseases that Bowdler and colleagues had omitted to mention, and that major environmental differences negated at least some of the practical methods that had proved effective closer to home. The acquisition that England chiefly coveted, nonetheless, was the prize of the West Indies. The islands in the Caribbean were seen as an essential gain on economic grounds and were viewed with only one clear objective, that of making money. So, in spite of minor setbacks, from the 1600s, the twin concepts of a transatlantic colonial empire and lucrative commercial takings enjoyed a happy marriage that would continue until the early part of the nineteenth century.

The needs of mercantilism provided a convenient excuse for whatever colonial misbehaviour took place in ousting, subjugating, shackling and periodically murdering indigenous populations. The first tenuous defence had been that colonists were also spreading the Christian message. By the time of the post-Cromwellian Restoration, however, the explanation about Christian (and Protestant) enlightenment had not gone away but it had been largely overtaken by more secular justification. Britain decided that she did not actually need to explain away her predation in the Americas with God as an excuse, and that the promise of cash benefits would do just as nicely. The subjugation of foreign territories formerly enjoyed by European rivals, most notably the French and the Spanish, was seen to possess long-term strategic and economic benefits. What was not taken by force could be negotiated into British hands through treaty and transfer. The Treaty of Utrecht, signed in 1713 to end the War of the Spanish Succession in North America, marked a turning point in the adoption of this strategy. British negotiators demanded and won massive concessions from the French, including the colonies of Nova Scotia, Hudson Bay and Newfoundland and the French half of the island of St Kitts. They also took over the lucrative *asiento* contract to supply slaves to Spanish America. This 'consent' resulted in the British acquiring total dominance over the West African slave trade to the Americas. The rationale that colonial seizure was of economic advantage to the British people had not been seriously promoted hitherto, but now it came to the fore and left the defence of spiritual enlightenment looking distinctly passé.

The British Empire thus came into being by varying degrees throughout the sixteenth and seventeenth centuries, although it would not receive its name formally until the Act of Union in 1707 that brought together England and Scotland. During that time it was largely an empire concentrated in the western hemisphere but, even so, by the eighteenth century the control of territory far beyond Britain's shores had reached such impressive dimensions that it proclaimed her position as the worldwide imperial power par excellence. To be British, therefore, was also to be part of the engine of an empire that had reached the top of the world order. Having fallen into disuse after the retreat of the Romans in ancient times, the name 'Great Britain' gained popularity under these heady circumstances and came to represent the spirit of the people. The title was applied formally to England, Wales and Scotland after the Union of Crowns in 1603. It was carried on by order of James I who believed that it would serve as a cohesive influence, moving his diverse subjects to a sense of belonging to a new multiple and powerful kingdom. In reality the expression had been in vogue for some time before that to distinguish this island from Britannia Minor, or Brittany in France, and also, perhaps, to emphasise national independence, not least from the pope. The poem 'Rule Britannia' summed up all the patriotic and insular emotions of the age. Penned by James Thomson (1700–48) and set to music by Thomas Augustine Arne in around 1740 it is still trundled out lustily on the last night of the Promenade Concerts in the Albert Hall, although today it amounts to no more than a bit of light-hearted jingoism and a dimming remembrance of past glories. In the eighteenth century, however, when a new sense of British national identity was blossoming, the words rang out with a far more vivid and immediate reality. 'Rule Britannia! Britannia rule the waves!'

At least this was the way the situation looked in the heady nationalist fervour of the age and it brings us to the matter of British military strength and its effectiveness in guaranteeing security. Beneath the veneer of prowess and invincibility, all was not well. In spite of her global dominance, by the time that the abolition debate got under way, Britain had become increasingly unstable and strategically vulnerable. Hers was not the only imperial presence in Europe. Powerful and envious neighbours, most notably France and to a lesser extent Spain, posed a constant threat. Since the 1650s Britain's answer to security at home and abroad had lain in control of the high seas, because as an island nation she had learned certain hard lessons. Since the time of Roman occupation the unwelcome experience of successive conquests across the divides of the English Channel and the North Sea by an assortment of European adversaries had taught the value of building a strong and protective maritime force. This naval strength was put to the test convincingly when Philip II of Spain ordered a fleet of 130 ships to invade England in 1588 on the excuse that he had received divine authority to launch a crusade against Protestantism. God, so history records, settled on the side of the English in the decisive sea battle at Gravelines and from that point in time 'Britannia' could indeed lay claim to ruling the waves. Having built and maintained a supreme naval force, successive English and British monarchs used it effectively in the acquisition of colonial territories. But once an empire is constructed, the builder is then faced with the task of keeping the ramparts intact. In spite of impressive size and formidable reputation, the English navy found that it could not meet all the demands placed upon it and so its role became increasingly defensive. The navy was committed to policing both sides of the Atlantic. Its men-of-war were required to keep American possessions safe from acquisitive hands and at the same time to ensure that English trading interests were kept happy on the west coast of Africa. This was no easy job. The Dutch, already there and well established, were running a lucrative slave-trading operation and when it became English policy to oust them from this position through the establishment of successive Royal African Companies, valuable sections of the English fleet were engaged in protracted skirmishes. These took place both with the Dutch and with privateers throughout the 1600s in order to safeguard slave-trading interests.

Not only was the English navy required to guard positions thousands of miles away from home shores on both sides of the Atlantic, but from 1700 onwards, the country was also faced with a formidable military force just a few miles across the English Channel. The French army was destined to become the largest in Christendom and it was with this mighty adversary that Britain became engaged in protracted conflict from the end of the seventeenth century until the early decades of the nineteenth. In practice the threat from France meant that the bulk of the British armed forces was needed at home for defence against invasion from Europe and not for securing, much less gaining, colonies in far-flung parts.

During the eighteenth century, however, distant military commitment was precisely what the country faced. Britain's armed forces overseas became severely stretched through involvement in a sapping succession of wars, most of them waged in the American theatre. She experienced military gains and losses on one front or another for more than sixty years and this amounted to a massive burden on her resources. The War of the Spanish Succession, popularly tagged 'Queen Anne's War' and waged from 1702 to 1713, affected the British colonies and British business across the Atlantic. The conflict had been triggered through the ambitions of Louis XIV to increase French hegemony over Europe. After the Spanish King Charles II had died without an heir, Louis proposed a Bourbon successor to the Spanish throne in the shape of his grandson Philip V. Britain, along with the Dutch, the Holy Roman Emperor and most of the German states, saw this union-in-the-making as a major potential threat to their national securities. Their recourse when it was ratified was to commence hostilities.

In the compact between France and Spain, two powerful European kingdoms, France played the dominant role, and this posed a number of possibilities, few of which were music to the ears of the British. With the French taking the upper hand, the likelihood increased that she would attempt to expand her colonial interest over the Spanish West Indies. This, in turn, would generate revenue to help tip the balance of power in Europe still further to the benefit of the French. Anticipating trouble from each other, both Britain and France promptly dispatched large naval contingents to the West Indies and the opposing forces became enmeshed in spasmodic, though never-decisive skirmishes for control of Caribbean territory.

In 1739 Britain found herself at war again and her adversary was Spain. This time the quarrel revolved around colonial issues in the Americas. Relations between the two countries were already strained because of differences of opinion over the legitimacy or otherwise of British trade with Spanish assets in the Caribbean, and along imperial borders each side was sabre-rattling. As early as 1721 a Board of Trade report had identified the British possession of South Carolina to be vulnerable to military pressure from neighbouring Spanish-controlled Florida. The Prime Minister, Sir Robert Walpole, adopted a cautious position. He was against embarking on another round of hostilities, fearing the long-term consequences. If the British forces lost, it would be disastrous but, equally, if they crushed the Spanish-American Empire, the balance of power in Europe would be dangerously upset. Walpole's political opponents scented opportunity for strategic gains, however, and by October, fighting had broken out. The war was a failure for Britain.

In spite of her own setbacks, France did not lie down meekly following the Treaty of Utrecht and the threat from across the Channel constantly menaced British security. The next round of eighteenth-century hostilities involved the French and became known as the Seven Years War, from 1756 to 1763. Once more, the cause of conflict lay across the Atlantic. Britain was faced with the urgent need to secure her colonies in the north against French incursions taking place along the Canadian coastline. Britain was to emerge victorious from what turned into a full-scale and very messy war, but the triumph was short-lived. She may have secured her Canadian possession but shortly afterwards was destined to lose the rest of her mainland colonies in the American War of Independence that raged between 1775 and 1783.

Within ten years of British forces returning bloodied and defeated from North America, yet another threatening situation was to unfold. The parlous situation in Revolutionary France from 1793 to 1802, and the fight against Napoleon from 1803 to 1815, simply compounded the feeling that Britain and her imperial possessions were vulnerable from all sides, and the latest experience, too close to home shores for comfort, exerted a major influence on the attitudes of British people. When the prospect of a French Revolution headed by the proletariat loomed large on the horizon, the British moneyed classes became fearful of similar social unrest and bloodshed, and therefore realised that change in the way society was run needed to be addressed.

The first rumblings of a new humanitarian movement can technically be detected in Britain from the start of the eighteenth century, in the reigns of William III and Anne. Quaker workhouses provided at least a glimmer of social reform and informed voices had begun to comment on the dire conditions in the prison system. But none of this did more than scratch at the surface of human deprivation, nor did it alter the balance of power away from the hereditary elite. Such changes still lay some way in the future.

By the time the century was drawing to its close, however, the mood was stronger, though not harmonious. On one side of the coin the landowning and intellectual 'blue stockings' saw a danger in giving the lower orders too much licence. On the other a number of affluent intellectuals, including such notable socialites as Miss Hannah More, playwright and darling of the dinner-party circuit, became quickly converted to the notion that a reformed life of good works would store up credit in heaven, and also perhaps save her bacon were the guillotine to be erected in London. It was probably inevitable that this interest in 'pragmatic humanitarianism', charitable intent touched with self-interest, would extend to the conditions in the colonies.

The conflict of interests was reflected in the first lacklustre parliamentary debate on the slave trade that took place on 9 May 1788, within five years of the costly and humiliating ejection of Britain from America. All eyes were now turned to the security of the West Indian colonies and the much-needed cash they generated to replenish a seriously bare British war chest. An inquiry into the question of slave-trade abolition had shrewdly been placed in the hands of the Privy Council, a body private by nature and designed to advise George III, well known for his lack of sympathy concerning anti-slavery sentiments. This conveniently delayed matters. Equally it is more than a coincidence that the first fudged decision that 'the slave trade ought to be gradually abolished' came when the Commons voted by a majority of 145 on 2 April 1792, the eve of the French Revolution, when images of insurrection were stark and bright.

In the end the danger of a French Revolutionary sequel receded because the British Empire triumphed militarily, and with Napoleon at last having been vanquished at Waterloo, Britain dominated Europe from an unassailable position.

Her naval power was virtually equal to all the rest combined and the Congress of Vienna, convened in 1814, saw the end of any remaining European pretensions to challenging British imperialism and British domination of global commerce. But the climb to the imperial summit had been decidedly unsteady, with large parts of the route unplanned; sometimes it had been negotiated chaotically, and it had been not infrequently surmounted more by luck than judgement.[5] It also left the British government with a distinct sense of unease over the West Indian colonies. There might be scant prospect of French invasion or even of another Robespierre rabble-rousing in the English shires, but the risk of insurrection among the slave populations of the British-owned sugar islands, poorly policed and with the European presence vastly outnumbered by Africans, was a more distinct possibility. In the last decade of the eighteenth century, slave uprisings took place in Santo Domingo (which was to become known as the independent republic of Haiti) and Grenada. Under the rebel leader Toussaint L'Ouverture, the first significant orchestrated violence against white colonialists in Santo Domingo proved a sobering lesson. It also reminded Britain of the dangers of republicanism. In 1794 Toussaint, a former slave, had joined the French revolutionaries, carrying with him the whole body of Afro-Caribs and was made commander-in-chief of the island, forcing British withdrawal under a non-aggression pact reached in 1798.

If two of the elements of Britishness were empire and dominance of the high seas, the third and most essential of all, was trade. Britain had to generate massive amounts of revenue. She needed money to build and sail ships, to fill, feed and arm her fighting regiments. Imperial Spain had aimed at digging its bullion literally out of the ground and had conquered mineral-rich territories in Central and South America to obtain gold and silver. But Britain, France and other nations of Europe with an interest in empire-building had gone for the acquisition of monetary reserves through the less direct means of trade. During all of her imperial and military adventuring, Britain's colonial business – underpinned by the strength both of her navy and her merchant fleet, but also providing the finance for these – remained of paramount importance. The popular sentiment, often gained through the shrewd pamphleteering of such contemporary writers as Robert Burton (who went under the pen-name of Nathaniel Crouch), was that the transatlantic colonies were essential to the economic well-being of the whole nation and that they needed to be cherished and defended come what may. The emphasis on trade was partly determined by Britain's size. In terms of population the British Isles possessed roughly a quarter of that of France so the British were, as Charles II put it, 'only considerable by our trade and power by sea'.[6] By the seventeenth century the West Indies and their smooth commercial functioning had become central to economic policy and by the mid-eighteenth the most important section of British overseas trade was that of the so-called Atlantic Triangle, although this is something of a misnomer. In reality a five-point network arose like a cat's cradle between the English merchant houses, the West African slavers, the West Indian plantations, the Spanish imperial possessions to the south and mainland North America.

The lands that had been seized both on and off the eastern seaboard of North America were not necessarily rich in precious metals, but the soils and climates of these budding transatlantic colonies were the key to other treasures that could be exploited no less effectively. The commercial enterprise of the network required the colonies to grow, harvest and export natural commodities of coffee, tobacco and, above all, sugar. Prior to the loss of the American mainland colonies, Britain imported these commodities and largely paid for them in kind by arranging with mainland merchants to provide the islands with foodstuffs, timber, textiles and so on, little or none of which were available locally. The islands paid for some of their imported goods by exporting rum and, for the balance, passed the bills back to London, which were settled by the export of manufactured goods from the mother country. Linked to this approximately four-way traffic was a thriving contraband trade, largely operated through Jamaica, with the Spanish islands and colonies to the south. It may have been illegal, but nobody was overly concerned because it was paid for by Spanish buyers in gold and the business proved highly lucrative. Estimates reveal that the bullion-earning exports from Jamaica, chiefly of slaves, had reached £100,000 by 1691.[7] It was not until 1760 that Britain reluctantly imposed anti-smuggling regulations to assist the Spanish in stifling such enterprise. The result was considerable damage to the West Indian 'middleman's' ability to take in British exports in the shape of manufactured goods and slaves. In the following five years the volume of trade fell considerably and the British government felt compelled to conduct a U-turn. This involved the establishment of free ports in the West Indies and, from the British side, legalisation of trade within the whole Central American area in 1766. Thus the Atlantic Triangle became, if anything, more vital to British interests, and the sugar estates of the Caribbean remained the hub of a complex network of movement in manpower, money and commodities.[8] In overall terms the system worked conveniently and generated the measure of revenue that Britain needed to fund the demands placed on the nation as an imperial power and international policeman. It also made some aristocratic colonial landowners exceedingly rich and it all hinged on slave labour. Both of these elements exerted a deep influence on the way the abolition debate was conducted and resolved.

The system on which British trade in the seventeenth and eighteenth centuries, and that of much of the rest of Europe, was based has since been described as mercantilism. First adopted formally during the Tudor period, to a modern business executive familiar with the principles of free trade and capitalism, the workings of mercantile trade would seem odd. Yet mercantilism amounted to the accepted economic theory of the day and although it had its critics it continued to be applied as the norm in Britain until the loss of the American colonies began to cast serious doubt on its effectiveness. In his standard work on the subject the contemporary writer Thomas Mun explained the theory that for the promotion of national power it was essential to improve economic resources. In his words, 'the ordinary means therefore to encrease our wealth and treasure is by forraign trade, wherein wee must ever observe this rule; to sell more to strangers yearly than wee consume of theirs in value'. Mun's theory, first published in 1664, was generally regarded as soundly constructed, along with several others on the same lines. So the influx of money resulting from exports was strongly encouraged while excessive imports were no less rigorously discouraged. When this tenet was effectively applied, the weighting in favour of export had the knock-on and popular effect of making more employment available in England. The crude view was that money, or bullion in gold and silver, represents the sole wealth of nations and their people. Others preferred the somewhat more subtle argument that possession of gold and silver, both as state treasure and as a private store of wealth, has more durability and effectiveness and therefore a value can be attached to these metals greater than that of other commodities. The logic continued that the way to increase reserves of bullion and gain maximum employment at home was by statutory regulation so as to produce a favourable differential of export over import.

In order to operate profitably the mercantile system indeed required substantial regulation of trade, effectively removing competition by creating protective tariffs and political barriers – in short, the creation of monopolies. The power that invested in the most effective monopoly to the disadvantage of its rival skimmed the cream, or so went the theory. But the application of mercantile principles resulted in some bizarre and costly economic decisions. In 1614, during the reign of James I, an alderman of the City of London, William Cockayne, persuaded the king to grant patents allowing cloth-makers to dye and finish all cloth for export, and prohibiting overseas sales of undyed and undressed cloth. The argument ran that this would bring more work for English textile workers and cream off an extra £700,000 a year in revenue. But the exercise proved a disaster. The English dyeing process proved lamentably substandard and the Dutch, the long-established European dyers, promptly prohibited cloth imports from England and began to manufacture their own. Much of the foreign cloth market was thus lost and took many years to regain.

In practice the mercantile system turned out to be the diametric opposite to free-trade commercialism. The pursuit of successful mercantilism demanded a mix of diplomacy and strong-arm tactics, and to implement both Britain relied on the strength of her navy. Merchants needed protection from enemy warships and privateers in times of conflict and, under more peaceful conditions demanded sea lanes free from commercial competition and encounters with pirates; that is, they required the navy to discriminate in their favour against other European powers by rigorous implementation of the Navigation Laws. They also wanted the colonies with which they conducted their trade kept free from external threat and internal unrest.

Security demands placed considerable burdens on the British armed forces and the merchants knew that their prosperity was far from guaranteed even under Pax Britannica. Perhaps nowhere was jitteriness more acute than around the sugar plantations, since mercantile trade with the West Indies provided the major source of the wealth, without which the British power base would clearly falter. In terms of value the most important import from British colonies by the mid-eighteenth century was Caribbean island sugar, grown, harvested, crushed, extracted and barrelled as molasses or turned into rum with the use of West African slave labour. By the early 1770s English ports were importing nearly 100,000 tons of sugar a year, mostly to meet the demands of the home market and those of British North America. The return trade proved no less lucrative. Britain supplied the West Indian colonies with slaves and with virtually all the goods and raw materials they needed for existence. In the 1770s the share of British domestic exports to the West Indies, East Indies, Africa and North America amounted to just over 50 per cent and the greater part of this involved commercial traffic around the Atlantic Triangle. The success of trade to America and the West Indies had a knock-on effect and was of immense significance in the employment of British shipping, running at about 153,000 tons by the same period. Ships were needed to carry the goods, whether sugar, rum, slaves or shingles for plantation house roofs, and ships were needed to uphold the Navigation Laws that protected British monopoly. As a member of the House of Lords, the Earl of Cholmondeley put it succinctly in 1738: 'The situation of our island and the genius of our people depended heavily upon the extent and security of British navigation and trade.'9

The legal basis of British security on the high seas lay with the Navigation Laws, which had been enshrined in the legislature of the Navigation Acts. The first of these acts, passed in 1660, legitimised a system amounting to an imperial trading monopoly. Supervised from 1696 onwards by a newly established Board of Trade, the acts provided a jurisdiction ensuring that all colonial trade, wherever it was carried on in the world, was undertaken in English or colonial ships and the cargoes could only be exported to England or, after the Union of 1707, to Scotland or the British colonies. Most European goods destined for the colonies had to be transported via British ports. Eventually some relaxation of the Navigation Acts took place, but essentially they remained in force until the nineteenth century.[10]

The tens of thousands of slaves who toiled in the West Indian plantations did not, of course, generate all of the profits to fund British imperial ambitions, military strength and mercantile trade, but they were responsible for a sufficiently large part to make them indispensable, particularly since the nature of their toil did not suit either the indigenous population of the islands or immigrant Europeans. Yet the fruits of the unpaid Negro sweat that watered the plantations, the products of the institution of slavery itself, was only one aspect of their worth. Their purchase, shipment and sale – the slave trade – contributed massively to the British economy. Its importance was summed up by Charles Davenant writing in 1709: 'It is acknowledged that trade (so difficult to be obtained, so easily lost) has been the source and chief foundation of the riches, strength, power and greatness of this kingdom. There being no branch of any foreign trade whatsoever, beyond the limits of Europe, so naturally adapted to the interests of Britain and the plantations thereunto belonging, as the Trade to Africa.'[11]

Initially several countries, including most notably Portugal, Holland and France, had handled slave-dealing between West Africa and the Americas. One of the early products of the French and Spanish compact that triggered the War of Spanish Succession in 1702 was the granting to France of the *asiento*, the legal contract to supply slaves to the colonies of the Spanish Empire in America. Under the papal deal struck with Portugal back in the fifteenth century, Spanish interests did not extend eastwards to West Africa, so she was not directly involved with the purchase and transport of African slaves. After securing the *asiento*, France enjoyed a domination of the trade that was to last for eleven years. Only in 1713 did strenuous diplomatic overtures towards Spain by the British government result in the contracts passing to Britain. This not only gave exclusive rights for British-owned ships to supply the Spanish colonies with slaves, it also included the permit, again exclusive to Britain, to send a fully laden merchantman annually to Spanish America. This was a not-insignificant concession, since in all other respects Spain refused to allow European countries to trade directly with her colonies. The yearly voyage of the *asiento* ship actually did nothing to prevent a thriving illegal enterprise and here the island of Jamaica played a key role. British ships out of Kingston regularly ran the gauntlet of the Spanish authorities in Caribbean waters in order to deliver contraband British manufactured goods in return for hides, other local produce and most notably gold bullion. According to one estimate, Spanish gold smuggled aboard British ships between 1748 and 1765 amounted to £3,255,654.[12] The handing of the *asiento* contract to Britain had effectively determined that she was now the sole slave-trader from West Africa, supplying both her own New World colonies and those of the only other major colonial power in the region. Accurate figures of slave shipments to the Caribbean are difficult to come by. They have often been wildly inflated and not only by anti-slave-trade lobbyists. In 1707 the independent British slave-traders petitioned Queen Anne for a better deal and dramatically inflated shipment figures in order to enhance their position vis-à-vis the Royal African Company. The independents put their yearly slave sales to the West Indies at 25,000 but Charles Davenant calculated the correct figure to be less than 20 per cent of this total.[13]

There remains a fourth component in that eighteenth-century sense of Britishness, and it is one that might seem to inject a discordant note. Britain regarded itself as the 'land of liberty'. Foremost in defining what it meant to be British, more than empire or military supremacy or trade domination, was a system of government and law that secured the identity of Britons as free people. The British claimed that it gave them a singular place among the nations and set them apart from the more absolutist systems of government that predominated in Europe. Britons were proud of the might of the British Empire and the sentiment was matched by no less pride in their liberty. To be English or British was also to be *free*. We should recall the next line of James Thomson's poem: 'Britons never, never, never shall be slaves!'

Individual freedom based on a peculiarly English system of law and government was the bedrock not merely of the nation but of the empire, or at least that was the way it was fondly imagined and proudly boasted. It was all conveniently traced back to the largely mythical 'ancient constitution', romantically attributed to Magna Carta and embellished with a dimly remembered hotch-potch of laws created before the Norman Conquest (nothing could possibly be credited to the French). To some extent the claim of liberty was now more accurate than ever before. Since the Interregnum under Cromwell, the Crown could no longer govern without parliament, and parliament was intended to protect the life, liberty and property of the people against the Crown. Although James II had pushed for pro-Catholic and absolutist policies, the Stuart dynasty had been ousted and William of Orange's Glorious Revolution with its Bill of Rights had served to reinforce a constitution of the people and the Protestant succession.

In which case, why did our forebears accept slavery so willingly and apparently with so little conscience? The nub is that although the British people had earned the right to liberty, or so went the argument, through their ancient heritage, they did not consider this liberty necessarily to be an entitlement for others. In fact aliens earned no rights to British justice or protection under British law and it is for this reason there was little discernible public conscience about the enslavement of West Africans. The latter were, in the eyes of most British people, beastly savages and a lesser order of human beings. Black African slaves were generally considered fortunate to have been released from the darkness and depravity of life in Africa where, according to a scattering of romantically drawn pamphlets of the day, ideas of law and justice were virtually non-existent, all kinds of wickedness were rife and God did not care to venture forth. New-found evangelism, however, needed to find a way around the apparent contradiction that possessing a human soul, however beastly, and being enslaved were compatible. They were able to quote John Chrysostom, who had declared, as far back as the sixth century, that the unpleasantness of being a slave was part of God's punishment of sin after the fall of Adam. But Protestants needed proper verification to come from the pages of the Bible and so later theologians came up with various explanations, based on the reading of Old Testament passages. One of these 'proved' that black Africans were the descendants of Ham, the younger son of Noah and father of Canaan. Ham had been denounced by Noah for revealing to his siblings that he had seen their father naked and in a drunken stupor: 'And he said, cursed be Canaan; a servant of servants shall he be unto his brethren.'[14] But the lot of such cursed folk could be ameliorated if their souls were first saved. Hypocrisy, most notably stemming from the aristocracy and the bulk of the Anglican clergy, had its way and, in reality, sentiments about liberty only ever had a peripheral impact in the slavery debate.

Throughout the eighteenth century, British liberty and the benefits of the British legal system chiefly remained the preserve of the upper echelons of society and both therefore depended largely on the lottery of one's birthright. In early societies there had existed two basic classes: an aristocratic minority that controlled government, bureaucracy, religion and money, and a mass peasantry that maintained the interests of the elite through sweated labour, while earning little or none of the benefits enjoyed by their masters. As late as 1700, throughout much of Europe including the British Isles, little had changed. The prevailing social system was still one in which land, money and political control rested with a very small element, which was the privileged aristocracy that had gained its position and pleasure largely through inheritance rather than solid enterprise or merit. When George I came to the throne in 1714 it heralded a new era known as the Whig supremacy, in the early part of which, two great statesmen, Stanhope and Walpole, carved out a dynasty based on the political theories of government promoted by John Locke.[15] Locke had proposed that all authority of the state derives from a voluntary contract made by its members and that the people bear responsibility for the actions of their government. When put into practice this presented a unique situation vis-à-vis other European nations. Unfortunately, however, there was a downside to Locke's arguments when they touched on his demand for rights of property. Locke had proclaimed that the cost of the poor amounted to a 'growing burden on the kingdom'. His suggested remedy was to force all the able-bodied poor to serve on His Majesty's ships and the rest to be sent to houses of correction where hard labour would set right their attitudes.[16] The property that Locke referred to was largely in the hands of the privileged elite that occupied positions of authority, and so the Whig parliamentarians found the excuse, through his theories, to look after their own social rights and to ignore those of the lower classes, sidestepping their duties to many of their less fortunate fellow citizens. When successive Whig governments were ousted by the Tories in mid-century, little would change.

Any tangible sense of identity, rights and destiny thus tended to be restricted.[17] There existed a solid middle class, largely of Whig disposition, which enjoyed some measure of civil liberty and rights. From its ranks, most of the petitioning against slavery would eventually come, but even towards the end of the century it still represented a small and largely ineffectual social group. Its influence was limited because it did not hold seats in parliament. The bottoms of the great landowners and squires mostly occupied these. As far as the eighteenth-century English peasant and labouring classes were concerned, liberty was a foreign word, because the concept of individual freedom when applied across the spectrum of society amounted largely to a sham. Though technically the masses working in agriculture and the newly emergent factories were not categorised as serfs, in reality their experience was scarcely different from serfdom. Eventually a new-found interest in replacing mercantilism and monopoly with *laissez-faire* would allow a few with sufficient wits to rise above their lowly station, but it also had its downside, leaving the less-adventurous poor at the mercies of a new breed of capitalist and often ruthless entrepreneur.

The poor could hardly be expected, therefore, to show any great concern over bondage in faraway places that few of them probably even knew existed, because their own lot in life, toiling in fields, mines and woollen mills, living in squalid and filthy hovels, and earning subsistence wages if they were lucky, bore strong comparison. In 1776 Adam Smith wrote of a civilised society that 'it is only among the inferior ranks of people that the scantiness of subsistence can set limits but that the liberal reward of labour naturally tends to widen and extend those limits. The wear and tear of a slave it has been said is at the expense of his master but that of a free servant is at his own expense.'[18] The problem with that argument in the harsh reality of the eighteenth century, as Smith was quick to point out, was that the wear and tear on the free peasant was as much at the expense of his master as that of the slave.

The Treaty of Utrecht that ended the War of the Spanish Succession brought massive concessions in favour of Britain on a worldwide scale. But these also had the effect of making the rich richer while the poor stayed poor, and so class-consciousness based on wealth was set to distinguish one person from another to an even greater extent. Unless born into the aristocracy, the landed gentry or the rich merchant classes, the Englishman's lot was not a particularly happy one and for the impoverished, regarded as a class apart, freedom probably meant very little. Destitution was rife in the eighteenth century and for the wage-earning peasant life was an unremitting toil from cradle to grave. Treatment of pauper children was particularly severe and many were sent to workhouses where an alarming number fell prey to basic lack of care and starved to death. In 1716 a House of Commons committee recorded that of 1,000 children christened in the London parish of St Martin-in-the-Fields, three-quarters died within the year. Between 1750 and 1769 London records indicate that 63 per cent of all children under the age of 5 died, and most were probably pauper children.[19] Many of the survivors found themselves in apprenticeships where they earned next to nothing and learned hardly more, aside from the ability to steal. The poor generally toiled up to fifteen hours a day in conditions of drudgery, with very few holidays except Easter, Whitsun and Christmas, their only other relief being drunkenness bought with cheap gin or beer.[20]

Yet it was not only the lower classes of the home country whose rights under law appeared tenuous. New World settlers may have considered themselves British, with inalienable claims to a European culture, but they were increasingly viewed in a different light as part of a ruse designed to distance the British government, many of whose members owned property in the Caribbean, from the brutal activities of the expatriates who ran the slave plantations. Thousands of miles distant, with their already alien institutions, the colonists' rights to British liberty and legal system, even to British identity, were being considered questionable by the mid-eighteenth century. Many people already saw them as 'miserable outcasts' from the British and European systems. In 1766 Benjamin Franklin defined them as having degenerated from British ancestry to such a degree as to become 'the lowest of mankind and almost a different species from the English of Britain'.[21] Two years later he categorised them not as fellow subjects but as 'subjects of subjects'.[22] The colonies, however, were also indispensable outposts of British economic might and the more the home government challenged their claims to British identity, the more the colonists became determined to demonstrate, however tongue-in-cheek, that they were wedded to British ideas of liberty and justice.

Along these complex currents were borne some of the seeds of the British abolition movement that developed during the latter half of the eighteenth century. One of the strategies of the abolitionists, many of whom had grown fat indirectly on the profits of slavery, was to instil in the minds of the British people that the slave-owning colonists were unworthy of claims to British identity and that no decent Briton would stoop to their levels of tyranny and oppression. Colonial expatriate identity thus became a serious issue because if Britain and her empire wished to stand for liberty, then the slavery in her colonies was dragging her in the other direction. Riding the same currents were the passions of those who believed that abolition would result in mayhem, the slaughter of the colonists and the collapse of the British Empire.

Chapter 4

NOTES OF DISAPPROVAL

I n the search for acceptable solutions to our attitudes towards slavery and its eventual demise we have created false heroes and missed simple truths. We have wallowed in cosy, if largely mythical, explanations that slavery was abolished through the triumph of a vaguely defined amalgam of Christian values and the British sense of fair play. The search for explanations of this nature has verged on obsessive, much of it seeking moral and frankly implausible answers. It is as if we have needed to purge ourselves by proving that our eighteenth- and nineteenth-century pro-slavery forebears were somehow different from us, more akin to the inhabitants of an idolatrous Jericho, awaiting Joshua's blast to avail them of the truth.

David Brion Davis set the tone in 1966 with *The Problem of Slavery in Western Culture*. He posed the ethical question of why, at a certain moment in history, a small number of men saw the full horror of a social evil to which mankind had been blind for centuries and were determined to attack it. In the wake of Davis's publication a well-constructed though heavily slanted book by another American writer, Edith Hurwitz, epitomised the genre more stridently. The preamble of her *Politics and the Public Conscience*, first published in 1973, assails us with a virtuous fusillade that leaves no doubt over the route that Hurwitz is to follow. 'The success of the British Anti-Slavery Movement indicates that there have been moments in British history when values have taken precedence over economics, when the spiritual triumphed over the material.' Although there has been a general dearth of interest from this side of the Atlantic in the last fifty years, one notable English historian, the late Roger Anstey, also based his arguments on the moral 'card'. Yet how effective was the moral pressure against slavery and, no less important a question, who were the real activists? To trace the rise of the objectors and why their ambitions were first thwarted requires another step back through some earlier periods of history.

The first detectable notes, if not of outright disapproval of slavery then at least of discrimination on ethnic grounds, emerged in Spain early in the sixteenth century. After the death of Ferdinand V in 1516, he who had authorised the first purchases of black Africans to work in Spanish-American mines, Cardinal Ximines briefly held the reins of government. Ximines retained an influential adviser, Bartholomew de las Casas, who had lived among Amerindians and was highly sympathetic to their plight. De las Casas persuaded Ximines that he should encourage the purchase of native Africans and develop a code of law for slave-trading in order to save Amerindians from the most flagrant excesses. Ximines did not retain control for long enough to take up the suggestions but when the Holy Roman Emperor, Charles V, inherited the Spanish throne later that year his approach was not dissimilar. He backed the slave trade, encouraging the purchase of black Africans in preference to Amerindians and, in 1542, some six years before his death, he instigated better legal protection for Indians in the colonies. In this respect the argument of David Brion Davis in support of a romantic sentimentality towards the native American finds support. The selectivity, however, seems to have been more pragmatic than humanitarian, designed to limit the possibility of further uprisings among a potentially disruptive Amerindian population. Occasionally other churchmen offered notes of protest against slavery. Before his death in 1521, Pope Leo X had complained that not only the Christian religion but nature herself cried out against the practice, but by and large the position of the Roman Catholic Church ranged from ambivalence to lack of interest over any suggestions of limiting or terminating the institution.

In England Queen Elizabeth I sermonised occasionally about the way in which Negroes might, or might not, be taken into bondage, while also opening her purse-strings to finance the slaving expeditions of Hawkins and Drake to West Africa. After his first voyage, Elizabeth cautioned Hawkins against carrying off Africans without free consent. 'It would', she once remarked, 'be detestable, and call down the vengeance of heaven upon the undertakers.' Her tone seems to have conveyed the sense of 'take them by all means but make sure that the way you take them is above criticism'. Hawkins seems not to have remembered the royal advice.

Aside from those directly involved in buying, selling and transporting, the English displayed virtually no critical interest in the slave trade or in the conditions prevailing in Hispanic America until their colonies in the Americas had become well established. Only then did a few first-hand accounts of the slaves' parlous situation begin to reach the public through occasional activist pamphlets. Such news was very spasmodic and, at the time, was generally considered little more than the unqualified ranting of religious extremists. A Church of England clergyman, Morgan Godwyn, is thought to have been among the first writers in England to publish an article expressly supporting the cause of abolition.[1] Penned in 1640, his pamphlet *Negroes and Indians Advocate* exposed the situation of 'these oppressed people of whose sufferings I have been an eye witness in Barbadoes'. In 1673 the English Puritan minister Richard Baxter, a clergyman of considerable influence who had been appointed one of Charles II's chaplains, but who was forced to leave the Church after the 1662 Act of Uniformity, published a *Christian Directory*. In this he delivered a fairly outspoken protest against the slave trade, even describing those involved as 'fitter to be called demons than Christians'. Less than a century later, in 1735, another on-the-spot reporter was John Atkins, ship's surgeon to the navy, who compiled an eye-opening description of the appalling conditions endured on the middle passage in his *Voyage to Guinea, Brazil and the West-Indies*.

The first collective voice against slavery was raised not in Britain but America. The credit for pioneering opposition must go to the American branch of the Society of Friends, the breakaway Protestant sectarians nicknamed the 'Quakers' on account of their practice of trembling with holy fear at the presence of God in their meetings. The early interest of the American Quakers in the abolition of slavery, however, does not reflect any major trend among the rest of the New World colonists during the seventeenth and eighteenth centuries. Their response was something of an aberration driven partly by their religious belief that all men are equal in the sight of God, but also by a level of pragmatism arising from the kind of commercial enterprises in which they had chiefly become engaged.

Launched in England by George Fox in the 1640s Quakerism had found its inspiration in Cromwell's Puritan revolution, many of its first recruits coming from remote parts of the north-west. Its members elected to deny aspects of the Scriptures and rely more closely on the 'inner light' of the soul to communicate directly with God. With little respect for social rank they also refused to recognise the authority of either magistrate or minister and were essentially pacifist, a position that made them less than popular among the English ruling classes. As the contemporary diarist John Evelyn noted, many found themselves thrown into gaol under the label of dangerous fanatics.

More importantly when considering their eventual stance over the slavery issue, the Quakers came under the general heading of 'levellers', a tag that they shared with Presbyterians, Methodists and other dissenters from mainstream Anglicanism. Quakers professed that if men were equal before God they should also be equal before the law and should not be made the victims of tyranny. Critical of human vanities they disparaged contemporary fashions for long hair, periwigs, painted faces and fancy costumes. When the monarchy was restored under Charles II, most Quakers saw future progress towards their ideal world as requiring political change, in order to erode the power of the moneyed classes and of the pro-royalist aristocracy that largely dictated the course of state religion. But a significant minority had its eye more closely on social concerns, and in America attention became directed towards the slavery issue.

New World Quaker settlers had sailed from England to Pennsylvania, and the founding father of the colony, William Penn, had been an early convert to Quakerism. Penn announced his personal aversion to slavery as early as 1668, calling it 'cruel, impolitic and unchristian',[2] and nor was George Fox blind to the problems it raised when he advocated that bondage be limited to a period of not more than thirty years. Both men, however, might be accused of weasel words, because Penn had bought and owned Negroes and he, like Fox, perennially accepted slavery as a necessary institution. It was to be the pronouncement of a group of immigrant Dutch farmers that set the tone when they attended the now-famous Germantown meeting in a small settlement of that name near Philadelphia on 28 April 1688. They gathered to address the issue of slave ownership and Francis Daniel Pastorius, the Germantown founder, issued the declaration: 'There is a saying that we shall do to all men like as we will be done ourselves; making no difference of what generation, descent or colour they are.'[3]

The Germantown meeting may have generated the first collective petition demanding the prohibition of slavery in an American settlement, but it has to be viewed as an isolated response even among Quakers, most of whom, in common with other colonists of the time, kept slaves. It is difficult to obtain statistics for the seventeenth century but mid-eighteenth-century official slave returns for the Pennsylvania counties of Chester and Delaware alone include the names of 237 slave-owning Quaker families.[4] In Weld's *Slavery As It Is*, providing another example, there is mention that Quaker slave-owners liberated 134 Negroes in North Carolina in 1776.

After the Germantown meeting, some sixty years passed before any substantial shift in American opinion became evident. In 1696 two leading members of the Philadelphia Society of Friends tried to introduce a ban on slavery and the slave trade at their yearly meeting. The attempt failed, although the assembly agreed formally to advise Quakers against importing any more slaves and to treat humanely those they might possess. This injunction was to become a regular feature of the yearly meetings and almost twenty years on, in 1712, the Pennsylvania legislature went so far as to attempt placing a prohibitive tax on the import of slaves. The British government was not slow to rule the move out of order but, as statistics reveal, American Quaker communities were beginning to regard slavery as socially unacceptable. In 1705 some 70 per cent of Quakers had owned slaves; fifty years later the figure was slashed to a mere 10 per cent. Nevertheless the Quaker mentality was strongly mercantile and transportation from West Africa was a lucrative enterprise, so that, as late as 1756, eighty-four Quakers were listed as members of the Royal African Company, including most notably the Barclay and Baring families of later banking fame.[5]

In England it was also to be a group of Quaker activists that initially spearheaded activity against the slave trade though, in common with their American counterparts, they experienced little success in the short and medium terms. The English Quakers were burdened with two major drawbacks quite apart from the awkward admission that some of them were profitably engaged in transporting slaves from West Africa as independent 'Ten Percenters'. To begin with they did not possess an organisational structure that would allow them to mobilise more widespread support in the country. Eventually the Wesleyan Methodists proved themselves far more competent in gathering sympathisers. The Society of Friends also met with strong resistance from an English establishment that regarded anyone who opposed or operated outside the Anglican Church to be untrustworthy and even un-English. This was one of the roots of parliamentary and ecclesiastical antagonism when it came to the abolition question that the Quakers were set to champion in England. The Society of Friends also tended to be linked with Presbyterianism and both were reminders of Puritanism, which the public by and large had come to detest thoroughly. Nonetheless the dissenters could still rely on considerable support, particularly among shopkeepers, artisans and yeomanry. Some 2,000 of the 9,000 church benefices up and down the country were held by Presbyterians and shortly after Charles II's coronation there were some 40,000 Quakers evangelising in the English shires, their numbers swelled by several hundreds more released from imprisonment.[6] Presumably with such numbers in mind when receiving a Quaker deputation, the king once announced, 'You shall none of you suffer for your opinions ore religion, so long as you live peaceably, and you have the word of a king for it.'[7]

Almost immediately under the Restoration monarchy the sectarians suffered a more serious setback. In 1662, after a lunatic-inspired anti-royalist plot of the previous year, the finger of blame was pointed squarely at Quaker schemers and some 4,000 of them were incarcerated. The incident also encouraged parliament to pass the Act of Uniformity that brought back benefices to episcopally ordained clergy, badly eroded by the Puritans. The Act allowed for nonconformism of a kind but discriminated against the dissenters by excluding them, one and all, from all positions of authority in Church and state. In the following year, the Quakers Act came down heavily and specifically on the Society of Friends, curbing much of their activity and ensuring that about 1,300 remained in prison. Quakers were seen to be openly rejecting allegiance to the Crown and it was rumoured that all manner of sedition was going on behind the closed doors of their meeting-houses. In consequence, after a third offence of gathering for worship or refusing to take the loyal oath, the decreed punishment was forcible removal to the colonies. Hence many either left England voluntarily in anticipation of persecution or found themselves transported as 'white servants' and it was this kind of experience that introduced them first hand to the harsh realities of the middle passage. One notable parliamentary petition tabled in 1659 reveals how seventy-two dissenters had been incarcerated below decks among horses during the entirety of a 5½-week voyage and that many had suffered severely in the tropical heat and humidity.[8]

Notwithstanding the Act of Uniformity, technically making dissent lawful, it was only in 1672 that the second Declaration of Indulgence lightened some of the burden placed on sectarians and reduced their numbers behind bars to about 500. Charles II suspended all penal laws against 'whatsoever sort of nonconformists or recusants' and approved places in which dissenters could worship publicly without fear of reprisal.[9] The Act was not well received and had the effect of stirring up public anger. Not until the latter part of the nineteenth century did nonconformists gain their full civil rights.[10] When the so-called 'Glorious Revolution' of William and Mary came in 1689, negating many pro-Catholic and absolutist policies retained by the Stuarts, most English people may have imagined that the turn of events would ensure religious freedom, yet dissenters were still deprived of their full share of the cake. Under the Toleration Act of that year, restrictions on their activities had been relaxed but they could not hold any office under the king, gain commissions in the army or qualify for university degrees at Oxford or Cambridge. Quakers among them were still offering passive resistance by refusing to take an oath of allegiance or pay tithes and were facing gaol terms by way of reward. The clergy were also being egged on to righteous indignation by a series of well-organised pamphlets labelling Quakers as godless troublemakers. In this they shared a bed of harsh discrimination along with Roman Catholics. What all this meant was that while the nonconformists were among the staunchest activists in the embryo anti-slavery campaign, their means of implementing political or social change, including any shift in government policy on slavery, were limited.

A scattering of European writers and poets started to expound their disapproval of slavery from the late seventeenth century onwards, although this rarely extended to criticism or moral opprobrium per se. Most notably the critics included the French commentator Montesquieu, who investigated the economics of slavery in his *Esprit des Loix*, published in 1748, and Francis Hutcheson, who wrote his *System of Moral Philosophy* in 1755. Two years later the British politician and philosopher Edmund Burke, in his *Philosophical Enquiry*, penned an appraisal of the slave unrest that was reportedly erupting from time to time in the West Indian colonial settlements. Burke put the blame firmly on the shoulders of the British government. A noted conservative and reactionary, opposed in principle to the adoption of modern ideas of democracy, he once observed that 'the Negroes in our colonies endure a slavery more complete, and attended with far worse circumstances, than what any people in their condition suffer in any other part of the world'. Burke's view of the world included a philosophy that God had chosen to give the human species a capacity to delight in the misfortune and suffering of others, but that this also opened the door to exercising occasional benevolence. His opinions were not exclusively directed towards black Africans and he is on record as having lumped the British working classes into the mass category of 'miserable sheep'. Certainly he felt that some improvement of the situation of Negroes in the West Indies would not go amiss, but was nonetheless a staunch supporter of slave-owners and slave-traders and was clearly appalled at any prospect of militant abolitionism surfacing.

A few churchmen raised their heads above the pulpit and delivered timely broadsides, though perhaps more in a spirit of religious cant than any sense of shame over shortcomings in Christian morality. In 1766 Bishop Warburton preached a sermon before the Society for Propagation of the Gospel, on the one hand severely admonishing the oppressors of miserable Africans, while in the same breath describing enslaved Negroes as 'savages in bonds', much as he might have lamented cruelty to a domestic animal. For the most part, however, there was little interest in their plight. Few people had more than the haziest idea of the conditions endured by black Africans on the middle passage, how the cargoes were obtained or the situation faced on arrival in the Americas. Had they been confronted with any of the less-salubrious details, such as those which would be published by the Quaker historian Anthony Benezet in 1771, it is still questionable whether they would have been overly concerned since, as far as the majority of the public were concerned, the black African was not a suitable subject for consideration beyond making sure that he was fed, watered and stabled.

One of the factors governing this seemingly cavalier response to the plight of others was that, with rare exceptions from the time of Goncalvez, black people lived abroad. The English landed gentry who enjoyed any kind of franchise in the affairs of the nation did not, by and large, have black African slaves in their backyards at home, nor did the politicians who represented them at Westminster. When slave ships were plying their trade out of London, Bristol and Liverpool, the fate of their human cargoes was altogether remote from daily life. The poor in England probably fared almost as badly and, in any case, had no say in the affairs of state. The affluent and the powerful viewed the Negro as a two-legged commodity with which to generate profit or loss, and with no more entitlement to rights than a horse or a dog. To no small extent this reflected the well-established view among a broad swathe of public opinion, that Negroes were not human but constituted some lesser species closer to apes than *Homo sapiens*. In a society where man's best friend was often his horse or his dog, this did not necessarily mean that cruelty was justifiable, merely that the Negro should be treated with the same firm discipline and under the same conditions as a responsible owner would provide for his domestic animals. The ambivalent mood about Negroes was summed up in a book by a churchman named Primatt, who recorded his disquiet but under the revealing title, *Dissertation on the Duty of Mercy, and on the Sin of Cruelty to Brute Animals*.

These elements, however, were not the sole reasons for lack of concern. Slavery was naturally a part of English tradition. Icons of power, respectability and esteem, like Elizabeth I, 'Good Queen Bess', had been openly supportive. The Stuart kings and Queen Anne had acquiesced to what was going on and had issued slaving licences to royal traders. Their Hanoverian successors were largely approving. In the colonies the aristocracy kept slaves; the pillars of the Church at home kept slaves. With hardly a dissenting voice speaking out against African slavery, Church and state alike had encouraged the institution for as long as anyone could remember. Up to the end of the eighteenth century and for some years after, therefore, few decent people saw anything wrong with the institution of slavery.

Which, then, were the key figures and organisations in Britain and America that set the anti-slavery bandwagon properly rolling? One of the chief American protagonists was John Woolman, a Society of Friends member, born in 1720 in Burlington County, West Jersey. This place had been a Quaker stronghold from as early as 1676. after controlling interest in the colony was sold to a group of London-based Quaker businessmen, and West Jersey was where William Penn had first made American footfall. During a visit to the South in 1746 Woolman developed a strong personal concern about the plight of slaves on the burgeoning Quaker estates of North Carolina. Unease seems to have first lodged in his mind when a terminally ill neighbour asked him to write out a will, and the testimony included the transference of slaves as part of the man's inheritance to his children. Woolman started to broadcast the basic question of whether the Society of Friends had any right to be involved in slavery. As recently as 1710 Quakers had constituted only about 2.5 per cent of the population in the Carolinas, but by the time of Woolman's visit they dominated some of the elected assemblies. The region attracted its share of English dissenters, many having responded to recruiting efforts in the home country, and a significant number of these had arrived via Barbados, where they had witnessed some of the harshest excesses of slavery in operation at first hand. Woolman did not receive an enthusiastic initial response and as late as 1730 Quaker merchants in cities such as Philadelphia were running lucrative enterprises importing and selling slaves. Paradoxically, though, the eventual support of his position towards the end of the eighteenth century by the wider community of Quakers may have been helped along by direct involvement with the market in slaves, giving a sharp and uncomfortable insight into the incompatibility of the slave system with Quaker humanitarian principles.

Woolman was doubtless aware of the conflict of ethics but he was also not slow in understanding that any meaningful appeal to his fellow sectarians against the practice of keeping slaves would be more effective if presented on economic grounds rather than purely as a humanitarian issue. In his diary he made a point of quoting a Quaker militiaman whose view it was that the untoward and slothful disposition of Negroes was probably more trouble than it was worth and that one of their own labourers would do as much in a day as two slaves. Woolman noted that free men, whose minds were properly on their business, found satisfaction in improving, cultivating and providing for their families; but Negroes, labouring to support others who claim them as their property, and expecting nothing but slavery during life, did not share the same inducement to be industrious. Quakers were, by and large, shrewd businessmen and logic dictated that it was better to tweak the strings of purses than hearts, particularly if slave labour was not vital to their commercial interest.

Significantly the main support for the Quaker anti-slavery movement in North America came initially from among small, rural communities in Virginia, Pennsylvania and New York. These areas had never been particularly dependent on slave labour since they were located too far north for successful growing of sugar or cotton. Their colonists were not overly concerned about the prospects of manumission (the freeing of slaves) and abolition since the production of grain crops with which Quaker farming families were engaged was not as labour-intensive as that of sugar. Though not as profitable as sugar production, grain made good economic sense because it could be sold readily to the sugar plantations of the South and the West Indies, none of which showed much interest in growing cereals for their own consumption. It did not, however, benefit the grain farmers economically to use slave labour.

By the 1750s Woolman was beginning to garner support among like-minded Friends. The 1758 yearly meeting of Friends in North Carolina concluded that Negroes had a right to liberty and that it would be appropriate to 'visit' such Friends as kept slaves with the intention of encouraging them to abandon the practice. The proposal was accepted without opposition and a 'visiting committee' was established. In the same year the meeting of Philadelphia Quakers registered unanimous concern about importing, buying, selling or keeping slaves and in the following year a more formal recommendation was extended to Pennsylvania Quakers against buying and keeping slaves. Woolman clearly felt vindicated in his one-man evangelical campaign and commented in his diary that he had 'at times in some meetings been almost alone therein. I was humbly bowed in thankfulness in observing the increasing concern in our religious society, and seeing how the Lord was raising up and qualifying servants for His work, not only in this respect, but for promoting the cause of truth in general.'

In 1760 the Philadelphia Quakers passed a declaration excluding any member who participated in the slave traffic, but obtaining support in the wider community proved more difficult. Leading Quaker families living in Rhode Island, for example, were still actively involved in slave-trading.[11] Old religious prejudices were hard to dispel. Quakers in support of the slave trade might have seen themselves as levellers ironing out society's secular ranks, but they retained the somewhat apocryphal conviction that Negroes were the offspring of Cain, their blackness being the mark which God set upon him after he murdered his sibling Abel. It was, therefore, down to Providence that they should be slaves, as a condition proper to the descendants of a man with a record so tarnished as that of Cain.

Passing the moral onus back to the British government was, of course, a useful way of assuaging consciences. An anonymous account published in the early 1760s is perhaps not untypical of the feeling being generated in some sections of the community, that the authorities in the home country were displaying hypocrisy and double standards over colonial slavery. 'It is a matter of astonishment how a people who, as a nation, are looked upon as generous and humane, and so much value themselves for their uncommon sense of the benefit of liberty, can live in the practice of such extreme oppression and inhumanity without feeling the inconsistency of such conduct.'[12]

Unable to persuade the colonial legislature to pass a statutory ban on the importation of black Africans, Woolman resorted to writing a pamphlet, published in 1762, entitled *Considerations on Keeping Negroes*. Although it was suggested at the Society of Friends' yearly meeting that the work be paid for with funds raised by the society, Woolman decided to cover the cost of printing from his own pocket and arranged for the material to be distributed freely. Unfortunately, although his efforts proved influential among Quakers, many of them choosing to liberate their slaves and employ them as freemen, he still met with only limited response elsewhere. Pressure on the British Crown nonetheless continued. In 1772 the Virginia assembly petitioned to stop the importation of slaves into America but the request was ignored and this was among the principal grievances aired by the colony before the opening salvoes of the War of Independence erupted three years later. Immediately before the conflict began, the Massachusetts assembly had also made several attempts to rid itself of slavery, but three successive governors, who insisted that they were acting on instructions from Britain, quashed the acts of the General Court. In 1773 another attempt was made by the Philadelphia Quakers, this time to levy an import duty on slaves, but this was rejected by the British parliament, determined that no hare-brained scheme dreamed up by a gaggle of colonial nonconformists would jeopardise such a lucrative trade. By 1775, however, with the American War of Independence in full spate, the newly formed Pennsylvanian government promptly forbade slave importation. Pennsylvania was to keep up the momentum towards abolition and this was shared by Massachusetts.

Thomas Jefferson, destined for election as the third president of the United States in 1801, was a committed abolitionist and as a lawyer on the threshold of his political career he made a significant speech at the first general congress of the colonies held in Philadelphia in October 1774. He declared that 'the abolition of slavery is the greatest object of desire in these colonies, when it was unhappily introduced in their infant state'. Jefferson's sentiments reflected the widely held, and to British ears dastardly, claim that slavery had been introduced into the American colonies against the wishes of the settlers by the avarice of British traders and with the connivance of the British government. Among the Articles of Association adopted by the congress was the declaration that 'we will neither import nor purchase any slave imported after the first day of December next, nor will we hire our vessels, nor sell our commodities or manufactures to those who are concerned with the slave trade'. Jefferson's more privately held views were not quite so liberal. A parcel of pamphlets bound into a rare volume discovered in the private collection of George Washington after his death in 1799 revealed that Jefferson questioned the mental capacity of the Negro and did not know if he possessed the capabilities and qualifications for equality of citizenship alongside the European immigrants. Jefferson inclined to the belief that Negroes were members of an inferior race and that freeing them among the white population was 'incompatible with the happiness of both'. He thought it better to emancipate them and speedily dispatch them out of the country under some sort of colonisation scheme, though he doubted if half a million liberated slaves could be effectively deported or, indeed, where they could be sent. Some took Jefferson's opinion seriously and at a later stage they actually formed a Colonisation Society with the aim of a type of ethnic cleansing. This group purchased the area on the West African coast that became known as Liberia.

In the following year, that of the Declaration of Independence, the first anti-slavery society was founded at the Sun Tavern on 2nd Street in Philadelphia on 14 April 1775. Acquiring the cumbersome title of 'The Society for the Relief of Free Negroes unlawfully held in Bondage', its original members were mostly, if not all, Quakers. The war put its meetings on temporary hold until 1784, but afterwards they became regular events and Benjamin Franklin was elected president with Benjamin Rush joining as secretary. Franklin's last public act was to draw up and sign the renamed Pennsylvania Abolition Society's petition to

Congress on 3 February 1790. He died just over two months later. In much of the rest of North America, however, a far more protracted chapter of events was unfolding.

It has to be said that not all colonies viewed the freeing of slaves with the same enthusiasm. In 1777, two years into the war, the North Carolina assembly passed a restrictive law actually making manumission more difficult and demanding the seizure of any slaves that had been illegally freed. In many instances these were being taken by traders and sold on to plantation owners in the Deep South, where slavery would not be abandoned for another eighty-three years. The public mood was changing, however, at least for the time being, although events to unfold early in the nineteenth century, including insurrections in North Carolina and Southampton, would bring a strong reversal of support. In 1780 Pennsylvania passed an act of gradual emancipation and Massachusetts became the first state to outlaw the institution of slavery altogether, a remarkable turnaround considering that in 1776 the number of slaves in the state was calculated at 5,429, of which about half were in Boston. Gradual emancipation was also incorporated in the constitutions of Rhode Island and Connecticut in 1784, and a Society for Promoting the Manumission of Slaves was organised in New York state in January 1785. There are, however, some commonly held misconceptions about where the strength of opposition to slavery was focused. It may be imagined that any agitation aimed at the plantation owners in the southern states was concentrated in the North and especially in Massachusetts. But this is not strictly correct and the main interest appears to have come from Virginia and Maryland.

In Britain and continental Europe, during the same period of developing American activity, criticism of the institution of slavery tended to be individual and declamatory and was, literally, far removed from any kind of effective action. Travel across the Atlantic at that time represented a voyage to another world and what happened in the Americas neither troubled the conscience of Britain and Europe, nor did it affect everyday life to any appreciable extent. The visitor to the docks of Bristol and Liverpool would be confronted by what must have seemed an unstoppable machine in the comings and goings of the awesome fleet of slave ships.

Nevertheless, London Quakers were warned against dealing in slaves as early as 1758 and various spokesmen, including the Methodists' founder John Wesley, the American Quaker Anthony Benezet, the evangelical preacher George Whitefield and James Ramsay, the rector of Teston in Kent, at one time or another commented on the slavery system through publications or personal campaigns. Benezet was influential not least because in 1771 he had been responsible for the publication, in Philadelphia and London, of a slim but powerful volume describing at first hand and in graphic terms the dreadful treatment of Negro captives on the West African coast and in the American colonies. He was not afraid to blast his readers with accounts of chilling punishments such as flaying alive and some other uncomfortable statistics including the calculation that of 80,000 Negroes in Barbados, 5,000 more than are born die each year, requiring the stock to be renewed every sixteen years.[13] Some five years later Benezet published another tract for serious consideration, this time directed more specifically at those in positions of power. He criticised the calamitous state of slaves, applying slightly dysfunctional grammar, 'How an evil of so deep a dye, hath so long not only passed their countenance is indeed surprising and charity would suppose, must in great measure have arisen from this, that many persons in government, both of the clergy and laity, in whose power it hath been to put a stop to the trade, have been unacquainted with the corrupt motives which give life to it.'[14]

Whitefield's is a curious but by no means unusual case of an evangelical who accepted black slavery and was even in favour of its establishment in Georgia, where it had originally been prohibited. He relied on the dogma that human sin is so vile that God saves only a predestined few and that slave-owners probably had the best chance of bringing their chattels to salvation. His criticism was directed not so much at the institution but the way it was managed. In an open letter to the people of Maryland, Virginia and the Carolinas, printed in 1739, he railed that when he had 'viewed plantations cleared and cultivated, many spacious houses built and the owners of them faring sumptuously every day, my blood has frequently almost run cold within me, to consider how many of your slaves had neither convenient food to eat, or proper raiments to put on, notwithstanding most of the comforts you enjoy were solely owing to their indefatigable labours'.[15] He preached energetically, tirelessly and no doubt changed some moral attitudes.

Wesley had gradually become an advocate of abolition since reading Benezet's publications, and in 1774 was to pen an influential tract of his own, *Thoughts upon Slavery*. In 1769 an English constitutional lawyer and Whig supporter called Granville Sharp had also circulated a pamphlet entitled *A Representation of the Injustice and Dangerous Tendency of Tolerating Slavery, or of admitting the least Claim of Private Property in the Persons of Men in England.* It has to be borne in mind, however, that the exhortations of these individuals only reached a very small section of the general public, since few people could read or write and such publications enjoyed a very limited circulation. The great mass of the population remained in a state of ignorance or apathy.

The interest of Wesley, and more particularly that of Sharp, was stimulated additionally by a well-publicised legal case concerning a black African whose name was James Somerset. The outcome set an important precedent, which was to be used as ammunition by both sides in the slavery debate. Somerset had been brought to England from Virginia in 1769 by his master, Charles Stewart, and, after a time, had absconded. He was captured and taken on board a ship, the *Ann and Mary*, destined for the colonies, where the intention was to resell Somerset as a slave. Granville Sharp took a personal interest and decided to employ counsel on Somerset's behalf in order to contest the right of Stewart to return him forcibly to Jamaica. To appreciate the context of the situation more fully we need to go back to some advice given in 1729 by the two most eminent legal minds of the day, the then Attorney General, Sir Philip York, Earl of Hardwicke, and the Solicitor General, the Hon. Charles Talbot. They had jointly rendered the opinion that a slave coming from the West Indies to Great Britain or Ireland, with or without his master, did not become free, his master's right and property in him did not become varied and baptism did not bestow freedom. Furthermore York and Talbot concurred that the master might legally compel a slave to return to the plantations. This opinion conflicted with the broad principle that it was the essential and constitutional right of every man in England to the liberty of his person, unless forfeited by the laws of England. Nonetheless York reiterated the position in June 1749, at which time he had attained the high office of Lord Chancellor.[16]

The opinion that a slave remained a slave even on English home soil was first put to the serious test in 1771 in the case of another black African, Thomas Lewis, a former slave owned by one Mr Stapylton. Lewis had been seized on Stapylton's behalf and rowed out to a Jamaica-bound ship, an incident observed by a local resident identified as Mrs Banks. Knowing of his interest to promote the slavery issue she approached Granville Sharp, who applied on behalf of Lewis for a writ of habeas corpus (the accepted means of testing the legality of an unlawful imprisonment). Lewis was freed under the writ but Mrs Banks insisted on bringing Stapylton to court and the case was heard before Lord Chief Justice Mansfield in June 1771. Mansfield relied on York and Talbot and ruled that since Mrs Banks now had Lewis 'in her possession' it was inadvisable for her to proceed further. In the aftermath Granville Sharp registered a strong protest at Lord Mansfield's ambivalent response, believing that this refusal of judgment against Stapylton would set an alarming precedent for future cases. Either a man in England was free, or he was not![17]

In the following year, on 7 February 1772, Mansfield, assisted by three lesser judges, also heard the Somerset case when it was brought before him. Granville Sharp took a close interest and agreed to pass over to the leading defence counsel, Mr Serjeant Davy, the detailed observations he had compiled during the Lewis case. In court Davy argued that villeinage had been effectively eliminated in England and that English law affected all people entering the country. Legally

Somerset had become a subject of the king the moment he set foot on English soil, was thus subject to the laws of England, governed and regulated in his conduct by those laws and also entitled to the protection they provided. Davy pressed Mansfield to rule on the critical issue of whether or not the laws of Virginia applied in England, since this was the main defence of Charles Stewart.[18] The case was held over and in the interim Granville Sharp wrote to the First Lord of the Treasury, Lord North, requesting him to use his influence to 'put a stop to the monstrous injustice and abandoned wickedness caused by slave holding'. The letter apparently elicited no response from the North government and the matter of judgment was repeatedly postponed by Mansfield. But on 22 June 1772, having paid due attention to York and Talbot, Mansfield concluded that the 'cause returned was sufficient by law' and he therefore discharged Somerset on the writ of habeas corpus. In doing so he made the crucial and historic observation that 'if the Negro Somerset was a man – and he should conclude him one till the court should adjudge otherwise – it was impossible he could be a slave in England'.

It would be naive to suggest that Mansfield's ruling in the case of Somerset marked the turning point in the course of the abolition, a moment in history when the British sense of morality and fair play swung into effect and triumphed over legalised inhumanity. Mansfield's view appears to have remained one that suggests that slaves, horses and cattle could be lumped under the same heading, a position that was to achieve prominence in another case a few years later. Lord Mansfield's ruling did, however, contain far-reaching implications, since it drew a distinction between the laws of England and those of the Crown colonies, in most other respects British territory subject to British rule. To have made the American mainland possessions or the British West Indies strictly subject to British law would have necessitated abandoning slavery, and in 1772 that prospect was unthinkable even for those most staunchly opposed to the institution. What it did mean, however, was that the British parliament could start to wash its hands of the dirty conduct of the colonial legislatures. This self-exoneration came to be used in the most cynical fashion by members of both Houses, who could express righteous indignation at the treatment of slaves but claim that the brutality inflicted by the plantation overseers was outside British control (even though the owners of the plantations *in absentia* were frequently members of parliament) and was the responsibility of the colonial assemblies. It reinforced the sentiment that colonialists were not really British at all and by the nature of their emigration had become aliens. In a manner not unlike our purging the misdeeds of our forebears with popular hagiographies that focus on the Christian do-gooding pillars of the past, eighteenth-century society itself required to indulge in an exercise of distancing itself from the errant behaviour of its expatriate brethren.

In spite of the outcome of the Somerset case, nothing of any note in the shape of progress towards launching an abolition movement took place in Britain for another decade. Aside from Quakers and a few other intellectuals, public indifference was solid. Then, in 1783, a small Quaker group, including George Harrison, Samuel Hoare, Thomas Knowles, John Lloyd, Joseph Woods and an American member of the Society of Friends, William Dillwyn, got together to formulate a plan of action. They presented a petition to parliament denouncing the slave trade and also agreed to encourage public interest in the plight of Negroes and the inhumanity of the system through newspaper articles. The coalition government of Lord North and Charles Fox responded to such eccentric nonsense by stating firmly that abolition of the slave trade was quite impossible. The business had become necessary to almost every nation in Europe and this most certainly included Great Britain.

With the coming to power of the Whig government under William Pitt in December 1783, succeeding the short-lived Fox–North coalition, the climate was seen to be marginally more liberalised. On 22 May 1787, having agreed among themselves the principle that 'the said trade was both impolitick and unjust', several of the Quaker group felt sufficiently emboldened to convene a formal meeting, announcing themselves as the London Committee for the Abolition of the Slave Trade. The founder members, including Woods, Hoare (who became the treasurer), Dillwyn, Harrison and Lloyd, were joined by Granville Sharp, suitably elected as chairman, a barrister named Richard Phillips with chambers at Lincoln's Inn, the publisher James Phillips, Philip Sansom, Joseph Hooper, John Barton and, most notably, one Thomas Clarkson. All, with the exception of Sharp, Sansom and Clarkson, were members of the Society of Friends. Later they were to be joined by a number of others, among whom was William Wilberforce. It is to these individuals and in particular Clarkson and Wilberforce that the story now turns, since with their arrival on the scene we come to one of the most commonly held misconceptions about the anti-slavery campaign.[19]

Chapter 5

PLAYERS AND PREJUDICES

stablishing who did what, and how effective or otherwise they were in doing it, amounts to a critical test in drawing out the true circumstances of abolition. In one respect the issue is about whether the anti-slavery activists, as an entity, constituted an effective pressure group that served to change the way in which parliament eventually voted. But, first, who were the key players and how well do we know them? It is on Wilberforce and Clarkson, the most prominent British trade-abolitionists, that attention now needs to fall. A critical investigation reveals something more than the influence they exerted on the sensitivities of the British public and on the parliamentary debate. It exposes considerable omissions and discrepancies, while amounting to a sobering tale of rifts, subterfuge and back-stabbings.

Gushing eulogies on Wilberforce and Clarkson are not hard to find. James Elmes, who published a monograph on Thomas Clarkson in 1854, described 'the zealous, indefatigable and persevering labours, faithful to the end, of that distinguished triumvirate of friends, Sharp, Clarkson and Wilberforce, to whose meritorious exertions the universal world is indebted for their great tribute to religion and humanity'. In their introduction to Wilberforce's life story, Robert and Samuel extol their father's most familiar characteristics as 'an infinite fund of anecdote, an unvarying fertility of wit, in constant readiness to please and to give pleasure'. Among modern analysts Edith Hurwitz declares that 'Anglican evangelicals under the leadership of William Wilberforce with the backing of non-conformist sects brought their cause into the political arena and from 1787 a new spirit of religion was active in political protest – the most enduring expression in the anti-slavery crusade.'[1] Quite so; but is such 'enduring expression' truly accurate in the way it has been presented?

In Britain it has been widely trumpeted in many popular books on the subject that William Wilberforce, the independent Member of Parliament for Hull between 1780 and 1825, was the driving force against slavery, and although his entry into the abolition struggle came later than that of Clarkson, it is perhaps sensible to pencil a sketch of him first because he is the better remembered.

William Wilberforce was born into a moderately affluent family in Hull, Yorkshire, on 24 August 1759, the third of the four children of Robert and Elizabeth Wilberforce. Among his siblings, all sisters, two would survive to adulthood. The fortunes of the family had declined somewhat during the previous hundred years but the Wilberforces were still very much part of the 'country gentlemen set' and William's grandfather, also a Robert, had been a prominent merchant in Hull. William Wilberforce's father died early and he was brought up from 1768 in the care of an uncle. During this time and through the ministrations of his aunt, a strong admirer of the preaching of the non-conformist evangelical, George Whitefield, he experienced a passing brush with Methodism. When William was about 13, however, his mother decided to remove him from this 'dangerous influence' and under her sole guardianship he entered St John's College, Cambridge in 1776, with an independent fortune and extensive landed property in Yorkshire awaiting him at maturity. It was at Cambridge that he decided to enter politics, moved to London and fell in with William Pitt. At a cost of nearly £9,000 he contested and won the parliamentary seat of Hull three years later at the age of 20. Politically Wilberforce's strategy in most respects was to play safe, although this may appear an unfair analysis in view of his radical stance on abolition. Nonetheless he stood as an independent and, while supporting Pitt generally, made his position clear that he would do nothing to bind himself to government policies. He was adroit at watching his own back, one of the reasons perhaps for delaying any agreement to raise the abolition issue in the Commons until after Pitt had done so.

From early in his adult life Wilberforce claimed to have inherited mental strength from his mother but to suffer from a 'delicate constitution', an impression bolstered by his diminutive, rather feeble frame and the weak eyesight from which he had suffered since childhood. These disabilities, however, do not appear to have limited him greatly. Though he complained constantly of poor health, his 'many bodily tortures' were not severe enough to affect a full social round, fraternising with the gentry and nobility. Wilberforce lived well and enjoyed playing the social host through much of his life. Inviting 'friends to supper' appears almost daily in his diaries. He clearly enjoyed travel, and alleged frailties do not seem to have deterred him from perennially journeying the length and breadth of the country on social visits, though when his travels might have included the prospect of venturing to the distinctly less-than-salubrious docksides of Bristol and Liverpool in pursuit of information about the slave trade, such excursions were conveniently left to others. Nor did a delicate constitution prevent him from marrying and raising a healthy family. On 30 May 1797 he wedded Barbara Ann, the eldest daughter of a wealthy Warwickshire landowner. Infirmities continued throughout his life but seem on occasions to have come and gone with almost miraculous speed. On 18 December 1808 his diary records another 'dangerous illness' diagnosed as lung inflammation. Yet within a week he was well on the way to recovery and making the most of the Christmas festivities.[2]

At times, and no doubt in company with much of his circle of eighteenth-century contemporaries, Wilberforce could be splendidly and even unwittingly hypocritical. Like many vain and arrogant men he was constantly at pains to stress his own humility, though occasionally the mask seems to have slipped. In his official biography an interesting early comment is attributed to him. 'The first years that I was in Parliament I did nothing to any good purpose; my own distinction was my darling object.'[3] Having discovered his evangelistic calling he professed to have shunned the moneyed and the titled, yet his social diary reveals a determined cronyism with precisely the kind of aristocratic set he is supposed to have turned his back upon. This is explained away through the tenuous claim that his 'general intercourse with society was now made subservient to the interests of the cause'. A more detailed trawl of his memoirs, however, suggests that the intercourse frequently did not touch on the abolition issue. Wilberforce lived for 79 years, reaching the same ripe old age as Granville Sharp, and died on 29 July 1833.

Much of William Wilberforce's life story is beyond contention, yet some aspects are harder to uncover because his correspondence and personal diaries largely became scattered, even during his lifetime. Some of this material he had ordered to be destroyed, and it was saved by chance in the latter years of his life. Such fragmentation, however, accounts for only part of the problem. In reality much of Wilberforce's esteem in the eyes of the public has been due to two publications completed some years after his death by his sons Robert and Samuel. They include a lengthy and rambling biography, *The Life of William Wilberforce*, and an extensive collection of letters, *The Correspondence of William Wilberforce*. It is, in particular, *The Life* that many hagiographers have kept at their elbows when wishing to promote the ardent view of a do-good Christian evangelist spearheading the abolition movement and ultimately receiving the victor's laurels. Unfortunately the 'source' compilations of what passes for Wilberforce's life history are as incomplete and inaccurate as they are politically slanted. It follows that subsequent approbation based on evidence that they contain may also be liable to distortion.

Claims from reputable sources cast doubt almost immediately on material in both of the original biographical works. In 1840, seven years after William Wilberforce's death, an eminent London barrister-at-law, H.C. Robinson, compiled a robust *Exposure of Misrepresentations contained in the preface to the Correspondence of William Wilberforce*, in which he observed that he was providing 'an explanation of some of the remarkable peculiarities in those works, as well as a correction of some of their gross errors'. Among the more plain-spoken mid-nineteenth-century periodicals, the *Edinburgh Review*, launched in 1802, observed that *The Life* is not so much a biography as 'with very short exceptions, an history of the Abolition struggle that emerges as a very rambling, confused account composed of desultory memoranda'. Unfortunately these 'desultory memoranda' were not always inclusive or accurate. Robert and Samuel Wilberforce are vulnerable to the criticism that they employed available source material selectively and frequently with bias, so that the resulting five volumes of *The Life* translate more as a disjointed panegyric than an objective historical portrait.

The question mark hanging over objectivity in no way suggests that William Wilberforce lacked moral fibre or denies that he developed an emotional and practical response to the plight of enslaved West Africans. But his was not, as his biographers would have us believe, the inspiration behind the abolition movement and if anything his contribution to the parliamentary debate may have played its part in retarding progress and protracting the timetable of abolition. The distortions have left their indelible mark so that the modern well-intentioned *Macmillan Encyclopedia* on my bookshelf states, mistakenly, that Wilberforce was 'a founder of the Society for the Abolition of the Slave Trade (1787)'.

The accolade of founder is correctly attributable to Thomas Clarkson. To many ears the name is as unfamiliar as that of Wilberforce is legendary, but it was a prize-winning Latin dissertation written by Clarkson in 1785, responding to a theoretical question about the legality of enslavement, that aroused the first serious interest among the British public. When this thesis was published in English in 1786 and 1788, under the title *An Essay on the Slavery and Commerce of the Human Species, particularly the African*, it served to excite anti-slavery sentiment at home into positive action.

Clarkson was born at the family seat of Playford Hall in Wisbech, near Cambridge, within a year of Wilberforce on 28 March 1760. He attended the local grammar school where his father, the Revd John Clarkson, was headmaster, and in 1775 went on to St Paul's School in London. He completed his academic studies for a Bachelor of Arts degree at St John's College, Cambridge, and it was there that he penned his now-famous Latin dissertation in response to the enquiry, *Anne Liceat Invitos in Servitutem Dare?* (is it lawful to make slaves of others against their will?). The choice of subject for this University of Cambridge Master of Arts essay prize was not merely plucked from the air at random, since it was framed by the Vice-Chancellor, the Revd J. Peckard (also referred to as Peter Peckard), whose liberal views about the plight of West African slaves were already well known. In 1784 Peckard seethed from his pulpit that the trade was 'a crime, founded on a dreadful pre-eminence in wickedness; a crime, which being both of individuals and of the nation, must some time draw down upon us the heaviest judgement of Almighty God, who made of one blood all the sons of men, and who gave to all equally a natural right to liberty, and who, ruling all the kingdoms of the earth with equal providential justice, cannot suffer such monstrous iniquity to pass long unpunished'.

Arguably Peckard chose to raise the profile of slavery by instigating a university prize on the subject and it was he who directed Clarkson to read Anthony Benezet's *Guinea* account as a starting point for his research. Having already won the Cambridge Bachelor of Arts essay prize in 1784, Clarkson went on to achieve the same result with his MA contribution the following year. He was then persuaded to translate his labours into English so that the work could benefit a wider readership, and it was published in the following year under the full title of *An essay on the Slavery and Commerce of the Human species, particularly the African, translated from a Latin dissertation, which was honoured with the first prize in the University of Cambridge, for the Year 1785*. It was this exercise that not only stimulated Clarkson's desire to do something about the slave trade but also brought him into contact with others of like mind. Both Granville Sharp and James Ramsay, Rector of Teston, had already published similar tracts and had campaigned to alert a wider audience to the injustices of the slave trade. Another early activist, the London publisher James Phillips, printed the English version of the essay and Clarkson's meeting with such people led him to launch the small founding group that came to be known as the London Committee for the Abolition of the Slave Trade. In 1786 Clarkson rented lodgings at the Baptist's Head Coffee House in Chancery Lane and some of the first meetings were held on the same thoroughfare in the chambers of another charter member, the barrister Richard Phillips.

It was Clarkson whose tireless efforts, sometimes putting him at personal risk, brought most of the 'inside information' that was subsequently cited by Wilberforce and other parliamentarians. Between 1787 and 1794 he travelled many thousands of miles in pursuit of evidence for use against the pro-slavery lobby. During a two-month period in 1788, for example, he covered more than 1,600 miles, often on horseback and at night.[4] He also negotiated with Les Amis des Noirs, the counterpart abolitionist organisation in France, and was responsible for meeting the Emperor of Russia in order to persuade him to back the cause. When his health declined he terminated his more active role for the London Committee but continued to attend meetings and was brought out of retirement for a while in 1805 when concern was raised over the lassitude of members. He retired to Ipswich, where he passed away on 26 September 1846.

Clarkson died without heirs, survived only by his wife, so he did not gain Wilberforce's advantage of literary offspring to compile his eulogy. Hence, details of his life are harder to come by, if only in that they are more diffuse. One of the most revealing of contemporary biographical sources is the monograph published by James Elmes in London some eight years after his death.[5] Elmes makes the succinct point, however, that his memoir is not a comprehensive study, the compilation of which belongs more properly to a relative or personal friend, but rather a sketch of that part of Clarkson's life devoted to the abolition struggle. We also have Clarkson's own major literary contribution to draw on, *History of the Rise, Progress and Accomplishment of the Abolition of the African Slave Trade*. Partly autobiographical, largely egotistical, this volume otherwise seems to be reasonably accurate.

Clarkson did, nonetheless, receive due commendation from politicians and poets alike. Among the latter was William Wordsworth, who dedicated one of his 'liberty' sonnets 'To Thomas Clarkson, on the Final Passing of the Bill for the Abolition of the Slave Trade, March, 1807', having clearly seen whence the driving force behind the abolition of the slave trade had come.

> Clarkson! It was an obstinate hill to climb:
> How toilsome, nay, how dire it was, by thee
> Is known; by none, perhaps, so feelingly;
> By thou, who, starting in they fervent prime,
> Didst first lead forth this pilgrimage sublime,
> Hast heard the constant Voice its charge repeat,
> Which, out of thy young heart's oracular seat
> First roused thee – O true yolk-fellow of Time
> With unabating effort, see, the palm
> Is won, and by all Nations shall be worn!
> The blood-stained Writing is forever torn,
> And thou henceforth shalt have a good man's calm,
> A great man's happiness; thy zeal shall find
> Repose at length, firm friend of human kind!

It is in the published accounts of Wilberforce's life that discrepancies occur chiefly and they can be dealt with under two headings: his involvement with the London Committee and his relationship with Clarkson. According to the authors of *The Life*, Wilberforce was actively involved with the London Committee from the outset on 22 May 1787, and they note that 'the body grew into a valuable ally of William Wilberforce'. The committee minutes, however, reveal a different story. They record his name for the first time on 30 October 1787, when he requested some information about the slave trade and proposed that Granville Sharp, Samuel Hoare and Philip Sansom should meet him from time to time. It was not until 1789, though, that Wilberforce hosted meetings on a few occasions with some members of the committee. His diary indicates that they first dined together during March and April of 1789 and that these informal get-togethers across the dining table continued through 1790, terminating in 1791.

The second reference to Wilberforce in the London Committee minute books occurs on 16 February 1788 with the report of a conversation with Clarkson over a recommendation to the committee that it should provide evidence to be placed before members of the Privy Council on the inhumanity and impolicy of the slave trade.[6] On 8 April 1788 the committee asked Clarkson to contact Wilberforce about presenting a motion in the Commons. The response came after three months in a letter dated 8 July 1788. Wilberforce's advice to the committee was 'to avoid giving any possible occasion of offence to the legislature by forced or unnecessary associations'.[7]

On 24 February 1789 the London Committee again wrote to Wilberforce urging him to raise the subject of the slave trade in the Commons 'early in the present session'. To this Wilberforce responded in non-committal agreement on 3 March. During 1790, the minutes indicate that Wilberforce was not contacted by the committee other than with a request from Granville Sharp on 30 November that he should move in the Commons to obtain copies of the muster rolls of seamen employed aboard the slave ships trading from London, Bristol and Liverpool. After four months of repeated overtures by the committee, Wilberforce eventually reacted by moving for the muster rolls on 29 March 1791. It was not until 26 April, however, that he was elected to the London Committee, in company with Lord Muncaster, Charles Fox, William Smith and William Burgh. If the minute books deliver an accurate record, Wilberforce attended none of the meetings of the committee before 7 June 1791, although he did have periodic contact with some of its members.

Until they gained access to the minute books of the London Committee, Robert and Samuel Wilberforce seem not to have appreciated this situation during their compilation of *The Life*. Having made the assertion that 'from the first Wilberforce directed the endeavours of the Committee' they decided that some explanation was desirable. Attracting the readers' attention in a note, 'Vide MS: the Transactions of the Abolition Society', they set out to justify their father's absence from the affairs of the committee on the grounds of political expediency, revealing blandly that 'it was long indeed before his [Wilberforce's] name was openly enrolled among their [the Committee's] number, because his exertions promised to be more effectual by his being independent of them'.[8]

In reality Wilberforce was not invited to become a founder member of the London Committee, which would have continued to function effectively with or without his attendance. He was only approached four years later, in 1791, when the committee concluded that it should have a formally appointed agent in the Commons. Wilberforce was considered a likely candidate because of his professed Christian principles, his views on the slave trade, his standing as an independent MP and his powers of oratory. He agreed, reluctantly, 'if no one more suited could be found'. Wilberforce undoubtedly possessed an interest in the condition of slaves but there is no evidence that he directed or was even connected with the activities of the London Committee until some considerable time after its inauguration.

One also finds clear areas of disagreement concerning the extent of Wilberforce's personal contribution, even at a distance, to the labours of the London Committee. The spring and summer of 1788 amounted to a pivotal period in its early progress. In April of that year Wilberforce is said to have fallen ill from an unspecified 'digestive disorder' but despite his condition, according to the authors of *The Life*, the operations of the committee during this protracted period 'were directed by his advice'. Their version of events is significantly at odds with that of Granville Sharp, the committee chairman. The Sharp memoirs assembled by his biographer, Prince Hoare, reveal that during the 'important transactions' of the spring of 1788, William Wilberforce was 'deprived by illness of the power of attending or in any manner assisting the Committee in its anxious progress'. Sharp's recollection of events is supported in the minutes dated 22 April 1788, when Samuel Hoare, the committee treasurer, observed that Wilberforce's health had been reported to be so bad that 'he was not suffered to read any letters concerning the slave trade'.[9] In his study of Clarkson, published in 1839, Thomas Taylor also concurred that Wilberforce was sufficiently indisposed during 1788 that he could offer no assistance to the committee and that all the effort was borne by Clarkson, who was unceasing in his first-hand research and in pressing for petitions to be raised.[10] Yet although this malaise prevented Wilberforce from assisting the committee, he was apparently fit enough to embark on a long journey from Yorkshire to Bath in the west of England, and thence on to various other destinations that served his protracted convalescence.

The barrister H.C. Robinson, in his *Exposure of Misrepresentations*, perhaps most concisely sums up the objectivity, or lack of it, inherent in certain aspects of *The Life*. He makes the pithy observation that the biography is written 'in a spirit manifestly unfriendly to the great body of abolitionists' and that with few exceptions Robert and Samuel 'barely tolerate the survivors and representatives of the original abolitionists'. He adds the succinct point that the Society of Friends is represented in *The Life* 'most incorrectly as the allies of Wilberforce whereas they were the acting body whom he represented in Parliament'.

The accounts of Wilberforce's personal relationship with Clarkson are also beset with misconception. Clarkson and Granville Sharp developed a close bond from 1787 onwards that lasted until Sharp's death in 1813, but this cannot be said of the association between Clarkson and Wilberforce. Elmes's cosy description of 'that distinguished triumvirate of friends, Sharp, Clarkson and Wilberforce' is wishful thinking. Wilberforce and Clarkson would eventually meet within the London Committee, though not until 1791, and their backgrounds were sufficiently far apart to colour their relationship within the constraints of the eighteenth-century English social world. Awkward currents seem to have existed from the outset. Eventually these resulted in considerable animosity though not, it has to be said, predominantly from William Wilberforce, whose position, by and large, remained one of aloof distance. He conveyed the distinct impression that Clarkson was his social inferior and consistently exhibited reluctance to treat him as a friend until, perhaps, the very end of his life, when the tone of some isolated correspondence indicates that he mellowed. For much of the time, evidence suggests that Wilberforce was prepared to manipulate Clarkson as and when it facilitated the enhancement of his own position. It was, however, the conduct of his sons, Robert and Samuel, towards Clarkson that became both nasty and unjustifiable.

Not least among the reasons for coolness between Wilberforce and Clarkson was their difference in approach to Christianity. Clarkson had become allied with the nonconformists and, as Wilberforce confided in a 1789 letter to the intellectual socialite Hannah More, 'the increase of dissenters, which always follows from the institution of unsteepled places of worship, is highly injurious to the interests of religion in the long run'.[11] In Wilberforce's eyes 'unsteepled' was probably synonymous with 'unprincipled'. On more than one occasion he expressed the view that nonconformists could (and probably should) do nothing without the established Church.

The Life goes to considerable lengths to colour Wilberforce as a man of unflinching Christian strength and rectitude and the authors lay much store on his lifelong crusade to rid the country of vice and immorality. Other sources, however, reveal that at times the outward profession of Christian principles did not match the practice. That he was adept at priggish affectations when it came to religious observance is evidenced in a letter to his mother, dated 26 September 1797: 'May you learn to be at the same time conscious of your own demerits as a sinner, and of the love of God, who holds out the promise of pardon and acceptance to all penitent believers in Christ.' Whether Mrs Wilberforce senior responded to this display of benevolent advice from her son, his biographers chose not to disclose.

Nor did Wilberforce's Christian charity extend to those whom he recognised as rivals, and Clarkson undoubtedly fell into this category. He was not slow to use an opportunity, however small, to denigrate. On one occasion, writing to his friend

Lord Muncaster about the importance of raising petitions against the trade, Wilberforce could not resist a snipe at Clarkson's level of competence by saying, 'I mention this lest Clarkson, to whom I threw it out, should have failed to tell you.' Trawling the correspondence folios of both men I could find very little surviving evidence of letters passing between the two. There are, for example, none contained in the Clarkson Papers held by the British Library, nor do they occur in the personal papers of Thomas Clarkson in the collection at St John's College, Cambridge. Where examples do survive, Wilberforce does not describe Clarkson as 'a friend' until the very end of his life, unlike men of the social and political standing of Pitt and Samuel Thornton (Chairman of the Bank of England), whom Wilberforce regarded as his equals and with whom he corresponded in tones of fawning affection.

To what extent Robert and Samuel Wilberforce orchestrated the dearth of any Clarkson correspondence cannot be decided but it is probably of no small significance that throughout the extensive collection of letters in the edited *Correspondence of William Wilberforce*, there is also not a single document addressed to, or from, Thomas Clarkson. In his *Strictures on a Life of William Wilberforce*, Clarkson confirms that soon after Wilberforce senior's death, Robert asked him for the loan of any letters sent by his father. Clarkson sent all that he had, but obtained no acknowledgement of their receipt. None are included in the *Correspondence* and the very small selection published in *The Life* appear to have been inserted by Robert and Samuel with little relevance to their father's biography. The purpose seems to have been exclusively to denigrate Thomas Clarkson.

In the chapters of *The Life* covering the period from the end of 1791 one can detect the most severe digs at Clarkson's integrity. For a while, until the darker aspects of the French Revolution became clear, some of his publicly aired remarks may have been construed, rightly or wrongly, to be in sympathy with the rise of the proletariat across the water. On 3 December 1791 Samuel Hoare, whose support for Clarkson was not always consistent, wrote to Wilberforce voicing concern that the Church of England was gaining an erroneous idea that the dissenters fancied revolution, and that the abolition of the slave trade was somehow connected with this ambition. 'What has added to this apprehension', Hoare complained, 'is some inquiries of Mr Clarkson's whether there are many friends to the French Revolution, in letters which he addresses to different places . . . a moment's reflection must convince him that there is too much reason to fear that what may be only meant as his own private sentiments, will be construed into an opinion of our committee.'

To exploit what they perceived as a flaw in Clarkson's loyalties to the Crown, the brothers drew on hostile reactions from an assortment of third parties.

Dr Joseph Milner, a close ally of William Wilberforce, noted that he wished Thomas Clarkson were 'in better health and better notions in politics; no government can stand on such principles as he appeals to and maintains. I am very sorry for it, because I see plainly advantage is taken of such cases as his, in order to represent the friends of the Abolition as levellers.' Another letter, from the Home Secretary, Henry Dundas, appears to have been included because it contains the critical comments, 'what business had your friend Clarkson to attend the "Crown and Anchor" last Thursday? He could not have done a more mischievous thing to the cause you have taken in hand.' This appears to refer to a public meeting that registered moral support for the revolutionaries. *The Life* also includes a letter penned in a clear mood of exasperation from Wilberforce to Muncaster: 'You will see Clarkson. Caution him against talking of the French Revolution; it will be the ruin of our cause.'

One particularly vexatious piece of correspondence was included because it cast doubt on Clarkson's role as founder of the abolition movement. Wilberforce's friend Bishop Latrobe had written to a daughter in 1815 alleging that the *force majeure* in the abolition struggle was a West Indian woman whom James Ramsay had married when living on the island of St Kitts. Back at the Teston rectory she had become closely involved with the wife of Sir Charles Middleton, the MP for Rochester, and another patroness, Mrs Bouverie. According to the letter, 'God put into the heart of Lady Middleton to venture one step further and urge the necessity of bringing the proposed abolition of the trade before parliament.' Sir Charles, having neither received messages from on high nor made his parliamentary debut, reacted that the cause would be in bad hands with him, whereupon Lady Middleton proposed a letter to Wilberforce at Hull. Thus, by implication, the authors of *The Life* dismissed the London Committee in general and Clarkson in particular from being the inspiration for abolition.

Acrimony was perhaps rarely far from the surface but it would erupt openly in July 1793, when Clarkson was attempting to secure a naval captaincy for his brother. He asked Wilberforce to use his influence with the First Lord of the Admiralty, John Pitt, Earl Chatham, and when Chatham refused the application it appeared to Clarkson, one suspects with a degree of justification, that Wilberforce had done little to intercede on his brother's behalf. Given that Clarkson had invested an inordinate amount of labour over many years, often placing his life and limb in personal jeopardy, into providing on-the-spot information for Wilberforce to use in the Commons, it may have seemed a not-unreasonable favour to ask. Clarkson's subsequent letter to Wilberforce reveals true frustration and a measure of intemperance, which he was later to confess to: 'My opinion is that my Lord Chatham has behaved to my brother in a very scandalous manner, and that your own timidity [in failing to influence Chatham] has been the occasion of his miscarrying in his promotion.' The letter continues by referring to Wilberforce's 'own want of firmness in the matter'.

If the reply published in *The Life* is authentic, Wilberforce used the occasion to put Clarkson down in a manner that was cold, chillingly polite and at the same time offensive. He made the scathing observation that he was 'used to such remonstrances and fairly unmoved by them'. This might have been the understandable tone for a politician replying to a persistently aggressive member of the public, but hardly in dealing with the man to whom he was so deeply indebted. However, there remain certain unexplained wrinkles in the affair. Having digested the version of events conveyed in *The Life*, Clarkson penned a curious observation about Wilberforce's response. 'It is indeed a most beautiful letter and one of the best specimens of his writing in *The Life*, but I have no recollection of having received it as there printed, though I know that he wrote to me in the same general effect.'[12]

We may never be sure if Robert Wilberforce edited and rescripted his father's letter but that is clearly what Clarkson implies. Beyond question the sons manipulated the record by avoiding inclusion of correspondence on the subject that might have shaded their father's conduct differently. Shortly after publication of *The Life*, H.C. Robinson, the editor of Clarkson's *Strictures*, obtained a packet of eleven letters that had been loaned to Messrs Wilberforce and which had then been 'remitted to Thomas Clarkson's order' in London. The letters were addressed to Lieutenant Clarkson, on whose behalf the application had been made. Six were larded with tones of affectionate familiarity and in one, dated 28 December 1791, Wilberforce wrote, 'If I have any opportunity of serving you in the line of your profession I shall be truly happy to embrace it.' Robinson observes that the sentiment is not easy to swallow, since William Wilberforce was 'the bosom friend of the Prime Minister, who was brother to the First Lord of the Admiralty'. It would seem, therefore, that, on the one hand, these particular letters amount to little more than a disingenuous ploy to maintain their author in the best possible light, but on the other, if published they could have indicated to the more casual reader that William Wilberforce was a closer friend to the Clarkson family than the sons wished to convey.

That sensitive material was sometimes omitted can be gleaned by comparing details of the correspondence included in biographical material published by Messrs Wilberforce with the personal letters in the Clarkson collection. The Clarkson papers unusually include a letter that Wilberforce senior wrote to Mrs Elizabeth Clarkson on 12 March 1822 from his home in Kensington Gore. He refers to her last letter to him and responds, 'As you think it desirable that we should have a little private talk before we meet publicly and as it could not take place at our lodgings without exciting surmise, I take the liberty of suggesting, but merely for your consideration, whether you could meet me at my son's, No. 45 Brompton Row . . . or anywhere you like, [such as] Hatchards booksellers, 107 Piccadilly, as not exciting suspicion and we could confer in its back shop . . . the cause of the variation – the person you mention – has manifestly suffered from living in a Society where the standard of morals has been very low.'[13] The reason for this proposed meeting, or indeed if it ever took place, is not revealed nor does any mention of discussions between Wilberforce and Elizabeth Clarkson appear in *The Life* or the collection of edited *Correspondence*. The Clarkson family must have considered the letter important enough to be preserved in their dossier of papers and the conclusion must be either that Wilberforce destroyed the evidence for the meeting during his lifetime or his sons excluded it out of concern that it might compromise their father's image.

Conversely, when credit for Clarkson's efforts was, according to third-party recollection, contained in correspondence, there are hints of reluctance to publish it. In 1791 Wilberforce wrote to Archdeacon Corbett with a note of thanks for the support given to the abolition cause by way of a parliamentary petition raised during a meeting in Shropshire. According to Corbett's record this letter referred to praise extended equally to Wilberforce and Clarkson at the Shropshire meeting. Only Robert Wilberforce would know for certain if it was included in a package of material that Corbett sent to him during preparation of *The Life* and why, if so, it was not noted in the biography.[14]

Elements of Clarkson's *History of the Abolition* undoubtedly amounted to a source of grievance for Wilberforce senior in his later years. Ostensibly this was because, in his eyes, Clarkson had minimised the research material in the abolition campaign provided by his brother-in-law, James Stephen. Closer to the truth, one suspects, each man was an itch under the other's skin and Clarkson was no less capable of pomposity and self-righteousness than was Wilberforce when he had a mind, though unquestionably with more justification. There is little doubt, from my reading of the record, that much of the standoffish attitude displayed by Wilberforce stemmed from realisation of his personal limitations and from worry that Clarkson's achievements would eclipse his own place in the record.

The real enmity, however, came from Robert and Samuel, High Anglican churchmen both, with little time in any event for nonconformists. They set out to demolish Clarkson with vicious intent and their campaign to trash both his image and his *History* is an indication of the depth of concern that their father's prestige might be overshadowed *in memoriam*. When, in 1838, some thirty years after publication of his *History* and at the age of 79, Clarkson wrote his *Strictures on a Life of William Wilberforce*, they were largely a response to these attempts to discredit him. In a letter to Henry Brougham, a barrister friend associated with reforming causes and with the *Edinburgh Review*, he described the work as being 'the only one I have written with feelings of unmingled pain; for it is the only one I have written in defence of myself'.[15]

The Wilberforce-family knives were to come out against Clarkson in a particularly offensive manner over a matter of money. In the course of his work for the London Committee, often in distant parts of the British Isles, Clarkson incurred not-inconsiderable expenses, much of which he met from his own pocket. I have discovered occasional records that the London Committee advanced funds to him but often with a substantial shortfall. By way of an example of his outgoings he describes how, in order to prosecute the case of a mate aboard the slave ship *Thomas* over the murder of a crew-member, William Lines, he found it necessary to hire a messenger to travel considerable distances to round up witnesses and to pay for legal representation. When the prosecution foundered, he had to expend a further large sum in order to send the witnesses back again.

By the spring of 1794 Clarkson had spent much of his own modest capital in an entirely proper manner on undertakings for the committee, often at Wilberforce's behest. Various individuals who knew of the circumstances, including Wilberforce, agreed that it was justifiable to reimburse him with a sum of £1,500, particularly since he was now in a poor state of health, largely as a consequence of his exertions. Wilberforce had agreed, therefore, to set up a private subscription among affluent supporters of the cause in order to procure the money. Clarkson's initial letter requesting funds from Wilberforce stated, 'I should have explained this to our committee, but that you in your letter of instructions desired me to apply to you, should it be wanting.' His remarks touched on an agreement that the sum could not be met 'with propriety' by the London Committee, although in reality it was less a matter of good taste, more the fact that the committee's bank account was depleted. At that time the treasurer, Samuel Hoare, might have found difficulty in raising a tenth of the sum.

It appears, however, that when the need for action became severe and Clarkson was suffering obvious financial hardship, Wilberforce at first ignored his overtures to negotiate the sponsorship. Clarkson was now faced with the humiliation of sending out a volley of pleading letters. He wrote to Wilberforce, 'can you send me any news relative to Mr Samuel Smith; he promised me he would give if you signified your approbation of the thing. I should hardly like to leave London till Mr Smith has been canvassed; you have only this one thing to do for me.' Clarkson was also obliged to approach several of the people on the list personally, one of whom was Lord Muncaster. Muncaster responded sourly, not to Clarkson but to Wilberforce, intimating his distaste for Clarkson's apparent willingness to support the cause of the French revolutionaries. 'To the justice of this proceeding

I say nothing but its policy appears to me open to objection from the prevailing idea of Clarkson's prejudices, and the attempts made by our enemies to colour the cause with those alarming principles. Clarkson tells me I am down on your list and that it is your intention to apply to me.' Wilberforce made clear in reply to Muncaster that he found the whole business distasteful, commenting, 'I have only been restrained [from writing to you and others on the subject] by a certain feeling of delicacy.' He had thought 'that the money should have been lodged in the shape of a life annuity and the secretary of one of those bodies should have been told to write to Clarkson, word that a certain annuity due to him appeared in the books of the Society and asking where and to whom he would have it paid. All my fine scheme is at an end.' A now-desperate Clarkson again wrote to Wilberforce 'I must stay somewhat later in town. At least ten days and have only to entreat all the exertion you can give with convenience to yourself in this time. You do not know what ten days may produce particularly if we act together. There are some persons independently of those on your list to whom I mean to apply.'

Robert and Samuel Wilberforce not only published all of this confidential correspondence during Clarkson's lifetime but also made specific allegation in *The Life*[16] that Clarkson obtained the money 'by means of importunate applications'. When they advised Clarkson of their intention to publish, he pointed out that he would stand accused as a detractor and liar and would have to appeal to the public for restoration of character. In truth Clarkson had been left with no alternative because Wilberforce had failed to act, either through distraction or, more probably, lack of interest. The impression is gained that Clarkson's financial plight was of passing concern to Wilberforce, since his advancing debility meant that he had largely served his useful purpose. It must have been deeply embarrassing that this private correspondence was to be aired for the world to read, implying that the application amounted to importuning. Clarkson objected especially to the fact that the brothers intended to highlight a letter to Wilberforce in which he had named certain individuals who he felt could reasonably be approached for the sponsorship. At the close of a letter of 18 July 1834, Robert Wilberforce delivered a particularly mealy-mouthed riposte that he and his brother would endeavour to express themselves in a manner 'as free as possible from all insult', thus actually implying that insult could not be avoided.

Lord Brougham responded to Clarkson's distraught letter of 1838 concerning the £1,500 with a comment that he could not conceive the necessity of printing these confidential letters to Wilberforce, since they had no bearing on the recipient or the abolition and were 'only calculated to give you pain. Their printing tends to give a most untrue representation of your character.' Brougham also observed that *The Life* seemed to deny that Wilberforce had ever read Clarkson's *History* or, at best, 'done more than dip into it'.[17] The first volume of

The Life indeed includes the revealing statement that William Wilberforce 'looked into the book and saw enough to induce him to refuse to read lest he should be compelled to remark upon it'.[18]

Wilberforce was averse to doing anything that might draw attention among his well-heeled friends to the sheer magnitude of enterprise that Clarkson had conducted personally in the cause of the abolition movement. The sons' aim subsequently seems to have been to discredit Clarkson over any suggestion that he might claim for himself the honour due, in their opinion, exclusively to their father. This, in their flawed estimation, was the underlying thrust of Clarkson's *History*. In his letter of July 1834, Robert Wilberforce levelled a bald accusation at Clarkson that 'the impression which, as far as I can see, your history of that cause [the abolition] is calculated to convey is that my father was originally engaged in it by you and that he was subsequently a sort of parliamentary agent, of whom you availed yourself. Now, that neither of these statements is correct I have abundant evidence. I could hope indeed that the impression which your book conveys, was not that which you intended to give; but the erroneous conclusion, to which it leads, my father's biographer will be obliged to notice; he will be compelled to show both that Mr Wilberforce did not originally enter upon the cause at your suggestion, and that when he had taken it up, he was the principal, by whom its operations were directed.' The evidence is clear, however, that Robert Wilberforce's hostile reaction amounted to scarcely more than bluster and wishful thinking. That which he articulated so negatively in his 1834 letter is, in fact, closer to the truth than much of what is claimed in *The Life*.

Gathering together all the available evidence about the relationship of Wilberforce and Clarkson, it is probably fair to say that outright hostility never surfaced between them. The real acrimony stemmed only from the pens of Robert and Samuel, whose twenty-page preface to the *Correspondence*, in particular, reads as an unremitting assault on Clarkson, his competence, knowledge and character. In Wilberforce's final years he may have come close to an admission that he had treated his fellow abolitionist unreasonably. Like many influential but not overly talented men, he had exploited Clarkson, when opportunity arose, in order to further his own ambition of being the shining beacon of the abolition. At the close of the *Strictures* Clarkson contends that Wilberforce 'showed a warmth of friendship for me amounting to affection . . . putting me on a footing with one of his most intimate friends. All this I could have shown in many letters but the greater number has been destroyed.' Clarkson claimed to have preserved four letters from Wilberforce, although none has survived the passing of the years. In the last, written four months before his death and copied into the text of *Strictures*, Wilberforce addressed Clarkson as 'my dear old friend' and confessed that he was 'unaffectedly vexed by the idea of having treated you unkindly'. He talked at length about his children and seems genuinely to have wished to make amends for earlier shortcomings. The letter closed with the sentiment 'my dear friend, ever sincerely and affectionately yours'.[19] Whether Clarkson ever did possess those 'many letters', whether any of this reflects a sincere wish emanating from two elderly and obsessive men to bury the hatchet for posterity, we shall never know. Perhaps when all was said and done, each preferred the world to believe that the other had been his friend, not his adversary.

One aspect, though, remains essentially clear. Robert and Samuel Wilberforce's disdain for Clarkson, their passionate desire to place their father on a pedestal, receiving the sole honours, was equalled only by Clarkson's own deep and lasting resentment of their strategy to knock him down. At the close of the *Strictures* he observes that the brothers had access to the volumes of London Committee minutes, which can have left them in no doubt that he was the founding father of the British abolition movement, and he notes how extraordinary it is that they should have denigrated him in *The Life* as 'the agent of the committee seeking patiently for evidence'. He rejects emphatically the impression that Wilberforce was ever more than a complete stranger to the men that he, Clarkson, successively enlisted to the committee. He underlines the fact that for some years Wilberforce did not contribute to the interminable journeys, the correspondence, or the production of literature and newspaper articles that he had shouldered and which eventually undermined his health.

Some unresolved mysteries remain. Inserted in the flyleaf of the first of the three original London Committee minute books is a handwritten copy by 'F. Smith' of a letter from Richard Phillips to Thomas Clarkson, dated 18 August 1854. It includes the comment, 'I am much pleased that thou has found that important paper of the late W. Wilberforce's, trusting that when R. Wilberforce receives a copy of it, it will prevent his proceeding in the mistaken and vexatious line he had intended.'[20] Was this Wilberforce's absolution of Clarkson?

That Clarkson was the true driving inspiration of the London Committee for the Abolition of the Slave Trade may be gleaned from a quantitative inspection of the minute books. From its foundation in May 1787 until Clarkson's retirement in May 1794, a physically broken man, the minutes covering those seven years fill 523 folio pages. From July 1794 until the abolition of the slave trade was achieved in 1807, almost twice the passage of time, they amount to a mere seventy-six. Furthermore, from 1795 the entries change strikingly. Once immaculately and carefully inscribed, they become largely characterised as crude and hasty scribblings. One might deduce from this evidence alone, that the committee had lost its drive and its heart.

Chapter 6

THE ABOLITIONISTS

There is a mistaken belief, promoted by some modern historians, that the abolitionists were the key players in securing the cessation of Afro-Caribbean slavery; that new-found morality swept through parliament and public alike with a fervent white heat; that the vogue of practical Christianity, lit by such choice gatherings as the Clapham Saints, shone like a triumphant beacon; and that all this cut through the darkness of outmoded and near-pagan behaviour. Unfortunately the bare reality of the abolitionist movement reveals that it amounts largely to wishful thinking.

It is necessary to dispense with some basic mythology. Officially the London Committee for the Abolition of the Slave Trade was not about freeing slaves and it is important to bear in mind that in the eighteenth and nineteenth centuries the slave trade and slave emancipation were wholly discrete issues as, for that matter, was ownership of slaves. The London Committee was established for precisely the purpose indicated, namely to get rid of the trade. The committee was launched in 1787 and after the Act of 1807 it existed in name only until it was finally dismantled in 1819. Whatever private sentiments its members may have nursed about liberty for West Indian slaves they kept to themselves. The committee had nothing to do with, and never publicly supported, emancipation. A number of considerations must have come into play. Not least was an undercurrent of public sentiment, discernible since almost the beginning of the century, that although the use of slaves on the sugar plantations was right and proper both economically and morally, the national benefit of the slave-trading exercise had become open to question.

Serving as slave-shippers to the world may have looked fine at face value but on closer inspection it did not make a great deal of economic sense, and as early as 1713, voices had been raised, especially against the wisdom of the *asiento* deal with Spain. The contemporary eighteenth-century economics pundit Malachy Postlethwayt complained that the contract lost Britain the substance in exchange for the shadow and could hardly have been contrived with less benefit to the nation. Among his arguments was that the deal with Spain's court had ruinously deprived Jamaica of its right to trade into the South Seas while entitling Britain to the questionable benefit of selling 4,800 Negroes to Spanish colonial buyers and delivering a paltry 5 tons of goods to Porto Bello once a year. Much of this stock then rotted under lock and key in royal Spanish warehouses. Postlethwayt considered that the French had been altogether more astute in unloading the *asiento* on to England having made their fortune out of it to the impoverishment of the entire Spanish Indies, and having overdone the trade to such an extent that it was little value to any successor.[1] Fifty years on, reminders of such comments must have echoed with an uncomfortable ring of truth. In 1788 the Privy Council recorded the sobering detail that of the annual British export of slaves from Africa, two-thirds were sold to foreigners – in other words handed over to Britain's competitors in the plantation business.

Understanding among the abolitionists was that in the prevailing social and political climate towards the close of the eighteenth century, they stood as much chance of emancipating colonial slaves as they did of obtaining universal adult suffrage. Interestingly the absence of political power for women benefited the lobby backing the trade. Had women been entitled to the vote when Mary Wollstonecraft published her pioneering *A Vindication of the Rights of Woman* in 1792 things might have turned out differently. When pressure for slave emancipation was mounting at the beginning of the 1830s, the protests raised by such sororities as Ladies of Lyme Regis against Slavery reached the tables of the Houses of Lords and Commons in some volume. But even then the effect is questionable and one suspects that there such petitions sat, largely unread and unloved by ruddy-faced, landowning backbenchers with other things on their minds.

The London Committee was starkly aware that any hint of a plan to assault the institution of slavery would have been fruitless and would have damaged its cause. It would have been pitted against too much powerful influence in the make-up of both houses of parliament. The Upper House in particular represented a formidable body of opposition to any talk of emancipation. Many of those on its benches, as Lord Westmoreland once conceded, owed their personal fortunes and their Westminster seats to slavery.[2] A sizeable number also owed these benefits to the trade itself but, nonetheless, the slave trade was seen to be vulnerable. Abolitionists viewed it as the softer target and the committee was at pains to stick firmly to the line that the trade alone was the quarry.

One is also tempted to believe that at heart the members of the committee were not overly concerned about emancipation. The adverse conditions under which slaves were kept no doubt bothered them, but slavery was part of an English tradition that most people, the majority of trade-abolitionists included, probably accepted without any great qualms. The committee correctly discerned that abolition of the trade was the critical issue and that good economic arguments could be drawn out in its favour. It must have also nurtured the long-term view that the outlawing of the trade would cut off the supply of the slave-owning plantations. If statistics of mortality against birth rates in the West Indies provide any measure, their 'life blood' would be drained within a measurable period and the colonial slave system would collapse.

So what were the tactics of the London Committee for the Abolition of the Slave Trade and how effectively was it set to operate? Thomas Clarkson and Richard Phillips had been sitting down together for some time before the official launch of the committee. Clarkson notes in his *Strictures* that they were 'accustomed to work together every night, Sundays excepted, at his chambers at Lincoln's Inn at the latter end of 1786 and the beginning of 1787'.[3] When the members first came together in May 1787, an eclectic mix of dissenting Quakers and evangelicals, they decided sensibly that their first objective ought to be the development of a subscription list among the more influential and well-off members of the public, drawing in any members of parliament that showed signs of sympathy. In an age of mass media and global electronic communication we cannot readily appreciate the extent of eighteenth-century problems in 'getting the message across'. Public meetings would generally attract local audiences and therefore require ad hoc mobilisation in towns across the country in order to be effective. Pamphlets were expensive to print, and their production, in an era when typesetting was immensely cumbersome and had to be originated from manuscript, took time to complete. But once they were published, to whom did one distribute them? No mailing agencies existed and many people were illiterate, so encouraging a subscription list not only brought essential working revenue but also resulted in a nucleus of known supporters on whom to call. It was decided, therefore, in order to attract subscribers, that the committee would first publish a summary of what little was known about the trade, including an insight into the methods of abduction on the West African coast.

Very early in its operations the London Committee understood that it would be a mistake to focus exclusively on religious and moral arguments and this essential element of the tale has been overlooked or perhaps not appreciated by writers claiming that the abolition of the trade was brought about through humanitarian pressures. On 15 January 1788 the committee drafted an internal report making certain recommendations, 'For though it can by no means be admitted that the greatest commercial advantages ought to preponderate, when opposed to the greatest dictates of religion and morality, yet the committee are not insensible of the natural influence which interest has in biasing the judgements of men and much important it is to convince the public that the commerce of this kingdom and even the interests of the slave holders will be advanced by the success of our endeavours.'[4] The same report went on to lay stress on the fact that British trade to West Africa, already reasonably profitable, could be made much more attractive commercially if the relationship with the local communities was based not on spreading 'distress and divestation' but 'peace and civilisation'. In a report dated 15 April 1789, the committee returned to a similar line of argument stating, 'There is no reason for any description of his Majesty's subjects to be alarmed at the proposed abolition of the slave trade under a delusive fear that a decline in the cultivation of the sugar colonies will be the consequence.' In July 1790 it reported that it had been established, beyond contradiction, that 'Africa is capable of supplying articles for an honourable and beneficial commerce from her own produce.'[5]

The 'distress and divestation' afflicting West Africans was a factor that Wilberforce paraded to excess, but it was also a significant element in the abolitionists' strategy. Clarkson's view in his *History* is that local African despots and unscrupulous European entrepreneurs should share the burden of blame evenly and that Africans who preyed on their fellows were guilty in equal degree to the European traders who encouraged their sense of greed and that there was no morality evident on either part.[6] The accusation was laid out in a London Committee statement of 24 May 1787, which added that 'slaves are acquired by [local tribal] war, for which arms are furnished by Europeans. Since the introduction of the trade all crimes are punishable by slavery.'[7] First-hand evidence at this level was readily available from a number of sources. The adventurer John Barbot, writing in 1732, had said, 'the trade in slaves is in a more peculiar manner the business of kings, rich men and prime merchants, exclusive of the inferior sort of blacks. The king goes and ransacks some of his enemies' towns, seizing the people and selling them for such commodities as he is in want of which commonly is brandy, guns, powder, balls, pistols and cutlasses.' In its report the committee singled out the King of Dahomey as an unusually guilty party.

Information was gathered mindful of the need to provide impressive reading for public consumption. Statistics about numbers of captives and rates of attrition were always going to be effective. The annual exportation of West Africans bound for the Americas was estimated by the committee to be about 100,000, of which more than 20,000 allegedly died en route during the middle passage, and as many again expired during the process of 'seasoning' in the West Indies. There is no indication of whether these figures were accurate, beyond the inference that they came from Anthony Benezet. He apparently drew on an earlier work, Anderson's *History of Trade and Commerce*, in which it was stated that 'England supplies her American colonies with Negro slaves amounting in number to above one hundred thousand every year.'[8] Limited committee funds were immediately earmarked to print 2,000 copies of an initial summary, including these various details, for distribution along with a pilot print run of 300 copies of Clarkson's prizewinning Cambridge University essay, for which James Phillips, the publisher on the committee, was paid £30.[9]

The members of the London Committee were quick to appreciate the desirability of adapting their campaign to the intended audience. What moved parliament or Crown did not necessarily touch the heartstrings of the public in the same way. Members of parliament and the wealthy aldermen of slave ports were less likely to suffer sleepless nights troubled by moral conscience than risk to their status and their wallets. A sizeable number of parliamentarians faced the prospect of financial ruin should either trade abolition or emancipation eventually come about. But the more discerning public, it was believed, was in a mood to be attracted by arguments based on moral expediency. The more emotive material elicited a strong response when circulated and ongoing strategy was to appropriate hard facts that would support the arguments of the committee in the eyes of the public.

Lurid details of atrocities and the gruesome conditions endured not just by slaves but by British seamen were likely to garner greater reaction from those asked to sign petitions than economic arguments. To this end and to obtain first-hand evidence, Clarkson volunteered his services to trawl the seedier dockside quarters of the big English slave-trading ports. It was resolved on 10 June 1787 that he would travel to Bristol and thence north to Liverpool in order to collect information from various quarters, including the custom houses that held details of voyages and their manifests. Clarkson was to be accompanied on the Liverpool leg of his trip by a former slave-ship surgeon, Alexander Falconbridge, who had written a pamphlet, *Account of the Slave Trade on the Coast of Africa* and who was to send reports back to the committee. The name caused some problem for minutes secretaries, who tended to record phonetically as Fawconbridge or Fauconbridge, but I assume they were referring to the same individual. The committee allowed him £10 (equivalent to about £395 in 2005) for this expedition and advised Clarkson to exercise caution on expenditure.[10]

On arriving in Bristol, Clarkson took the opportunity to shake the hands of as many influential local citizens as possible and earned assurances that petitions against the trade would be raised not only in Bristol but in Bridgwater, Monmouth, Gloucester, Worcester, Shrewsbury and Chester as well. He was introduced to several Quakers, including Harry Gandy, who had lived for some thirty years in the West Indies and had made two voyages to West Africa as the master of a slaver before retiring from the trade. Gandy was, therefore, in a good position to provide Clarkson with an amount of first-hand information. Clarkson had also deduced that there might be value in promoting the idea that West Africa could provide many more vital commodities than human cargoes, and wherever possible he started to gather a collection of locally manufactured goods. These eventually included gum, wax, ivory, an assortment of tropical timbers, cotton, cayenne pepper, locally woven and dyed textiles and other products that would constitute evidence presented to a Commons select committee on the slave trade in 1790 and 1791.[11]

Statistics about the loss of seamen aboard the slave ships was, however, Clarkson's main objective. He and others in the committee discerned, accurately, that blue-stocking readers were likely to be more sympathetic to the welfare of British sailors aboard slave ships than their African cargoes. Already it was rumoured that the death rate among the crews of these ships was higher than in other vessels but no hard evidence was currently available. With this in mind it had been agreed that procuring copies of the muster rolls, effectively the crew manifests, for vessels operating from the ports of Bristol and Liverpool was desirable in order to establish how fatal the trade was to those it employed. These documents revealed figures for the numbers of seamen going out and coming back in ships trading to Africa.

The extent to which the people of Bristol opened their arms to Clarkson is in some doubt. He maintains that in general they received him warmly, but Bristol was very much a child of the slave trade and its businessmen had grown fat on the proceeds. The port had matured into what was seen by many as not merely a wealthy, but also a model, city. The contemporary writer Joshua Gee noted that 'the magistrates of Bristol have that city under such excellent regulation that foreign beggars do not appear; they are not troubled with obnoxious sights so common to us'. According to a civic list of 23 June 1755, 237 members of the African Company resided in Bristol, slightly more than in London and Liverpool combined, and the wealth of its merchants was prodigious. Edward's *History of Jamaica* estimated the purchase price of slaves in the British West Indies in 1791. An able-bodied adult is said to have fetched about £50 in harbour auctions. Boys and girls could be obtained for slightly less, at £40–7. The price paid on the West African coast at that time was slightly under £22 a head, so the profit on a voyage was likely to be considerable. Bristol and Liverpool shippers could also undercut their London competitors by 10–15 per cent and, although from the turn of the 1790s the number of slaving ships operating out of Bristol steadily declined in favour of Liverpool, interest there remained powerful right up to the time of abolition. In a heated Commons debate of 1791, a local Bristol member, John Baker Holroyd, Lord Sheffield, declared the arguments of the abolitionists to be 'downright phrensy [frenzy], raised perhaps by the most extraordinary eloquence',[12] and Clarkson noted that when news of rejection of one of

Wilberforce's Commons motions reached Bristol in April 1791, the church bells 'rang out with merry peals'.[13]

Allegedly attempts were made on Clarkson's life more than once during the trip and from the outset he encountered hostility and considerable reluctance to disclose evidence. On 3 July 1788, however, he had learned that a slave ship, the *Brothers*, was lying in the Bristol roads waiting to sail, but that its captain was unable to obtain an adequate crew. Word spread along the dockside that on its previous voyage thirty-two sailors had died, at least some of them as a consequence of inhuman treatment by the captain. To obtain confirmation, Clarkson used a local contact to gain access to the vessel's all-important muster roll. He also established that one member of the former crew, a free black African called John Dean, had come in for exceptionally brutal treatment over some passing misdemeanour. It was alleged that his punishment had involved being stripped and spreadeagled face-down on the deck, his flesh ripped open with hot tongs and boiling tar dropped onto his back. Clarkson eventually tracked down a London solicitor who had represented Dean in court and who confirmed the allegations, advising that the captain of the *Brothers* had been convicted and forced to pay substantial damages. The captain had, nonetheless, retained his command, which was the principal reason for the reluctance of seamen to join the crew on another voyage.[14] This was abolitionist fuel!

To an even greater extent the reliance on the business was true of Liverpool, which by the end of the eighteenth century could lay claim to being the greatest slave-trading port of all, handling well over half of the entire European traffic and nearly three-quarters of that in Britain. Clarkson's reception was largely unwelcoming and it was not until November 1787 that he was able to write to the London Committee to describe any of the lethal circumstances of shipboard conditions and of the cruelty perpetrated by the captains and officers of slave-carrying vessels. It would have been surprising if his entrée had been any more cordial. Sir James Picton, in his *History of Liverpool*, estimated that when the bill to regulate the slave trade was tabled in 1788, the town was making profits of around £300,000 a year on the enterprise, in which many of its businessmen had invested heavily. One merchant declared that he had sunk £30,000 into the traffic and would be ruined if the bill became law. Any Liverpudlian who came out in open support of the trade, particularly from among the clergy, was amply recompensed. When the Revd Raymond Harris wrote a pamphlet confirming that God had backed the legality of the trade in sacred writings, his open channel on the divine word was rewarded to the tune of £100. Neither Liverpool nor Bristol, therefore, was overly keen to open its closets to strangers poking their humanitarian noses into local matters, wherein profits from a single contract could exceed 100 per cent. Among accountancy figures of round-trip voyages that have been preserved are those of the Liverpool-based ship *Ann*. Six shareholders had fitted her out in 1751 at a cost of £1,219. She then assembled a crew and carried a British export cargo valued at £385 to West Africa. The slaves picked up there were shipped to Antigua and sold. The master brought back bills of exchange to a value of £2,006, from which sailors' wages and other sundry charges amounting to £138 had to be deducted. Merchants in Antigua later remitted a further £1,519 as the proceeds of sales on six-monthly terms less commission. The total net profit for the trip came to £3,287. On the next voyage of the *Ann*, completed in 1753, the 'produce' generated £8,000 against an initial outlay of £3,153. When the trade was at its height in the last decades of the century the average return on any given voyage out of Liverpool was reckoned at roughly 30 per cent and the town was making net gains of £260,000 a year from the traffic (over £10 million in 2005 terms).[15]

Clarkson was also seeking clear evidence of atrocities on the West African coast and he pieced together details of a massacre that had taken place in the town of Calabar (now part of Nigeria) in 1767. In the eighteenth century Old Calabar was an important centre for West African slave exports and the information he gathered took the form of original depositions made by a witness and recorded in the case of *The King v. Lippincott and others*. At the time of the atrocity six British ships were anchored in the Calabar river. A tribal spat had brewed up between local factions involved in slave-dealing, and the captain of one of the vessels, the *Indian Queen*, had offered to mediate. His intention was, more precisely, to capture the ringleaders of the dispute and either butcher or haul them on board to boost his cargo. The circumstances resulted in a slaughter when the crews of the slave ships engaged in a vicious manhunt and killed Calabar residents virtually indiscriminately.[16] From Clarkson's point of view the report amounted to valuable ammunition for the London Committee to disseminate, illustrating the barbarity and injustice of slave-dealing at the point of origin.

One of the most notable instances of cruelty to stock the abolitionists' armoury involved another case heard in the courts some years earlier. In March 1783, Gustavus Vasa, a black former crew-member of a slave ship called the *Zong* visited Granville Sharp to recount an alleged case of mass murder. His story provided for the kind of graphic disclosure that, had a tabloid press existed at the time, would have liberally fuelled its front pages for weeks. Granville Sharp indeed exploited the opportunity by circulating detailed accounts to all the London newspapers.

Vasa reported that 133 members of the captive human cargo of the *Zong* had been deliberately drowned in order to facilitate an insurance swindle. The master, Luke Collingwood, had sailed from West Africa in September 1781, commanding a Liverpool-registered vessel that was severely overcrowded, with 440 slaves aboard. During the Atlantic crossing a number died and others became sickly. Drinking-water was also soon in short supply as a result of the overcrowding, and Collingwood's response was to commence throwing the dead and the enfeebled overboard together. This strategy was intended to minimise the insurance losses to the owners on the basis that underwriters rejected marine insurance claims if slaves died of natural causes en route but not if they were lost accidently. Collingwood had arrived off Jamaica, mistakenly believing it to be Hispaniola. When he realised his error and sailed on, the water position was critical and he continued to throw slaves overboard in batches even though rain fell in the Caribbean on the day before he disposed of the last. Sharp brought a charge of murder and the case came before Lord Chief Justice Mansfield, with the Solicitor General appearing on behalf of the owners. That Clarkson and Sharp were facing an uphill task in the longer term must have been clear in their minds from the experience of the immediate outcome. The defence argued the right of a vessel master to throw overboard as many slaves as he thought fit, provided he exhibited a powerful reason. It also argued that this was a case involving chattels or goods rather than human beings and that, for the purpose of insurance settlement, they constituted goods or property. Mansfield directed that 'so far from the guilt of anything like a murderous act, so far from any shew or suggestion of cruelty there was not even a surmise of impropriety and that to bring a charge of murder would argue nothing less than madness'.[17]

The reporting of incidents such as that of the Zong and the Calabar massacre was valuable to the London Committee and its aim was to use the evidence that Clarkson was gathering in the most compelling way in pamphlets and reports. But members also recognised the maxim that a picture paints a thousand words, particularly when trying to rouse public sentiment. One of the first positive moves in this direction was to approve the use of a seal depicting a black African supplicating in chains above a motto posing the question: 'Am I not a Man and a Brother?' This was to prove so successful in attracting attention that in March 1789 they settled upon a similar promotional venture in the shape of a sketch depicting the sections through a slave ship and revealing the excessively cramped conditions. Eventually 500 of these, printed on wooden plaques, were delivered to members of the House of Commons, and another 500, more tastefully executed in copperplate, found their way to addresses of Their Lordships.

The main thrust of activity, however, remained the production of reports and other articles designed to increase awareness of the issues. The London Committee frequently circulated its abolitionist literature through the agency of local dissenter organisations. But the material was often blatantly propagandist and the humanitarian angle, including graphic details of the 'horrors' of the middle passage, risked becoming exaggerated to any discerning eye. Eric Williams points out that as an exercise it smacked of ignorance or hypocrisy or both. There is no dispute that slave-ship cargoes were packed in like sardines, each man with less space for movement than he would have enjoyed in a coffin, because the underlying aim was profit. They did indeed suffer extremely uncomfortable experiences, including brutality, during the weeks at sea, because comfort was not foremost in the minds of the shipowners whose view of their charges was that they were scarcely different from horses or cattle. But mortality was fundamentally down to disease, and this was liable to affect slaves, indentured white servants, crew and free passengers alike.[18]

The sheer volume of abolitionist publications distributed is an indication of the value placed upon them. By the summer of 1788 more than 30,000 copies of summaries and reports had been authorised. In addition the London Committee had printed 14,000 copies of a letter by the Dean of Middleham eloquently deploring the trade, and a further 21,000 pamphlets and booklets penned by various eminent abolitionist authors. The cooperation of the Dean of Middleham must have been found especially valuable, since one of the objectives was to gain the support of the established Church of England in the debate. The London Committee was still largely composed of dissenters and the Anglican Church generally did not support their views, not least because the Anglican clergy owned slaves: The Anglican Society for the Propagation of the Gospel ran an efficient plantation endowment on Barbados.[19] When the 1788 debate on regulating the trade went into committee, the immediate concern of the Bishop of London was not providing much-needed improvement in the conditions for the slaves languishing below decks, but what kind of compensation would be afforded to shipowners whose vessels had already sailed or were on the African coast. Not all of the senior Anglican clerics were unsympathetic and some even broached the taboo subject of emancipation. In February 1788 the London Committee received a paper from the Bishop of Peterborough containing 'many valuable hints respecting the future emancipation of slaves in the West India islands', and in the same year, clergy in the established Church sponsored slightly less than a quarter of petitions against the slave trade. From the viewpoint of the dissenters this was an important gain because it presented a means of lowering mutual distrust.[20] In April 1789 it was noted that the Bishop of St David's had pledged his support.[21] Such bonuses, however, were not commonplace. Many Anglicans remained wary about the degree of public support that they might lose by joining the anti-slave-trade bandwagon and only slowly, from the 1790s, did the entrenched position of the Church begin to be eroded under the impact of popular evangelism.

By August, upwards of 100 petitions had been presented to the Commons. But it came at the cost of severely depleting the London Committee's limited financial resources. This demanded substantial new injections of cash. Not least among the monetary requirements was a need to finance the attendance of witnesses before the Privy Council committee that was currently gathering evidence on the issue of the trade.[22] Subscriptions having gradually started to materialise, the money was chiefly employed to defray the expense of printing and distributing large numbers of graphically worded pamphlets to the public and to MPs. It was also used to support local petitioning, but donations never reached a level that would have permitted the London Committee to launch major campaigns beyond these limited objectives. The British public was willing to put its name (when capability allowed) to pieces of paper extolling worthy causes, but less keen to give money in support of the suffering African. There were exceptions. A letter from 'Mrs Bull' of New Palace Yard, London, enclosing £10 (about £400 in 2005 values) in November 1787 was not untypical of the amounts received. Larger donations arrived in the mail less frequently, among them 100 guineas subscribed by Manchester Society of Friends on 29 December of that year.

In January 1788 the money available in the London Committee's account permitted the printing and distributing of 5,000 more Summary Review pamphlets and 2,000 of Clarkson's essay, with consideration given to publishing a new revised edition of Anthony Benezet's book on Guinea. The decision was also reached to increase the committee to a maximum of thirty members. By early 1789, donations of between £50 and £100 had become more frequent, but by the summer of the following year, cash levels had still run seriously low, with a treasurer's balance of just £94 14s 10d showing. Faced with insolvency, the committee placed advertisements in all the London newspapers in a fresh attempt to drum up support, but it was in much the same impoverished financial condition at the close of 1791 and its measure of cash liquidity was not destined to improve.[23]

In spite of restraints and the tendency to overdramatise the more lurid aspects of the transatlantic passage, the pamphlets brought awareness of the trade to a wider audience and almost from the outset allowed petitioning to begin more actively. In the absence of anything approaching an inclusive voting system, the raising of public petitions was a peculiarly eighteenth- and early nineteenth-century vogue although it tended to go through peaks and troughs. For the abolition, the process had commenced in Manchester in 1787, where a city with fewer than 50,000 inhabitants managed to raise about 10,700 anti-trade signatures, a fairly remarkable result to set the precedent. If the measure of petitions tabled provides a gauge, mass public interest in the anti-slavery campaign reached peaks in 1788 and 1792, but after this the gathering of names on animal skins started to go out of favour as British politics became more polarised. Governments were increasingly disillusioned with the romance of popular politics and from 1795 successive ministries were openly discouraging public petitioning and even imposing legal restrictions.[24] In reality, after 1792, there was no general call for petitions until 1814.

Forces were marshalled predictably and speedily to cast aspersion on the professed aims of the London Committee in the face of growing popularity. Already in the spring of 1788 London was buzzing with salacious gossip that the abolitionists amounted to an anti-royalist fifth column that, given half a chance, would liberate slaves en masse to the detriment of the British economy. Soon after, they were being linked with the extremist founders of the radical Jacobin Club in France and accused of sympathies with the republican revolutionaries. This had been at the root of much of Wilberforce's irritation with what he saw as unwarranted public comments by Clarkson. Out of concern to combat the adverse criticism at local level, in the summer of 1788 Clarkson proposed the establishment of committees in the different counties of Great Britain, but the worry about misrepresentation of the London Committee's true aims remained. I have already mentioned the interesting snippet underlining the degree of paranoia among the members, discovered in the committee minutes of 10 June 1788. An unnamed person among those present appears to have referred to the 'evil of slavery', but this comment has been emphatically deleted by the minutes secretary and replaced by 'evil of the slave trade'.[25]

By April 1789 Clarkson's demanding personal investigations around the slave ports had materialised into a substantial file of evidence, which was submitted to the Privy Council committee sitting to examine the slave trade, excluding for reasons of security the names of witnesses and ships. Appended to this file were two concisely worded summaries, signed by Granville Sharp on the instruction of the London Committee:

From the diminished supply of African slaves during the time of war, from the numerous instances of plantations in the West India islands which have flourished without any purchase of slaves for many years, from the acknowledged deficiency on the part of the planters in protecting and promoting the increase in population of slaves and more particularly from a consideration of the natural and universal progress of population when unchecked by oppression, there is no reason for any description of his Majesty's subjects to be alarmed at the proposed abolition of the slave trade under the delusive fear that a decline in the cultivation of the sugar colonies will be the consequence.

and, moreover,

That the trade to Africa for slaves inasmuch as it occasions a loss of seamen in a proportion more than double that of all the other branches of commerce from this kingdom is a national injury.[26]

Clarkson's drive to set up local committees in order to dispel scandalmongering met with only limited response and his enquiries revealed another potential threat to the abolitionists' aims. It was being rumoured that the slave-traders of Bristol and Liverpool might transfer their bases of operation to Ireland, where opposition was considerably more muted and where after 1782 the legislature enjoyed complete independence from the rest of Britain and could permit freedom of trade. Control there rested largely with absentee landlords holding seats in rotten boroughs and present in the British parliament in sizeable numbers. Clarkson's fears were also raised over coffee-shop chatter that Liverpool merchants were preparing a bill that would provide answers to 'every reasonable complaint against the slave trade' in order to secure legislation regulating the trade but not abolishing it. On returning to London he urged that the complaints should be pointed out even more explicitly, not just to the members of the Privy Council committee but to the wider audience, believing that the British public would respond sympathetically to details of how violence played a large part in obtaining slave cargoes, and the extent of mortality on the middle passage. He therefore set to in compiling another essay entitled *On the Efficiency of Regulation or Abolition*.[27]

Not long after he completed his tour of the western ports, in 1789 Clarkson's indefatigable energies were called upon once more, on this occasion to try and rally support in France. He had been about to set off on another information-gathering trip to the north and east of England but it was concluded that his experience would be better employed in meeting the French representative of the London Committee, Brissot de Warville, who was closely involved with its counterpart, Les Amis des Noirs, which had agreed in August 1787 to act on behalf of the British organisation. In practice Clarkson's trip met with very limited success and the French remained largely reluctant to express any outright hostility to the trade. They were perhaps more preoccupied with the imminent prospect of social upheaval on their own doorstep and, as Seymour Drescher has remarked, we cannot look to France for sources of abolitionist inspiration.[28]

In 1790 matters started to take a downturn for the committee and the initial impetus was lost. By this juncture, meetings were often so poorly attended that on 18 May a meeting had to be called off because only three members, insufficient for a quorum, were present. A similar cancellation was forced on 25 May. The cash balance in the committee's bank account had also run dangerously low, to the extent that it was again obliged to place advertisements in

all the London newspapers to solicit funds. The position was keenly reflected in
the report of the committee on 20 July which concluded, 'At commencement of
this Society it could not be foreseen that the prosecution of its great object would
require so much time and expense.' Considerable expense was, nonetheless, still
being incurred, of which by far the biggest drain was that resulting from the
collection and dissemination of evidence. Income is rarely identified in the minute
books but the treasurer's entry for 20 July 1790 lists expenses as:

Stationery, printing and books	£103 7s 11d
Collecting information etc.	£1,177 19s 2d
Secretarial salaries	£63 6s 2d
Coal and candles	£36 14s 11d[29]

The position had changed little when, on 26 April 1791, the committee
recruited parliamentarians to its ranks in the shape of Wilberforce, Muncaster,
C.J. Fox, W. Smith and W. Burgh. Little is recorded of Burgh but it is clear that
Wilberforce and Fox were invited in because of their influence at Westminster.
William Smith was also valuable as an ally. A professed dissenter and MP at
various times for Sudbury, Camelford and Norwich, coming from a well-to-do
family of wholesale grocers, he supported Pitt, before switching allegiance to the
Foxites. In 1798 he would make a personal if unsuccessful stand in parliament to
improve conditions aboard slave ships by limiting numbers and guaranteeing
minimum space per man.

To what extent Muncaster's election to the London Committee served any
constructive purpose, however, is questionable. Lord Muncaster, otherwise titled
Sir John Pennington of Ravenglass, Cumberland, was an early friend of Pitt,
enjoyed an intermittent parliamentary career of no great consequence and,
when the mood took him, followed a desultory interest in the slave trade. This
made him a crony of Wilberforce, who claimed that they were 'tuned to the
same key' and he was almost certainly invited to join the committee at
Wilberforce's behest. Theirs was a harmony that certainly did not include
Clarkson, whom Muncaster seems to have regarded more as the penny whistle of
the ensemble. A pamphlet attributed to Muncaster, *Historical Sketches of the Slave
Trade*, was regarded as a useful source of some information, but on the whole he
seems to have been a typical product of eighteenth-century aristocratic breeding
with whom Wilberforce would have curried favour – flashy, pompous and
habitually indolent. He apparently never rose in the House to speak on the
subject of the trade and, on at least one occasion, was reprimanded about his
repeated absenteeism from Westminster. Frances Horner, a member of the so-
called 'Ministry of all Talents' assembled after the premature death of Pitt on

23 January 1806, described him waspishly and probably quite accurately, as 'half-saint, half-debauchee and whole raff'.[30]

By 1792 the London Committee was displaying all the signs of having lost its heart and its way, and this mood was to continue. Meetings became more and more infrequent and lacklustre, with poor attendances. The flow of donations largely dried up and pleas for money were a monthly occurrence. Failure of a parliamentary move for abolition in 1791 and the generally desultory state of progress clearly diminished the enthusiasm of members. The minute books reveal that from July 1792 onwards the committee was meeting less than once a month, in contrast to previous regularity. Suggesting, as Seymour Drescher does, that in 1788 when the London Committee had barely been formed, that 'it allowed Pitt to squeeze through the first bill to regulate the trade' or that 'in 1792 the abolition campaign contributed to the reversal of the 1791 parliamentary decision' simply does not hold water. One of the few incentives conducted with any degree of success was a public relations exercise to discourage English households from purchasing West Indian sugar and rum. Yet even this campaign was not managed with any degree of confidence and achieved only limited results. On 20 June 1793 the committee drew up a strategy including the different measures to encourage abstinence from West Indian sugar and sugar derivatives, and Clarkson claimed ambitiously that 300,000 families responded to the call. Yet by 5 August the committee had decided that 'the expediency of recommending disuse of West India sugar and rum be suspended for the present'.[31] The move had come at a particularly inopportune moment if it was intended to discomfit the British sugar industry. The revolution on the island of Haiti in 1791 had already resulted in a shortage of sugar exported from the West Indies, with a consequent sharp rise in prices. The raising of righteous noses at the commodity among housewives in the English shires did not trigger a glut and, in any case, such was the demand for sugar across the Channel that rates of re-export from Britain to continental Europe virtually trebled, quite negating any efforts of the abolitionists to worry the refiners.

The malaise among the abolitionists lasted for a decade. It was only from 1804, for the last three years of the trade abolition debate, that the London Committee became infused with a degree of renewed enthusiasm and even this fell far short of the heady fervour that pervaded meetings in early days. On 14 May 1805, the minutes reveal fresh concern about the continuing 'lassitude of committee members'. So few members were turning up to meetings that a resolution was passed censuring those absent on more than three consecutive occasions (members of parliament excluded). Those who declined to make an appearance for six months or more would be asked to resign. On the other hand, new committees had eventually been founded in key strategic towns, including Bristol, Tewkesbury, Gloucester and Worcester.[32]

The incentive, drive and the early enthusiasm of the abolition movement had, however, been reduced to virtually nil. When the critical moment of triumph arrived on 25 March 1807, when it was learned that the royal assent had been given to abolition of the trade, the news did not result in a wild party for the tired remnant of the committee. Granville Sharp drafted a letter, the tone of which, if rhetorical extravagances of the day are any measure, was fairly low-key. Sharp declared, 'We request that you communicate this very satisfactory intelligence to the friends of the Abolition in your neighbourhood and we trust the success which has hitherto attended their exertions will encourage them to continue their co-operation with this Society in its endeavours to promote the observance of the Act.' In reality, however, the committee was only to meet on seven more occasions in as many years and was officially wound up on 9 July 1819, when the balance of its funds, £120, was handed over to John Thornton, the treasurer of the recently appointed African Institution.[33]

Edith Hurwitz claims that abolitionist effort caused the collective conscience of a large number of British Protestants (Roman Catholics were experiencing too many problems of their own concerning emancipation) to be influenced by the anti-slavery movement because it claimed to be inspired by the revealed word of God.[34] This may be true, but what Hurwitz fails to comprehend is that public conscience, sincere as it may or may not have been, did not sway the opinions of those in power any more than protest movements affect governments today, unless they actually pose a threat to the survival of that government and its prospects in re-election. To claim, as she does when discussing the eventual emancipation, that 'the abolitionist movement coerced political leaders, forcing men and parties to bow to their demands' paints a romanticised and largely overblown scenario. What brought about the eventual change of heart in the corridors of power was not public protest, although it would be foolish to deny that this amounted to an added consideration, but a raft of more-gritty arguments. After the abolition of the trade was achieved, another twenty-six years were to pass by before parliament voted for slave emancipation of a kind, and this required a quantum shift in economics and in the make-up of the parliamentary body.

Writers have claimed that the London Committee played some kind of decisive role in the eventual shift from the pro-slave-trade stance among a majority of British opinion. But they appear not to take into account the history and progress of the committee. The abolitionists did manage to raise public awareness of the situation, albeit through literature at times somewhat larded in terms of the levels of atrocity committed by slavers, and it was instrumental in the gathering of a sizeable number of anti-trade petitions tabled in the upper and lower houses of parliament. But it would be misleading to suggest that any of this went very far in swaying parliamentary opinion and it probably exerted no more than a marginal influence on the debate.

The image of anti-slavery petitioning was not exactly squeaky-clean. It had been dented by rumours of fraud and 'backhanders' and this tended to raise additional worries among the members of the London Committee. One of the most formidable opponents of the abolitionists, the Liverpool MP Banastre Tarleton, accused local activists in Edinburgh of encouraging schoolboys to sign, thus boosting figures, and his complaint proved partly justified.[35] There were also rumours that more-impoverished signatories occasionally had the pen placed in their hand along with something extra by way of a financial reward. The absence of a voting franchise for any more than a privileged few of the population was a true impediment and the energies put into gathering names on paper often counted for very little, particularly when viewed by landlords responsible only to ghostly tenants residing in rotten boroughs.

In those decades of the late eighteenth century when petitioning was tolerated, lists of people protesting on any kind of issue, including, incidentally, many supporting the pro-slave-trade lobby, were being tabled daily. A trawl of Hansard reveals that William Cobbett's parliamentary day records included details of petitions as a matter of obligation, but they are usually tucked away in the small print. Judging by the lack of reaction to most of these pleadings in the day-to-day business of parliament, most politicians probably neither knew nor were overly concerned about what they contained or who had signed them. Public opinion slowly gained greater recognition in the way legislation was crafted, but it was only after 1814, when the move towards emancipation was taking shape, that petitioning as a strategy began to create any more of an impact on ministers.

In summary, if the energies of the London Committee for the Abolition of the Slave Trade left any lasting mark on British history, it was to bring the salient issues to the attention of the public in a way that had not been achieved hitherto. Its activities fuelled anti-slave-trade sentiments but also fired up those of the slavers in response. It facilitated the delivery of a measure of public protest to Westminster and for a brief moment managed to translate public revulsion over the slave trade into action through the high-street boycotting of West Indian sugar. But it did not force the hand of parliament. This was down to other considerations.

Chapter 7

PARLIAMENT AND THE TRADE

In his analysis *Capitalism and Anti-Slavery*, Seymour Drescher highlights three important features marking the history of the campaign to abolish the trade. These include emotive incidents such as the case of James Somerset and the *Zong* atrocity, the subsequent launch of the London Committee against the trade and the decision by William Pitt the younger and William Wilberforce to bring the issue before the British parliament. Yet to what extent did the influence of Wilberforce move hearts and minds of MPs and, of no less critical significance, was Pitt truly committed to abolition or did he use his considerable abilities in government to manipulate the situation and so ensure his own political survival? Some of the answers to these questions are to be found in the day-to-day details of parliamentary matters recorded in the pages of William Cobbett's *Parliamentary History* and the subsequent Hansard's *Parliamentary Debates from 1803*, although these verbatim reports reveal only part of the story. Nonetheless parliament is where the 'buck stopped' over abolition and it was there during the often dreadfully long-winded and tedious exchanges that crucial decisions were made during the twenty-year period between 1788 and 1807.

We can dispense with a few more myths about who did what. During the decades of wrangling about the cessation of the slave trade a number of notable protagonists emerged. Men who represented plantation interests or stood as the MPs for slave-trading centres like Liverpool and Bristol spearheaded the pro-slavery lobby. One of the most formidable speakers on behalf of the trade was Colonel Banastre Tarleton, a lawyer by training who had turned to a successful army career. As MP for Liverpool he consistently assailed what he considered to be the mistaken philanthropy of abolition. Bamber Gascoyne of Childwall Hall, Liverpool was no less a staunch defender of the slave-traders, as too was Richard Pennant, Lord Penrhyn of Caernarvon, godson of the Chief Justice of Jamaica, owner of large estates on the island. Matthew Brickdale and John Baker Holroyd, Lord Sheffield, were also supporters, both having sat at different times as MPs for Bristol. These were influential and persuasive orators, backed with hard cash. The chief abolitionists, though generally nursing reservations of one sort or another, included William Wilberforce, the volatile Charles James Fox, leader of the parliamentary opposition against Pitt in the early days, Edmund Burke, a former spokesman for the Rockingham Whigs characterised by Gibbon as 'the most eloquent and rational madman I ever knew', and William Smith, at various times supporter of both Pitt and Fox and MP for Sudbury, Camelford and Norwich. The pro-abolitionist camp also listed the philanthropist Thomas Babington and, in the later stages of the campaign, Lord Howick and Sir Samuel Romilly, the Chancery lawyer who first took his seat as an independent in 1806. Somewhere in that grey area between these two largely polarised camps stood a group including Pitt, who in 1788 held the position of Chancellor of the Exchequer, Henry Dundas, the Home Secretary, and Sir William Dolben, the MP for Oxford University and Northamptonshire. On the whole, Dundas' sympathies tended to err on the side of the colonists. Dolben had become convinced of the 'crying evil' of what was taking place in British ships but was enough of a pragmatist to advocate a 'third way' of regulating the trade rather than pursuing wholesale abandonment. While these men collaborated with Wilberforce in principle, the quartet did not always see eye-to-eye in the practical application. Lastly there existed a rather larger body of MPs, the minor players who supported one side or the other, often without a great deal of consistency, and who spoke occasionally in debate.

William Wilberforce's public entry into the abolition struggle was less auspicious than some writers have suggested. Away from parliament Wilberforce was not closely involved in the gathering of public support because, as Seymour Drescher concedes, when the campaign was begun, in 1788, he positively discouraged any public meeting by the London Committee and the movement developed beyond his control.[1] In theory Wilberforce was indisposed for a lengthy period of time from April 1788 with 'digestive disorders', during which he first retired to Bath and then moved around the country, visiting estates of various friends and acquaintances for the purpose of convalescence. Nor did appreciative cheers accompany his eventual debut into the parliamentary debate. On the contrary the occasion was marred by controversy and immediately criticised as being ill judged. After Thomas Clarkson returned to London from his fact-finding travels to Bristol and Liverpool, and submitted the evidence that he had collected, the London Committee decided that the campaign must go to Westminster without further delay. Wilberforce, however, reluctant to expose himself to hostile reaction by presenting an anti-slave-trade motion in the Commons and, in any event, still absent in Bath, decided to approach William Pitt with a proposal that the matter be referred to the king. Wilberforce's reasoning seems to have been that George III would then place the onus of responsibility on the Privy Council. No doubt equally wary of launching a fraught Commons debate on the subject, Pitt agreed to follow Wilberforce's suggestion and so it was that a Privy Council committee was formed. His Majesty's Order in Council, dated 11 February 1788, was to call witnesses and to examine the issue 'concerning the present state of the Trade to Africa, and particularly the trade in slaves; and concerning the effects and consequences of this trade as well in Africa and West Indies, as to the general commerce of this kingdom'.[2]

The involvement of the Privy Council proved an unpopular decision among parliamentarians across the spectrum, irrespective of whether they nurtured abolitionist sentiments or not. Seen to be a defunct remnant of the era of absolute monarchy, the council was widely believed to consist of a body of men interested only in currying favour with the king, largely out of touch with the real world, and in no way representative of legitimate government. By the late eighteenth century the cabinet was largely taking over its role, and whether such a committee was ever likely to be effective in moving towards legislation is highly debatable. Generally speaking, from 1788 to the final years of emancipation in the 1830s it could be reckoned that the more elevated the social standing of individuals in positions of authority, the stronger their support of slavery and the trade. At the head of the established order for almost twenty years, George III stood implacably against any move towards abolition, as did the Duke of Clarence, the future William IV. As late as 1807 Clarence was still adamant that criticism of the conduct of planters and slavers was unsubstantiated.[3] Clarkson had already reported difficulty in obtaining witnesses to attend any potential board of inquiry because of their fear of recrimination and, of these, an even smaller number was prepared to appear before the Privy Council. Out of forty-seven people to whom Clarkson had been introduced, only nine were persuaded that, if necessary, they should give evidence.[4]

Among the most vociferous objectors to the handing-over of authority to the Privy Council were Charles Fox and Edmund Burke. Wilberforce came in for much resentment over the recommendation and in his diary he complained, 'I have been blamed for this decision; as if I had suffered the first favourable feelings to our cause, which existed in the country, to die away.' Under increasing pressure to take such an important issue back into government hands, Pitt felt obliged to bring it to the attention of the Commons in May 1788.[5] It was, therefore, Pitt rather than Wilberforce who opened the slave-trade debate. By way of justification for asking members of the House to deal with such a vexatious matter, Pitt pointed to the various petitions that had been presented on the subject. Thomas Taylor, in his biography of Thomas Clarkson, notes that Clarkson was introduced to Pitt in February 1788 and that he had been instrumental in obtaining more than 100 petitions. The details of these public reactions appear not to have been preserved but they were obtained largely through Clarkson's efforts around the various towns and organisations he visited.

On 5 May 1788 William Pitt, Chancellor of the Exchequer, rose, proposing to move a resolution, 'that the House will, early in the next session, proceed to take into consideration the circumstances of the slave trade'. In his opening parliamentary address on the subject on 9 May, he prudently recognised two lobbies, the one conceiving that the African trade should be stopped altogether, the other that it merely needed reforming through new regulations. He avoided the more contentious titles of 'abolitionist' and 'pro-slavery'. By handing the matter to the Commons he managed to take some of the sting out of the Privy Council involvement, but then advocated no further discussion until the next parliamentary session, when the House would be asked 'to take into consideration the circumstances of the slave trade complained of in various petitions'. Pitt had thus made the first move in an orchestrated policy of postponement that would hold good for twenty years. The response from the Whig benches was generally less than favourable, the House erupting with aristocratic growls that the characters of planters were being blackened and their conduct grossly calumniated. One notable voice of support, however, came from Charles Fox, who declared that Pitt's proposal had 'laid him under considerable embarrassment having intended to bring something forward in the House respecting it'.[6] Fox had been approached by Clarkson and other members of the London Committee and persuaded to pledge support.[7] But Fox, too, appears to have been a canny politician, keeping his lips sealed on what might turn out to be political suicide until he had a better idea of who his teammates were.

Meanwhile, any notion of impartiality among members of the Privy Council board of inquiry was severely tested when it was revealed that the first witnesses paraded before it included men whom Africa merchants had deputised. Originally the board went under the full title of Lords of the Committee of Council appointed for the Consideration of all Matters relating to the Trade and Foreign Plantations, but it rapidly became known as the Board of Trade. Its standing committee began to hear witnesses on 13 February 1788 and submitted their report almost a year afterwards. But by that juncture the committee had interviewed a limited number of individuals and most of these turned out to have been acting on behalf of the planters and traders. Some witnesses were examined with laboured thoroughness; others were questioned in a more perfunctory manner. Close reading of the report indicates that this depended largely on whose interests were being represented. On 25 February 1788 the committee interviewed two people who had been put forward by the London Committee for the Abolition of the Slave Trade. These included Harry Gandy, who had travelled extensively in West Africa, and Alexander Falconbridge. Gandy was able to give first-hand experience of slavery conditions, although he had encountered these not in British operations but in Danish-held islands off the coast; for his part Falconbridge gave weight to the

widely held assertions that Negroes were being kidnapped from their villages, often
in the small hours of the night. Their Lordships, however, were openly disbelieving
about much of what they heard. Thomas Clarkson also appeared before the
inquiry board, very briefly, on 11 June 1788. Virtually no questions were put to
him and there was clearly little sympathy for his position or interest in the
conclusions drawn from his tours of Bristol and Liverpool. Other abolition
sympathisers such as Thomas Eldred, who had been employed in an African
merchant ship but had considered the trade unlawful and resigned, experienced
similar dismissive attitudes.[8] Only James Ramsay among the abolitionists was
interviewed at any length. He submitted a report deploring the treatment of
Negroes in the West Indies, which included such pithy comments as 'It is
exceedingly rare to see a grey-headed Negro . . . almost the only instruments used
in managing the slaves are the whip, beaustick, dungeon and chains.'[9]

Strikingly different was style of interview enjoyed by a Liverpool delegation
consisting of Robert Norris – a Carolina planter – and various African merchants,
including Charles Spooner, James Penny and John Matthews. The committee
received this delegation on 27 February 1788 with Benastre Tarleton in
attendance to provide moral support, and it continued to give evidence until
11 March. The interviews here were extensive, cordial and went into considerable
detail, but were exclusively with a pro-slave-trade interest that did not avoid an
opportunity to present its own version of events. Even more slanted in favour of
the traders and merchants was a succession of interviews conducted from 1 April
1788 with a witness named Stephen Fuller, supported by the planter and pro-
slavery historian, Edward Long. These exchanges continued for several days,
notwithstanding the fact that Fuller prefaced his evidence to the committee with
a comment, 'I have spared no pains to get your Lordships every possible
intelligence, yet I look upon the answers I have now the honour to present as
imperfect and in some instances possibly erroneous.'[10] When it was the turn of
Long he delivered evidence that might have raised eyebrows even among the most
ardent of pro-slavery supporters. Long advised that 'Negroes are addicted to
eating dirt' but that they lived an opulent life. To emphasise the latter, he related
an anecdote about a planter in the parish of Westmoreland, in Jamaica, having
fallen on hard times and being sued for non-payment of accounts. 'His Negroes
assembled before his door and, expressing their concern, they offered him a large
sum of money which they had brought ready tied up in bags made of old
stockings and said, if the money was insufficient, they could borrow as much
more among their friends and relations.'[11]

MPs on both sides of the divide were soon openly murmuring that the
involvement of the Privy Council amounted to little more than a crude delaying
tactic, since it was in possession of no public petitions and little more background

information. As John Pollexfen Bastard of Kitley near Plymouth protested, 'Who knows anything of what is doing by the Committee of the Privy Council or what progress they are making?' Fox also vehemently lamented their involvement but, more to the point, the Commons had found an excuse to delay the debate. The device of 'putting matters off six months' became a refined and successful tactic of the pro-slave-trade lobby. When questioned in the 1 April debate on whether inquiry by the Privy Council amounted to a loss of time, Pitt responded with an obscure observation that, far from it, time had been gained. On hearing this, Mr Pollexfen Bastard was on his feet, not about to permit such evasion to pass under his nose unchallenged. 'We cannot attend to your petition today,' he declared waspishly. 'Tomorrow we hope to have a holiday; and we must defer inquiring into the allegations of your petitions till next session.'[12]

It was agreed that in the current session any debate should be confined to a less vexatious issue of regulating the trade in such a way as to make life more tolerable for the slaves aboard middle-passage vessels. On 21 May 1788 a motion was brought in by Sir William Dolben 'for the relief of those unhappy persons, the natives of Africa, from the hardships to which they are exposed in their passage from the coast of Africa to the colonies'.[13] He believed that if a bill were introduced with the less contentious object of alleviating hardship during transportation, while keeping clear of the trickier general question, the House would have no objection to dealing with it straight away. Dolben was wrong in his estimation. What amounted to the first African Slave Bill was proposed in the Commons on the premise that the number of slaves carried in vessels should be proportional to their tonnage, but when the matter went into committee during the following month it earned vigorous opposition. Pro-trade members complained that any reduction in the number of slaves aboard each ship would ruin the business because the vessels would be carrying less than economic cargoes. Pitt presented the appearance of sitting strictly on the fence, quick to point out that nobody could dispute the principle involved but almost in the same breath cautioning that the facts on which the bill was allegedly founded were vulnerable to dispute. He dashed Dolben's hopes at a stroke by stating that he could not 'agree to any regulation the bill might contain, which opposed indirectly the trade itself, when the general question of its abolition was not before the House'. Charles Fox challenged Pitt's reluctance to accept the facts on which the bill was founded and Fox was probably justified in doing so. Much of the hard statistical evidence obtained by Clarkson on his visits to the slaving ports and currently laid before the Privy Council is likely to have also been communicated to Pitt in their February meeting. It is difficult to see how Pitt, renowned as he was for close research into any issue on which he was to speak, could have disputed these particular findings with conviction.

During the first reading on 26 May, Bamber Gascoyne exploited Pitt's ambivalence when he rose to protest that the bill could not pass without bringing forward a premature discussion of the general question. William Young of Delaford Park, Buckinghamshire, the first son of the Lieutenant Governor of Dominica, echoed Gascoyne, also certain that Dolben was not aware of the wide field for discussion and inquiry that his proposals for shipboard regulation would lead to. The Bristol MP Matthew Brickdale insisted that the introduction of regulations should not be agreed hastily. The Attorney General joined a growing chorus for delay, protesting that as no notice had been given to bring forward the motion and since the House had been taken by surprise, the motion should be withdrawn.[14]

In June the issue was handed back into parliamentary committee and the political climate became less congenial than the weather. The acrimony intensified when Dolben, in the chair, proposed a specific amendment that the maximum number of slaves carried should amount to five men per 3 tons of every ship of up to 150 tons burthen weight (a ship's carrying capacity), with three men to 2 tons in all vessels above that weight. Richard Pennant for the slavers became virtually apoplectic. He declared that the proposal, if accepted, would bring the entire trade to a grinding halt and offered the timely reminder for those ignorant of the fact that two-thirds of the commerce of the country depended upon it. He flatly denied that cruel practices had ever existed in the trade and was looking to full and sober discussion, not snap decisions.[15] It would have been surprising if Pennant had taken any other position, representing as he did a strong and wealthy coterie for whom money talked and which had used its affluence to purchase votes and parliamentary seats. Among this affluent pack there existed a degree of nepotism. Richard Pennant, for example, was able to count blood ties among the leading West Indian families of the Beckfords and Dawkinses. William Beckford, in particular, inherited vast wealth in the 1730s and became the most powerful West Indian planter based in England, using part of his capital to build the opulent Fonthill estates in Wiltshire.

When he made his major contribution on 28 May, Pitt clearly chose his words with care. 'In my mind the best mode Parliament can adopt will be to keep the subject entire till the next session, and I therefore wish to make as little alteration in any part of the conduct of the Trade as possible, but, if upon inquiry, it is proved that it is carried on in a manner free from abuse, merely to take care to see that it should so continue to be carried on till the next session.'[16]

When the discussion of Dolben's proposed regulation reached the Upper House it fared still worse. Implacably opposed to any measure that would undermine the trade, the great landowners sitting in the Lords generally took an unsympathetic view. Among the peers of the realm, rivalry with the French was a sensitive issue and as relations between the two countries progressively soured, political leverage could be gained by placing emphasis on the disastrous benefits that would accrue to the foe across the Channel if this or that action was taken. The Earl of Sandwich noted gravely that the French would not give up the trade, and since all seamen engaged in the African trade were at risk of being lost to Britain, the French were set to pick up the rewards. This kind of fighting talk was guaranteed to stir jingoistic sentiments and by the end of June, after the bill had been returned to committee, the consideration of amendments was put on hold until the end of the parliamentary session. Finally, however, the regulation motion was accepted, the logic winning through that to agree on some measure of improvement in shipboard conditions, difficult to verify and well nigh impossible to enforce, would silence the abolitionists for the time being. On the last day of the session the measures received a reluctant royal assent.

It was only after this opening gambit that Wilberforce chose to wave his own abolitionist flag in any significant fashion, almost a year having passed since Pitt had launched and delayed the parliamentary discussion. On 19 March 1789, under mounting pressure from the London Committee, Wilberforce moved that the House should resolve itself into committee to consider the subject of the slave trade in its wider context. As Dolben had correctly anticipated, the proposal came in for cross-party opposition and, again, delaying tactics were brought into play so that Wilberforce did not obtain leave for his debate until 12 May.

If his first major speech critical of the slave trade was intended to stir parliamentary hearts and minds in favour of cessation, it fell somewhat short. At the opening of the full Commons debate Wilberforce delivered a rambling three-hour oration that appears to have been tedious even by the rhetorical standards of the day. In it he digressed into the immorality of seizures on the West African coast, the shipboard conditions, the survival rates in the colonies and the greed of Liverpool merchants. One of Wilberforce's more persistent weaknesses, unlike Pitt, was that the strength of his research did not always match his ability for rhetoric. Immediately after he had sat down, Richard Pennant rose majestically to attack the validity of much of his argument, pointing out that Wilberforce had 'misrepresented so many articles with regard to the West Indies in respect to its population and other matters that no reliance could be placed on the picture he had chosen to exhibit'. He had also, Pennant alleged, misquoted Mr Long, a prominent and respected author on Jamaican history, concerning maintenance of birth rates on the islands. Wilberforce had overlooked many things essential to a fair statement of the case. He had displayed great ingenuity as well as eloquence but had made scarcely any assertion that was not contradicted by the report of the Privy Council. Another of the pro-slavery lobby, Thomas Powys, promptly agreed with Pennant that the evidence Wilberforce had presented was partial, incomplete and unsatisfactory. Whether entirely fair or not, these early attacks on Wilberforce's credibility left the deeper impression on MPs that day. He was also still seen as the culprit for the much-resented involvement of the Privy Council. Alderman Newnham, representing interests in the City of London, insisted that its report should not be made a ground for proceeding in the House and a colleague, Mr Rolle, added his voice of disapproval. Any evidence emerging by way of the Privy Council, he declared, was unparliamentary and irregular. Thomas Powys, MP argued that it amounted to a deviation from the usual rules of parliament and that the evidence the report contained was not competent.[17]

The upshot was that Pitt had successfully manipulated a breathing space and during the year of 1790 progress on terminating the British slave trade was virtually non-existent. A parliamentary committee overseen by Wilberforce was established to hear the evidence of witnesses who might have first-hand evidence for and against the trade, but its tediously pedestrian pace merely aggravated the lack of impetus. So slow was the progress of the committee that it actually encouraged cries of 'foul' from the pro-slave-trade members, anxious for the issue to be sorted out and buried more speedily. In April of that year a frustrated Bamber Gascoyne demanded to know how many more witnesses Wilberforce intended to call and whether they would impeach the veracity of witnesses called by the other side. Wilberforce could not provide a clear answer. Time employed, he responded vaguely, would become measured by information obtained. Not to be so easily fobbed off, Gascoyne requested the House to consider 'the destructive consequences of this, more than any other which had lately engaged the attention of Parliament, seeing that delay in the business was intended'. Alderman Newnham, with his London backers at his heels urging that the matter be disposed of, asserted that further evidence was unnecessary and that everything had appeared to convince the House of the impracticability of abolition. Charles Fox, however, supported Wilberforce against restricting the time given for examination of evidence.

Months passed, another year's end came and went with procrastination still the order of the day, and by February 1791 the supporters of the trade on the Commons committee had gained the ascendancy. William Smith bemoaned the fact that out of eighty-seven sitting-days in committee, fifty-one had been commandeered by opponents of abolition, while only twenty-six had been taken to examine witnesses in favour. The backers of Liverpool merchants, headed by Banastre Tarleton, had used twenty-one of these sessions in cross-examination. In April the House resolved into a fresh committee but, by this date, Wilberforce recognised that the odds were increasingly stacked against him. He reluctantly accepted that further adjournment of a full debate was unacceptable. His strategy was to let fly another stultifying and interminable speech focused largely on the manner in which slaves were obtained on the West African coast. Tarleton responded by reminding members of the committee that parliament had always countenanced the trade, and its sanction could not, without a breach of the faith, be withdrawn. Abolition, he asserted, would destroy a trade that employed annually upward of 5,000 sailors in more than 160 ships and earned £800,000 in export revenue. This was more the kind of stuff that MPs could savour and get their teeth into! Even Charles Fox, perennially unpredictable, now advocated that any notion of immediate abolition was unwise. It was he who for the first time in the Commons proposed that the matter should be put on hold for the foreseeable future and that two, three or four years hence, as the House might think expedient, was more appropriate. Thomas Grosvenor, who had come in as MP for Chester in 1790, enthusiastically echoed much of Tarleton's assault on Wilberforce and summarised neatly that it was 'not an amiable trade, but neither was the trade of a butcher an amiable trade, and yet a mutton chop was, nevertheless, a very good thing'. Members of the Commons committee chuckled over a little light relief and it was agreed that further committee work was altogether necessary. Delaying tactics again triumphed.

In spite of clear warning signs, Wilberforce doggedly opted for confrontation and brought a full abolition motion before the House. On 19 April 1791 the debate got off to a particularly inauspicious start, having been opened by Sir William Young. Young's father, the Lieutenant Governor of Dominica, owned lands in Tobago, Antigua and Vincent, and this background placed him solidly in the pro-slave-trade camp. A supporter of Pitt, he nonetheless held rigidly conservative views and stood in opposition to parliamentary reform and any regulation of the slave trade. Young made an obligatory polite acknowledgement of Wilberforce's passion and eloquence before proceeding to demolish him. In 1789, Young reminded the House, Wilberforce had declared confidently that if Britain led, other nations would follow. Wilberforce had deluded himself, and facts proved that the nations in Europe were actually making fresh exertions to extend their trade. Expressing deep caution over abolition, Young was reiterating a widely recognised argument that Britain could abandon her part in the trade but not abolish it. In the ensuing exchanges, Wilberforce was supported by Pitt, William Smith and Charles Fox but, in addition to Young, he faced solid opposition from Sir John Russell and Banastre Tarleton. Russell hammered home the message that abolition would prove visionary and delusive. It was, he said, a feeble attempt, without the power, to serve the cause of humanity. The trade would simply be taken up by other nations and the only acceptable solution was regulation. Tarleton reminded the House (as if any needed reminding at this stage) that the trade had enjoyed royal assent since the reign of Elizabeth I. He flatly denied earlier claims by Wilberforce that mortality rates among slaves reached 50 per cent and asserted that they had never exceeded 1 per cent in Liverpool-based ships. Ten times that figure, he declared, had perished among regiments sent to the West Indies or the Americas. Tarleton also raised the not-invaluable spectre of the St Domingue revolt, asking to what this could be imputed but to the question of abolition. When put to the test, Wilberforce's motion failed by a considerable majority of 163 to 88, lost by 75 votes at 3.30 a.m. on 19 April 1791. The defeat was the first of many bitter pills for the abolitionists.[18]

After such a prominent setback, Wilberforce abandoned any further attempts to reintroduce a fresh motion during the remainder of the session, knowing that the mood of parliament was becoming increasingly hostile. Across the English Channel, the French were plunging ever deeper into the anarchic mire and the insurrection in St Domingue, for which abolitionists were promptly blamed, had resulted in a further hardening of attitudes among MPs. Fears of a similar crisis unfolding in Jamaica loomed large and even Wilberforce conceded that it would be prudent to defer tabling any new motion until the following year. The merchants and planters applauded loudly; the abolitionists pondered their fate.

On 2 April 1792 the Commons committee was assembled again to renew its discussion of a possible schedule. William Dolben took the chair and while Wilberforce declared that he was prepared to renew his application for immediate abolition, despite the setbacks of the previous year, the Home Secretary and leader of the Scottish parliamentary lobby, Henry Dundas, proposed to introduce the word 'gradual' into any future resolution. During this meeting Wilberforce took an opportunity to spell out his resistance to emancipation.[19] In response to a rumour that it was 'my design and that of my friends to propose, besides an abolition of the trade, the immediate emancipation of the Negroes', his denial was robust. It was, he declared, an intention that he could never have entertained for a moment. He was 'exceedingly sensible that they [the black Africans] are in a state far from being prepared for the reception of such an enjoyment'.

Away from Westminster, the London Committee also noted that the pro-slave-trade lobby was organising a smear campaign along similar lines, and felt sufficiently pressured that in January they paid for advertisements in the London press refuting such allegations: 'The views of this Society having been industriously misrepresented by a report that the emancipation of the Negroes in the British Colonies is the object of their exertions, they think it incumbent upon them again publickly to declare that they have uniformly adhered to the original purpose of its institution, namely the abolition of the trade to the coast of Africa for slaves.'

During the debate in committee, Pitt's ambivalence was more clearly revealed. He appeared to support Wilberforce on the desirability of immediate abolition of

An idealised eighteenth-century engraving depicting a family of caribs on the island of St Vincent. *(Courtesy of the Special Collection of Bristol University Library)*

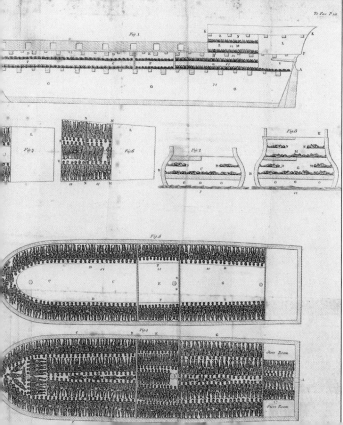

A schematic plan of the Bristol-based slave ship *Brookes* showing the stowage of slaves on four decks. *(Courtesy of the Special Collection of Bristol University Library)*

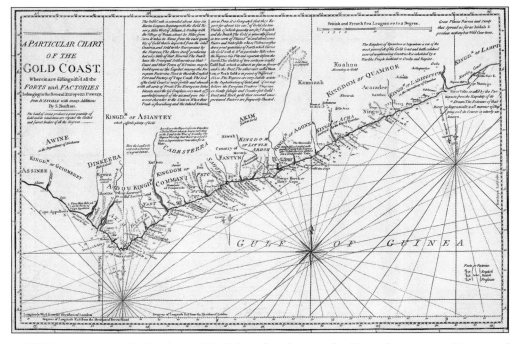

A 1794 map showing the locations of English trading forts on the West African coast. *(Courtesy of the Special Collection of Bristol University Library)*

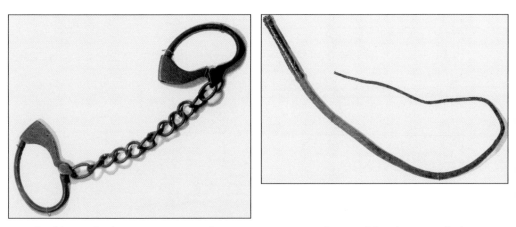

Leg shackles and whips were among the instruments most favoured by slavers and plantation overseers for the effective control of slaves. *(Courtesy of the American Museum in Britain)*

A painted model of typical servants quarters in Alabama in 1833. *(Courtesy of the American Museum in Britain)*

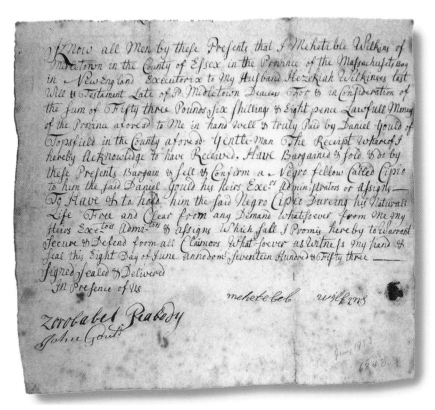

The Bill of Sale relating to an eighteenth-century Negro slave named Cipo in Massachusetts. *(Courtesy of the American Museum in Britain)*

The driver's whip unfolds its torturing coil.
"She only Sulks——go, lash her to her toil."

Contemporary nineteenth-century cartoons depicting the popular image of Afro-Caribbean slaves being taken from West Africa and employed in American plantations. *(Courtesy of the Bodleian Library, Oxford)*

O my great massa in heaven,
Pity me, and bless my Children!

This image depicting a black African supplicating in chains proved a powerful abolitionist tool when published. It aroused strong public sentiment of resistance to the trade. *(Courtesy of the American Museum in Britain)*

Portrait of Thomas Clarkson by A.E. Chalon. *(Courtesy of P.A. Houston private collection)*

The earliest known Charleston servant tag, No. 184, found in New York State where slaves were often smuggled out of the south. *(Courtesy of the American Museum in Britain)*

THE

ANTI-SLAVERY REPORTER.

No. 103.] NOVEMBER 15, 1832. [Vol. v. No. 12.

CORRESPONDENCE BETWEEN SIR C. B. CODRINGTON AND T. F. BUXTON, ESQ., ON THE SUBJECT OF SLAVERY.

1. *Address of Sir C. B. Codrington to the Electors of Gloucestershire.*

Gentlemen,—Unwilling at all times to intrude myself unnecessarily on your attention, I feel that I should be doing my duty neither to myself nor to that man with intentional malignity termed my *slave*, if I did not in such times as these endeavour to open the eyes of the misled anti-slavery Buxtonites. Gentlemen, *if I were merely, like Mr. Buxton, to make assertions which I am convinced he will not venture to say he himself believes, I should deserve no credit for such assertions.* I will therefore state that only which, from a residence on the spot, I have been an eye-witness to; or which, extracted from letters in my possession, I will vouch for the truth of. I have lived among my Negroes, and seen their comforts, and I will assert (defying all contradiction), that a more happy and contented class of beings never existed, until cursed with the blessings of the Anti-Slavery Society. Still, gentlemen, I will say that no man can be more desirous of their emancipation than myself, because no man would be more benefited by it, if it answered its desired object.

Gentlemen, my family have, for a century and a half, held under the Crown an island in the West Indies, eleven leagues N. of Antigua. The Negroes, in 1825, having within the preceding twenty years doubled their numbers, amounted to about 430 : their number, at present, exceeds 500. I have an agent on the island called a governor, who, with two overseers, form the whole of the male white population upon an island eleven leagues from the nearest land, among a Negro (or slave) population exceeding 500.

Mr. James, in 1825, states the Negroes to be happy and contented, although under the greatest subordination ; and, in proof, he mentions his having frequently slept in the woods (pirates frequently landing), by the side of his horse, surrounded by 100 to 150 of them ; and having often swam out to wrecks, followed by these *cruelly-treated slaves*, in seas where no boats could live;—that he was in the habit of leaving his wife and daughter on the island, when going on business to other islands (in fact, he has actually gone to England on one occasion), although there was not on any door a lock, or on any window a fastening. In fact, he writes, "the greater part of them would lay down their lives to serve me. Scarcely (he adds) does one of your vessels go to Antigua without a quantity of poultry and salt fish to sell, and in good seasons an immense quantity of potatoes. Many of them have ten or eleven acres of land in cultivation, the produce of which, of course, is their own property." My agent, gentlemen, in the present year (1832) writes, that the father of one of my slaves will not allow his daughter to be emancipated, thinking their present state preferable to emancipation ; he states fully and convincingly the benefits which would accrue to me from general emancipation, but adds his conviction that not a fourth of my Negroes would be alive at the end of two years.

Gentlemen, I could add much more ; but I have already trespassed

An 1832 title page from the *Anti-Slavery Reporter*, one of the key publications of the Anti-Slavery Society, including a letter from Sir C.B. Codrington, of Codrington estates notoriety, defending the humane institution of slavery. (*Courtesy of the Bodleian Library, Oxford*)

The emancipation medallion of 1834 showing liberated slaves dancing joyfully, with sober politicians on the reverse. *(Courtesy of Bristol Museums and Art Galleries)*

Detail from *A Harlot's Progress*, plate 2 of 6 by Hogarth. *(Courtesy of the Special Collection of Bristol University Library)*

Portrait of Thomas Fowell Buxton. *(Courtesy of the Bodleian Library, Oxford)*

"He now proceeded to chop off George by the ankles! It was with the broad axe! In vain did the unhappy victim scream and roar! He was completely in his master's power. Not a hand among so many durst interfere. Casting the feet into the fire, he lectured them at some length. He chopped him off below the knees; George roaring out, and praying his master to BEGIN AT THE OTHER END!"

A contemporary cartoon describing 'the inhuman phase of slave life'. *(Courtesy of the Special Collection of Bristol University Library)*

A nineteenth-century cartoon depicting liberated slaves refusing to be taken in by a politician from the south campaigning for their votes. *(Courtesy of the American Museum in Britain)*

the trade. Yet he also urged against bringing in a fresh motion to the effect and then did nothing to dissuade Dundas from introducing the amendment in favour of gradual abolition that effectively amounted to a wrecking strategy. In this debate a typically ambivalent Dundas was for protecting the trade. In 1782 he had become treasurer of the navy, an organisation heavily dependent on the slave trade for financing but also one on which the slavers were no less dependent for protection. Dundas thus spoke for a considerable lobby of colonial patronage.

In spite of his overt backing for Dundas, it was in committee that Pitt rendered one of his most memorable speeches in favour of immediate abolition. In an eloquent delivery he described the slave trade using his now famous analogy of 'that noxious plant by which everything is withered and blasted, under whose shade nothing that is useful to Africa grows'. Pitt's speech was delivered shortly after he had had a meeting with Granville Sharp, and was probably intended as a sop to public opinion in general and the London Committee for the Abolition of the Slave Trade in particular. He must have been aware in advance that anything he said would not impede the progress of Dundas's amendment, and when it came to the vote, the incorporation of the all-important word 'gradually' to Wilberforce's original motion was supported by an impressive majority of 230 to 85.

In the committee rooms, predictable arguments began to emerge over just what was meant by gradual abolition. John Baker Holroyd considered that any future date for cessation of the trade before 1800 would be unworkable. The Earl of Mornington thought January 1795 to be the ideal cut-off point. The Speaker, Henry Addington, no friend of the abolitionists, proposed a compromise of 1796 and this was eventually agreed by a slim majority of nineteen. The Lords pursued further wrecking tactics, throwing out the amendment and supporting the original motion for immediate abolition, appreciating that Commons rejection would shortly follow. In the Lower House, to keep the fires of prejudice stoked, Lord Carhampton voiced the personal opinions of many that Negroes only wanted to 'murder their masters, ravish their women and drink all their rum'.

The full Commons debate reopened on 23 April 1792 and Dundas laid out the revised terms of his proposition in more detail. These included the fudged condition that from 1 May 1792 it would be unlawful for any ship to leave a British home or colonial port for the coast of Africa for the purpose of taking on board Negroes, unless such ships shall have been previously employed in the African trade or previously contracted for that purpose. After 1 May 1793 it would be unlawful to carry more males than females, a move clearly designed to ratchet up the slave birth rate in the colonies. After 1 January 1800 the importation of African Negroes into British colonies in ships owned or navigated by British subjects would become illegal. The last condition conveniently skirted around the prospect of other nations taking on the slave trade and supplying British colonies. Fox and Wilberforce stuck to principles and supported immediate abolition. Pitt, however, praised Dundas's candour and consistency of reasoning, and it seems that, as usual, nobody knew precisely where Pitt stood.[20] Between 3 May and 8 May, the House of Lords stymied the programme and again returned the original, unworkable motion for immediate abolition to the Commons.

The rules of a game between the two Houses were becoming tried and successfully tested. Had Wilberforce chanced to win the debate in the Commons, the Upper House would predictably have thrown out the bill for *immediate* abolition. In the Lords, until the very end in 1807, the proportion of peers against abolition in any shape or form was consistently greater than the strength of opposition in the Commons. From 1792 onwards the clear strategy of the Lords was to introduce delaying tactics complementing those employed in the Lower House by batting motions to and fro, and in this they proved highly successful. However, the idea of gradual abolition was finally accepted as a compromise measure with a closing date of January 1796. The logic of the pro-slavery lobby seems to have been that a lot could happen in four years and that during that time the abolition momentum could well be lost. In any event it gave the planters and the slave merchants time to develop a cogent strategy. The rationale was astute. The abolitionists had won a meagre symbolic victory but it was far from substantive. The slavers could exploit the postponement to increase the numbers of slaves imported into the West Indian islands. Moreover, as political promises for the future frequently turn out, 1796 would come and go without change, when fears of social upheaval grew on the home front along with concerns about events unfolding across the English Channel.

Much sentiment from that time forward was affected by the momentous changes taking place in France. In September 1792 the National Convention of Jacobins proclaimed a republic and 1793 saw the outbreak of war between Britain and France. In February of that year, with the French in mind, Wilberforce tabled a fresh Commons motion to prohibit British merchants from supplying foreigners with slaves. Unfortunately the anti-slavery movement had become tainted with a distinct whiff of radical Jacobinism, and British vulnerability played heavily on the minds of MPs. In the Commons on 26 February 1792 Sir William Young lost no time in exploiting the mood. He had, he declared darkly, toured most of the British possessions in the West Indies and obtained good first-hand evidence that landowners might not remain loyal 'if constantly irritated, outraged in their character and injured in their property'. This was enough to send a nervous tremor through the House. In the Lords the Duke of Clarence informed fellow peers that the promoters of the abolition, including William Wilberforce, were either fanatics or hypocrites; the Upper Chamber nodded sagely. MPs in the Lower House considered that more-important issues were at stake, and Wilberforce's plea for a debate 'Thursday next' was replaced by the phrase 'this day six months'. He got no further when he attempted to reintroduce the motion in September. The wider public also seems to have been increasingly wary or apathetic, having more-pressing concerns to think about. Any effect that petitioning might have had ran out of steam. Furthermore, Wilberforce disagreed with Pitt over the execution of the war and was all for suing for peace. This did nothing to enhance his image with fellow MPs, who regarded his appeasement policy towards the French and his ardour for abolition to be linked. In the Lords on 11 April the pro-slavery Earl of Abingdon chose to exploit the anti-French sentiment when he compared the principles underlying the chaos that had unfolded across the English Channel with the British campaign to abolish the slave trade. The proposition was clearly founded on French principles and the French 'new philosophy'. All of this worked against Wilberforce, whose energies were probably not altogether on the job in hand, since he was distracted by the prospect of work on a book entitled *Practical Christianity*, due for publication in the spring of 1797.

Some hope of success came in May 1793, when a motion was agreed to debate curbing the foreign slave trade. A sufficient number of MPs had come around to the view that prohibiting British entrepreneurs from assisting the French was desirable. But when Wilberforce moved for a bill to limit and regulate importation of slaves to British colonies, the application was smartly rejected. The bill halting supply of slaves to foreign powers was eventually passed by narrow margin in February 1794, but these were poor years for the abolitionists. Wilberforce tried again for total abolition in 1795. There were, he warned, over 100,000 more Negroes in the West Indies than had been there in 1792 'now most justly the object of terror and alarm'. Already, tens of thousands of slaves were trained in the use of arms and rattling them in the direction of the British from French-held islands such as Guadeloupe. But by then the trade-abolition cause was seen to be losing what little support it had previously enjoyed in parliament and without even the limited value of public petitions to use in the Commons chamber, Wilberforce's campaign was halted, with the weight of evidence increasingly loaded against him. The year 1794 had seen the end of the Haitian uprising, with Toussaint L'Ouverture proclaiming an independent, black republic. Was it Wilberforce or his opponents to whom the country should look as the authors and causes of encouraging slaves to revolt? Who was it that had excited jealousies and doubts by filling the imagination of slaves with notions of grievance and wrong? MPs were in little doubt over where the finger of blame should be pointed. In 1795, with a little help from the French, the more-disastrous predictions of the pro-slave-trade lobby seemed to be coming true. France enfranchised all the Africans in her own colonies and sent an envoy in the form of Victor Hugues to proclaim their freedom. The French were clearly hopeful that this would trigger rebellion in the British Caribbean colonies.

Wilberforce doggedly pursued his dream of a total-abolition bill each year from 1795 to 1799 but it was regularly thrown out, not least because of the continued blocking tactics of Dundas, Gascoyne and Tarleton. The pro-slave-trade lobby were now relying on 'war sentiment'. On 18 February 1796 Dundas opposed Wilberforce because, were his motion to be agreed, 'it would endanger the peace of the country'. He begged the House only to attend to the nature of the war [with the French] in the West Indies. It was not, he asserted, 'a war for riches or local aggrandisement, but a war for security'. Tarleton adopted a similar theme a few days later, reminding ministers that they had given commissions 'to many gentlemen for raising black regiments. By the Bill these regiments will be emancipated. The disturbance in the West Indies renders the present period very unfit for the abolition.'[21] Not surprisingly, the original 1796 deadline for abolition of the trade came and went without change. The war had provided the pro-slave-trade lobby with useful ammunition, since they could argue that any bill to abolish the trade would aggravate distress already caused by the French conflict. Liverpool merchants had built ships specially constructed for the trade and at great expense. They would lie useless and the government would have to indemnify shipowners and merchants for losses. Black regiments would be let loose to do as they wished and West Indian property would be destined for utter ruin. These were persuasive arguments and, as Pitt admitted in the House, during four years since 1792, far from slowing, the trade had actually been carried on at a higher rate than at any previous time.

On 18 February 1796 Wilberforce rose in the Lower House and bemoaned the continuing policy of the French to emancipate slaves in their own territories and encourage insurrection elsewhere. But his overall strategy was heavily criticised by Henry Dundas, who suggested that the mode adopted by the abolitionists tended to retard the object they had in view rather than promote and accelerate it. He reiterated that any other method of abolition than introducing gradual regulations based on the ages of those imported from Africa would fail. He made the astute observation that Wilberforce was actually further from attaining his end than he had been in 1788, when he first rose to speak on the subject. He considered the whole issue best put on ice until the termination of the war with France. Pitt, on the other hand, appeared, at least in the short term, to be shifting his stance in support of immediate abolition. The question before the House, he noted succinctly, was whether it would at last agree to do that which it had four years earlier pledged itself to the world to perform.[22]

In March and in a mood of rising desperation, having seen most of his friends in the House desert him, Wilberforce proposed a date for abolition of 1 March 1797. Familiar and powerful arguments came from Tarleton and Addington and his proposal was promptly rejected. Dundas reaffirmed that it was not the proper time for abolition and that it would prove unworkable unless other nations complied. West Indian property was currently valued at about £20 million and much of that money rested on credit from British bankers. For his part Pitt returned to enigmatic mode, claiming that the general state of affairs 'made it advisable to alter the time and manner of abolition'. According to Wilberforce's memoirs, such was the level of indifference among parliamentarians that when his 1796 bill was thrown out at the third reading, it was because most of his supporters had forsaken the lobbies and spent the evening at the opera watching Portogallo's new comic production, *I Due Gobbi*. One suspects that Dundas was among the opera buffs since, according to Cobbett, he was not a happy man that night. 'I have found myself called upon, in discharge of public duty, to come down to the House this evening, not without considerable personal inconvenience, to oppose a measure which, if carried into execution, would not only not be productive of good, but the cause of much mischief.' By 1797, in spite of the fact that the subject had been before the House for nine years, the Commons was rejecting proposals even to discuss trade abolition in committee. The remedy, as Charles Ellis, one of the anti-abolitionists proclaimed, was 'civilisation of the West Indian Negroes and their better regulation'. The Commons nodded almost as one. There was, however, one new emergent voice during this difficult time, that of Thomas Fowell Buxton. When, in future years, it came to the question of emancipation, he was to prove an infinitely more compelling and gritty speaker than Wilberforce had ever been.

Wilberforce's reliance on rhetoric was becoming an object of jibes and he was not infrequently accused of hypocrisy. A particularly damaging hurricane had hit the Caribbean in 1780 with the loss of some 15,000 lives. Obscurely Wilberforce proclaimed that this tragedy amounted to divine vengeance inflicted on the West Indian islands in consequence of the traffic. One waspish MP, Bryan Edwards, promptly enquired of Wilberforce if he had taken the trouble to consider how many widows and orphans had their last stake in the islands. If he was truly desirous of exercising his humanity he might do better to walk the streets, where he would meet a race of blacks as worthy of his benevolent attention as those in the West Indies, namely the child chimney-sweeps. Wilberforce was not alone among eighteenth-century politicians in exercising dual standards; he simply made them more obvious than most.

In 1798 Wilberforce's latest bill was thrown out by only a slim margin of eight, which might have suggested that the gap had narrowed dramatically, until one finds that only 156 MPs went into the lobbies, compared with the 321 that had participated in the 1792 vote. July 1799 saw a bill agreed by the Commons that would prohibit trading for slaves on the coast of Africa within certain limits, but it was quashed decisively in the Lords. The Duke of Clarence claimed that he had privileged information that a petition to this end had come from the Sierra Leone Company. Founded in 1791, the organisation had been given the mandate to 'promote African commerce and civilisation', Sierra Leone having been chosen largely on the strength of evidence from two explorers, the Andalusian geographer Leo Africanus in the sixteenth century and Mungo Park in the eighteenth century. They reported that inland, away from the corruption pervading the coastal towns, native culture was advanced by several centuries over that seen elsewhere in West Africa. Clarence insisted that, while claiming that cessation of the trade would result in commercial disaster, the Sierra Leone Company was actually attempting to procure total abolition.

On 5 July 1800 Wilberforce outlined fresh plans in a letter to an unnamed friend. Immediately after the shaky peace with France that was being crafted through the Treaty of Amiens, discussions should take place with all European powers except Denmark, which had already agreed to enforce abolition of the trade. Wilberforce believed that the negotiations being conducted in Amiens provided a once-in-a-lifetime opportunity to get all the slaving nations to abolish by mutual agreement. This would negate, at a stroke, one of the main arguments of the anti-abolitionists, such as Lord Hawkesbury, that the trade would be conducted by other nations if Britain abandoned it unilaterally. Napoleon Bonaparte, however, saw to it that Wilberforce's hopes failed, when he summarily dispensed with emancipation in the French-held territories in the Caribbean.

Pitt's administration fell early in 1801 and the Speaker of the House, Henry Addington, Lord Sidmouth, was asked to form a new government on 14 March. Sidmouth had never professed himself to be an abolition man and the experiment, in his view, would be far too hazardous. Yet on 2 January 1802 Wilberforce wrote a seemingly obscure letter to Sidmouth, advising that he intended to give up as the 'active and chief agent in terminating the trade' and that he hoped to see Addington take over. It was hardly surprising that he did not receive a favourable response, and two months later another predicted crisis came to fruition for the abolitionists that must have made Addington even more resolute. As Napoleon's French fleet arrived in the West Indies to confront Toussaint L'Ouverture in Haiti, a rampaging mob of well-armed and trained Africans proceeded to massacre white colonialists in Guadeloupe. Europe was backing Bonaparte to thwart the prospect of a black empire arising in the Caribbean. Meanwhile, the British press was doing its part to stir anti-abolition sentiment. On 31 April 1802 the *Morning Chronicle* ran a lurid and well-timed report of atrocities committed by Toussaint's

Negroes in Haiti before Napoleon's force had a chance to intervene; Britain needed to be on the side of colonial law and order.

Pitt was returned to power on 26 April 1804, albeit with a greatly reduced majority caused by the revolt of Addington and others. The latest anti-slave-trade bill passed its third reading in the Commons but was routinely quashed in the Lords. In his vulnerable political position Pitt was reluctant to take further risks by introducing a new bill during the session, with the likelihood of dividing the House. Wilberforce wrote again to Addington, urging him, if he would not support total abolition, then at least to make himself the voice of a party committed to suspension for five years. But Addington was not to be moved and even Pitt recognised the concern of the West Indian lobby that if suspension of the trade took place it would never be restored. In June, important Irish support for the abolition cause was lost, the West Indian lobby having persuaded many that it would amount to an invasion of private property.

On 30 May Wilberforce resorted to shock tactics in order to demonstrate the level of prejudice that existed, although in doing so he is likely to have stirred the fires on both sides. He quoted from Long, the knowledgeable author on Jamaican history whose opinions he seems variously to have valued and despised, that 'The African Negro is incapable of civilisation . . . they have no moral sensations . . . they have no settled habitations . . . and they have no pleasure in the beauties of nature . . . an Ourang Outang husband would by no means disgrace a Negro woman.' But the strategy to stir up humanitarian outrage may well have generated a reaction contrary to the one Wilberforce intended, since it gave the pro-slavery lobby further ammunition supporting their argument that Negroes were subhuman. They could wave their hats and cry, 'I told you so!' With the Commons bored at hearing Wilberforce's brand of pious rhetoric, constantly regurgitating the same overblown arguments, support for abolition was reduced to the low ebb of a mere forty MPs.

In a debate of 7 June, Pitt reinforced the message that among informed persons there was no thought of emancipation of the Negroes in the West Indies, but one of the numerous good effects of the abolition of the African trade would undoubtedly be to ameliorate their condition. Lord Castlereagh, the Hon. Robert Stewart, declared that arguing about the humanity of the issue was pointless; what mattered was practicality and Castlereagh probably aired the sentiment of many other parliamentarians when he said, 'I have always looked to the West Indies with serious apprehensions, as being a channel which exposes us to all the calamities of war, of climate, and of the dangers arising from the discussion of rational humanity.' It was his firm opinion that an international guarantee was the only basis for abolition of the trade, lest the national interest suffered by unilateral declaration. Earl Temple, Richard Nugent Grenville, took up the cry.

Without some form of guarantee that the rest of Europe would not commandeer the trade after Britain dropped it, the purpose of humanity would be out of British humanitarian control and in the hands of others who would exercise it with cruelty.[23] The sentiment, from a peer tagged by his less-charitable contemporaries as 'Lord Grenville's fat nephew' is again fairly typical of the free-and-easy hypocrisy that was rife in British politics of the eighteenth and nineteenth centuries. As the historian A.N. Wilson puts it, three or four generations of Britons could be seen to be in denial about many issues where a twenty-first-century observer sees clear cause for moral disapprobation. People could be thick-skinned, breezy and able to live without too much hesitation or procrastination.[24]

The applause that Castlereagh and Temple received did not please Wilberforce, who viewed the pair of them as further obstacles in his path. In 1805 he introduced a new abolition motion and this time the riposte came principally from Gascoyne, keen to revive the spectre of emancipation in the minds of his fellow MPs. Everyone must see, he declared, that the ultimate object was freedom for the Negro. Was not the West Indies a favourite object of Bonaparte's and would he not eagerly seize the advantage? The House shuddered collectively, Gascoyne moved that the second reading of the bill be delayed and Wilberforce was beaten again. But in 1806 the British political scene was thrown into disarray when Pitt died prematurely and unexpectedly. The government was dissolved and power passed into the hands of William Grenville, Henry Petty, Charles Fox and others, the so-called 'Ministry of Talents'. The change of administration was crucial because Grenville and his allies, largely unsympathetic towards abolition of the trade in the past, now shifted their opinions in its favour and offered to put the weight of the government behind a new bill. Addington's camp remained implacably opposed, considering that it was more appropriate to improve the moral fibre of Negroes by instructing them in the virtues of Christian life. But on 15 September 1806 Charles Fox, one of the key parliamentary figures, and another major player in the abolition debate, followed Pitt to the grave. The government was again thrown into confusion with a second dissolution of parliament in short order and a Whig government under the leadership of Addington was returned.

In 1807 the anti-slave-trade bill was trundled out again, but on this occasion there was no William Pitt in charge and Hansard reveals that Wilberforce also carried out his declared intention not to continue leading the parliamentary abolition lobby. He absolved himself from his usual prominent role, only spoke later in the debate, and then briefly by comparison with his more familiar marathons. The motion was presented by Lord Howick and the keynote speeches came from him and from Sir Samuel Romilly, who made, it was said, a 'brilliant and effective oration against slavery in general and the slave trade in particular'.

Howick dispensed with rhetoric and laid out some hard economic facts. The proportion of capital embarked in the African trade was, on the average of the ten years preceding the year 1800, one twenty-fourth part of the whole capital of the export trade. That had been reduced to a still lower proportion by the operation of the slave carrying bill and other bills that now prohibited importation of slaves into colonies conquered from the enemy. What remained now was only a remnant of the trade for the supply of the old British colonies. There remained in the trade a capital that was less than half of one per cent of the whole export trade capital – about £250,000. There was also now evidence that the populations in the West Indies could support themselves. In 1805, he noted, the excess of deaths over births in eight parishes of Jamaica was only 258. In Dominica, Bermuda and the Bahamas, births exceeded deaths by that time, and in most places in North America the population was increasing of its own volition. This time Gascoyne's response largely amounted to bluster.[25]

The bill was carried to the Lords and moved by Lord Grenville. Even at that stage, however, a number of high-ranking peers, including Clarence, remained staunchly opposed. In one of the last Lords debates on the subject, on 5 February 1807, the future king argued that, on personal observation, there was not the least foundation in fact for the charge that had been brought against the planters of ill treatment of their slaves. When the Africans in the islands found that no fresh importations took place, they would naturally enquire the cause, and when they found that the trade was abolished and declared contrary to justice, humanity and sound policy, would it not have a material effect in their minds with respect to their own situation?

The House of Lords nevertheless agreed Grenville's motion on 23 March 1807 and congratulated itself. Managing to overlook their Lordships' implacable resistance during the last two decades, the Bishop of Llandaff declared the decision to be an act of national humanity and justice. The Duke of Norfolk announced magnanimously that they had performed one of the most glorious acts that had ever been done by any assembly of any nation in the world.[26] Abolition of the slave trade thus received royal assent, and with it Addington's government was brought down. Such are the bare facts of the Westminster debate on abolition of the trade, but this does not yet explain all of the underlying reasons for the change of heart that came about in the spring of 1807.

Chapter 8

CAUSE AND EFFECT

At face value the British parliamentary body, in both the Upper and Lower Houses at Westminster, spent much of the nineteen years from 1788 to 1807 robustly blocking the abolition of the slave trade, whereafter it executed a smart U-turn and voted in favour. In the lost debate of April 1791, those backing immediate abolition stood at eighty-eight. In the all-important deciding committee vote of 6 March 1807, the number rose to 175. Whether this was purely because of MPs changing sides or in part to the increased efficiency of abolitionists in getting their supporters into the division lobby is not clear, and only limited information about swings one way or the other can be gleaned from interim voting patterns. By and large the Commons attendances for abolition debates were low, and therefore hardly representative. When, in 1799, for example, Wilberforce renewed his regular motion for a debate in committee and this was rejected by a majority of eighty-four to fifty-four, only a limited contingent of parliamentary MPs took part. No matter how extensive the trawl of parliamentary minutes, setting out to glean a convincing explanation purely from these more public records yields unsatisfactory results. The real influences and currents lie beneath the overt face of the debate, coloured, as it was too often, with rhetoric.

It is clear that the principal Westminster players were William Pitt, Henry Dundas and William Wilberforce. Wilberforce, however, can be neither labelled as the real architect of eventual success nor, conversely, blamed entirely for the extraordinary lack of progress during the drawn-out period of just short of twenty years. Of the trio, it is on Pitt that the scrutiny should fall most closely, because he bears the heaviest responsibility for manipulating the situation. William Pitt was probably never truly sympathetic to the cause of the abolitionists and a degree of significance might be attached to the fact that the bill to end the trade was not passed until after his death. Ostensibly he wore a cloak of humanitarianism, which suited him in presenting a beneficent face to the world, but throughout the abolition debate his position in the Commons remained largely ambivalent. When he supported Wilberforce on the issue, enthusiasm rarely showed in his contributions. On other occasions he was either absent from the chamber, or influenced the delaying of pro-abolition motions. At one time in 1792 he actually voted with the West Indian lobby.

Pitt chose deliberately to orchestrate a sense of uncertainty about whose side he was on. He created this air of ambivalence partly to protect his own back from the shafts of the abolitionists, partly because as the arch-pragmatist he had a clear view that abolition of the trade would adversely affect British interests and British security. He was canny enough to know that supporting abolition might amount to political suicide. Pitt was a born survivor, whose interest lay in maintaining British power and British security in exceptionally troubled times. From 1793 until 1815, Britain was almost constantly at war with France, much of the conflict concerning colonial issues. The government machine that Pitt controlled during a remarkable span of office was often insecure but it was held together, to no small extent, by his reputation for political shrewdness. Part of that acumen lay in care to avoid siding with one camp or another and to exert authority subtly. In reality Pitt was something of an autocrat and although he was keen on the principle of cabinet government, he tended to treat cabinet meetings more as a sounding board, while conveying to his ministers the impression that they acted with a degree of autonomy. He liked to work on the basis of precise information and would rarely reveal his hand unless he was assured of success. But virtually everything that moved in government needed Pitt's consent and, not infrequently, he reached important policy decisions outside cabinet with two of his closest cronies, his cousin, the influential Buckingham MP William Grenville, and the Home Secretary, Henry Dundas.

Unwilling to rush into policies that he considered professionally risky, Pitt built his reputation from 1786 onwards as a man of calm and far-reaching vision. The abolition debate was hazardous territory and he was for remaining on the fence for as long as possible. Five years earlier, Lord North, in opposition to Pitt, had declared that abolition was impossible, since the trade had become necessary to almost every nation in Europe. In April 1785 Pitt had motioned for parliamentary reform that might have redressed the balance on a range of issues, but his move had been rejected and he was well aware that with a powerful lobby of West Indian interest at Westminster, the make-up of neither the Commons nor the Lords favoured abolition. Before the parliamentary Reform Act of 1832, which came a quarter of a century too late for Pitt, the system of rotten boroughs allowed colonial representation to exert a disproportionate influence at Westminster. These boroughs amounted to areas that had become depopulated for one reason or another but still benefited from a parliamentary presence. In effect the MPs of such constituencies paid their way into parliament simply to obtain a seat and were answerable to nobody beyond their cronies and those whose vested interests they represented. The influx of 'colonial money', much of it amounting to the proceeds of slavery and plantation ownership, not only stimulated a boom in the price of parliamentary seats but also permitted the West Indian lobby to become entrenched in both the Upper and Lower Houses.[1]

Pitt's ambivalence did not escape criticism. The style of inconsistency that he demonstrated in his famous speech of April 1792, claiming to support immediate abolition while backing Dundas's package of gradual reform, led to accusations that he was indecisive and pursued no clear policy. In July 1797 the abolitionist James Stephen, in a letter to his brother-in-law Wilberforce, complained that 'Mr Pitt, unhappily for himself, his country and mankind, is not zealous enough in the cause of the Negroes, to contend for them as decisively as he ought, in the cabinet and more than this, in parliament.'[2]

Pitt was apathetic about ending the trade because he could envisage the dangers inherent in the broad picture, but there was also a more specific reason for procrastination. We need to backtrack and remember that towards the end of the eighteenth century Great Britain was plagued with a nagging sense of vulnerability on the world stage. In 1783 she did not feel particularly great and when the nation was vulnerable, so was Pitt. Britain had recently lost all of her American mainland possessions, aside from Canada, and at home and abroad the French presented an ever-present menace. France did not, however, amount solely to a military threat. The balance in the all-important sugar economy had also swung away from Britain in favour of France and she now dominated the European market for refined sugar. The chief factor contributing to the French economic bonanza was, to a great extent, the island of St Domingue (previously known by its inhabitants as Haiti, and nowadays consisting of Haiti and the Dominican Republic) and this became something of an obsession for Pitt. It lay behind much of his personal policy on the issue of the slave trade so that, as William Wilberforce's diary of April 1792 notes with chagrin, 'Pitt threw out against the slave motion on Saint Domingo account.'[3]

By the 1780s, St Domingue had achieved peculiar significance among the Caribbean islands in terms of its productive potential. It represented the richest single colony in all the European empires and in the 1780s its foreign trade was bigger than that of the entire United States. Coupled with Martinique, the island was responsible for two-fifths of all French foreign trade and involved two-thirds of the tonnage of its deep-water ships, even more if the coastal trade was taken into account.[4] It was also much larger than any of the British West Indian possessions, including Trinidad and Jamaica. Compared with most of the British sugar colonies in the region its soil had been exploited for a much shorter period, so was less depleted. Its yields were therefore higher and its production costs lower, with the consequence that the French now benefited hugely from cheap

Caribbean sugar exports. In his submissions to the Privy Council board of inquiry that sat through 1788, Stephen Fuller provided a comparison of sugar-production costs for Jamaica and St Domingue. At the time the British average yield was 800lb of refined sugar per acre. The proceeds of a 5¼-acre plantation of cane at the Jamaica market was calculated at £55 2s 6d. In St Domingue, the equivalent yield per acre was 4,231lb and the proceeds in the St Domingue market for one acre of cultivation were the same as that for five and a quarter in Jamaica. The profits earned were boosting France's exchequer and funding her war chest.

Fuller also noted, 'the French have purchased of late years, a great proportion of the Negroes they wanted from our traders on the Guinea Coast. They are customers also for Negroes at Jamaica and Dominica . . . the French also treat their Negroes worse and work them harder so the death rate is higher.'[5] The uncomfortable reality was that British ships were supplying French planters with slave labour so that they could beat down British sugar refiners in a strategic price war. The slave trade to the West Indies had thus begun to turn sour and Pitt was deeply conscious that, unless something was done about St Domingue and the other French-held islands, they would account for an irreversible downward shift in British Caribbean fortunes, while delivering still more muscle to a regularly belligerent neighbour.

Pitt concluded that he must undermine French naval and commercial interests in the Caribbean. He was convinced that if he could do so, French finances would suffer and French naval power, used so effectively in the American War of Independence, would be severely weakened. He also recognised that the revolutionary French might use any means to stir slaves into revolt if the British position on the trade were seen to be weakening. Pitt's initial scheme was to apply economic pressure, drawing on the resources of East Indian sugar to restore British market dominance, but this strategy failed because large-scale reliance on India proved impossible because of high import tariffs, which the West Indian lobby in parliament would not countenance removing. Pitt therefore turned to the military option.

Capturing French-held Caribbean islands would serve more than one purpose. It would restore an element of British pride that had been sorely dented by the loss of the American colonies. It would also hit French commercial interests hard and, with luck, would tie up and disable much of her long-range naval power. Pitt's aspiration was given a boost in 1791, when French plantation owners in St Domingue, fearful about their future welfare under a French revolutionary government, offered the island to the British and so in 1793, after the next round of Anglo-French hostilities had commenced, Pitt ordered an expeditionary force into action. Local British garrisons took a number of the smaller islands and thus achieved initial success with comparative ease, but they ran into more-serious resistance over the capture of Martinique. This demanded that additional forces, already stretched in Europe, be shipped out from Britain. Martinique eventually fell in March 1794, followed by St Lucia, Guadeloupe (for a brief period before it was retaken) and, by midsummer, the capital of St Domingue, Port-au-Prince. But the adventure against St Domingue was to amount to a costly failure. In the autumn of 1795 Pitt and Dundas assembled 27,000 men at Portsmouth and Cork in the biggest overseas military expedition ever mounted from British shores. It was to tie up 10,000 tons of British shipping and one-eighth of her deep-water resources, and in total, between 1795 and 1796, government ministers threw 35,000 troops into the battle for the island. Of these, 14,000 died in 1796 alone, felled by the combined perils of gunpowder, yellow fever and malaria. In the summer of 1795, predictions about French agitation of slaves on British-held islands came to fruition, triggering a messy, if short-lived, revolt in Jamaica.

Either Pitt had to win St Domingue by force of arms and claim the achievement of a glittering strategic prize, or wreck it economically. The disastrous outcome of the military adventure determined it to be the latter. Over a six-year period until 1799 Britain squandered vast amounts of money and manpower on attempts to take the island, now bristling with liberated, heavily armed, belligerent slaves, and in doing so, turned it into a wasteland. British military efforts dashed French superiority in the region once and for all but they also destroyed what Eric Williams rightly describes as 'the world's sugar bowl'. In 1799 Britain conceded the impracticability of military conquest, signed a non-aggression pact with Toussaint L'Ouverture and withdrew her forces. It brought to an end any aspiration to build a major new empire for Britain in the West Indies, and with it the emphasis on a slave-driven economy receded as covetous eyes turned to the prospect of fresh imperial gains in the East. In summarising the position, Pitt's closest parliamentary ally, Henry Dundas, observed astutely that 'Great Britain can at no time propose to maintain an extensive and complicated war but by destroying the colonial resources of our enemies and adding proportionately to our own commercial resources.'[6]

It was Pitt's preoccupation with St Domingue, more than any other single factor, that governed his attitude to the abolition of the trade. He possessed the clear understanding that it had to be the island or abolition, but it could not be both. While the extended campaign for control of St Domingue continued, he was under no illusion that abolition of the trade would be other than counterproductive. To restore full sugar production under something approaching peaceful conditions, the sugar plantations would demand 40,000 slave imports a year and although Pitt never revealed his view publicly, he must have been acutely aware that if Britain abolished the trade, any eventual conquest of

St Domingue would be pointless. Without the massive numbers of slaves needed to make the island economically viable it would amount to a useless piece of real estate that had been bought at politically unacceptable cost. It was only when the military options ran into the ground, when the adventure became irrevocably lost, that Pitt chose to play the 'humanitarian card', in the certain knowledge that the slave trade was now more a hindrance than a help to Britain. It had become, as an abolitionist cannily predicted in the parliamentary debate of 2 April 1792, 'the most destructive that can well be imagined in her interests'.[7] Pitt, ever the strategist, also saw political advantage in becoming Pitt the humanitarian. Then, and only then, was he willing to put his authority behind abolition of the slave trade. Humanitarianism was not, however, foremost in his mind. Britain effectively had control of the high seas. Available figures show that by 1805 the British navy had increased by a quarter, while that of France had almost halved. The logic ran that since the French remained heavily dependent on British slave-traders, abolition would serve to wreck what was left of their colonial economy. Pitt, as the French historian Gaston-Martin remarked dryly, was scheming 'in the name no doubt of humanity but also to ruin French commerce'. Gaston-Martin even volunteered that this was one of the motives behind swamping France with Clarkson's anti-slavery tracts and pumping liberal amounts of British funding into Les Amis des Noirs, the French abolitionist movement.[8]

Henry Dundas was also shrewd enough to appreciate and to go along with much of Pitt's policy. He too realised the immediate shortcomings of trade abolition and played a significant part in delaying the eventual outcome. Dundas, always loyal to Pitt since deserting the political camp of Lord North, was one of those trusted individuals, along with William Grenville, with whom policy decisions were often reached. With France isolated from her long-time Spanish allies through the machinations of the revolutionaries, and with French planters begging Britain for help in 1791, the time had been right. Determined to erode French colonial wealth and smash French naval power, Dundas was eventually made Secretary of State for War in 1794.

What then of the fourth element of the quartet that included Pitt, Dundas, Dolben and Wilberforce? One of the most hotly contested arguments about the impact of the various protagonists in the drive towards parliamentary abolition of the trade has been that concerning William Wilberforce. Conventional wisdom informs us that the Yorkshire firebrand stood head-and-shoulders above the throng, combining roles as a perfect model of practical, evangelical Christianity and an unflagging champion of the oppressed black African. A tone of toadying adulation often attaches to the man. According to more-sycophantic writers, Wilberforce is supposed to have masterminded, virtually single-handedly, the abolition triumph, and the Methodist leader, John Wesley, captured the flavour only a few days before his death when he wrote to Wilberforce on 24 February 1791:

> Unless the divine power has raised you up as Athanasius against the world, I see not how you can go through your glorious enterprise in opposing that execrable villainy, which is the scandal of religion, of England and of human nature. Unless God has raised you up for this very thing you will be worn out by the opposition of God and devils. But if God be for you who can be against you? Are all of them stronger than God? Oh be not weary of well doing! Go on, in the name of God, in the power of his might, till even American slavery (the vilest that ever saw the sun) shall vanish away before it.[9]

This romanticised portrait has been further glossed down the years since Wilberforce's death in 1833 by a plethora of fawning biographies. In the wake of the initial hagiography by his sons, Robert and Samuel, among the most significant works is an analysis penned by Reginald Coupland in 1923, entitled *Wilberforce*. One of the latest books, following much the same eulogising tone, is Kevin Belmont's *Hero for Humanity: a Biography of William Wilberforce*, published in 2002. Belmont's title sums up the general flavour. Many of the biographies are written from a Christian, often evangelical perspective, depicting Wilberforce as the unswerving visionary whose lifetime of saintly humanitarian zeal and determination led to the abolition of slavery. Yet is this a fair or accurate portrait?

That William Wilberforce was a God-fearing man is not in dispute. From his university days it is clear that service to his faith was a driving force in his life. He was undoubtedly among the first politicians in English history (though certainly not the last) to shout Christian values from the hustings and he earns credit for his reformist successes. But he was certainly not someone truly bent on freeing the African from shackles. If Wilberforce saw himself as a liberator of humankind it was probably not by way of consigning slavery to history, but strictly as a Christian evangelist seeking to bring light and grace into the heathen darkness. Wilberforce was a determined supporter of reform in the East India Company, and one of his less-well-publicised sentiments is a declaration that 'the first task of God and his Englishmen is to convert the Hindus of India to Christianity before concerning themselves about the abolition of slavery'. Wilberforce's ideas of Christian persuasion did not exclude quelling dissidence by whatever means, brutal or otherwise, and five years after his death the *Edinburgh Quarterly Review* of April 1838 appraised him as 'a man engaged in a conflict of sentiment with principle'. Like many in government today, Wilberforce's personal and political ideals ran on two sets of rails without being restrained by any of that brand of self-analysis that affects modern society.

In 1784 Wilberforce had become a fervent supporter of evangelical Christianity when he joined the Clapham Sect under its founder John Venn, the rector of Clapham Church in London. By and large these men and women were not the nonconformists that Wilberforce generally despised, the breakaway rabble of dissident agitators, but upstanding members of the mainstream Anglican Church. They were part and parcel of a new-found earnestness to change social and political norms, and in the closing decades of the eighteenth century this mood had begun to penetrate governing circles. Yet the drive towards what Wilberforce labelled as 'Practical Christianity' was also tinged with that brand of social hypocrisy that I have touched on already in places and that so greatly characterised the Georgian and Victorian eras.

The Clapham 'Saints', as they became known, paid lip service to social change but were generally of a staunchly conservative disposition, a privileged intellectual circle believing that the existing order was right and was not to be questioned. Theirs was a world in which the authority vested in the hands of the few over the many was a natural and even God-given arrangement to be jealously safeguarded. To stand aside and permit this authority to be undermined was to invite chaos. Nowhere, they could argue with justification, was the maxim being more clearly demonstrated in the 1780s and 90s than in Revolutionary France. The Claphamites backed abolition of the slave trade not out of recognition that it led to enslavement, not because its conditions were cruel, but because it interfered with the status of Africans in their home country. If a person was removed, forcibly and brutally, from his or her position in society, often from a family or local hierarchy, the Claphamites considered that it upset the natural order of things ordained by the Almighty and this was as undesirable in darkest Africa as it was in leafy south London. Wilberforce's objection to the slave trade echoed that of the Clapham 'Saints'. It was precise and clearly articulated on the grounds that if it forcibly changed the status and place of residence of a Negro (frequently from one world to the next), it became morally indefensible.

The Clapham Sect may have condemned the trade but it shut the door decisively on Negro emancipation and did so for the same underlying reason that it opposed the formation of working men's unions in Britain and disliked the ideology of Jacobinism across the water. In each case the outcome would be to overturn the obedience of one section of society towards its naturally ordained superiors and betters. The arguments of eminent pro-slavery writers like the planter and historian Edward Long were widely supported. In the February 1794 debate in the Commons, Sir Robert Peel of Bury, in the ascendancy as one of the great cotton barons of the north, had described any prospect of emancipation to be comparable to putting a sword in the hands of a madman. The natives of Africa were not yet sufficiently matured by civilisation to receive liberty and freedom.

With one exception, a notable gaffe by James Stephen, Clapham 'Saints' absolutely recoiled from the idea of Negro revolt.[10] For the Claphamites the ideal solution was not to extend rights to the underprivileged but to educate them in the ways of civilisation and to persuade employers, whether running Lancashire factories or far-off plantations, to move a little in the direction of benevolence and charity. By this they meant civilisation based on Christian values of marriage, family unity and regular churchgoing. That most formidable of late-eighteenth-century blue-stockings, Miss Hannah More, unsuccessful playwright turned philanthropist whose relentless Christian energies were lately channelled into good deeds, was keen to educate the poor and illiterate. Her purpose was to strengthen Britain's moral fibre and she aimed to achieve this through literary works, including *The Religion of the Fashionable World* (1790), *Practical Piety* (1811) and *Christian Morals* (1813). With the same ends in mind, she also set up local schools in order to equip impoverished pupils with an elementary grasp of reading. This, however, was where her concern for their education effectively ended, because she did not offer her charges the additional skill of writing. To be able to read was to open a door to good ideas and sound morality (most of which was provided by Hannah More through a series of religious pamphlets); writing, on the other hand, was to be discouraged, since it would open the way to rising above one's natural station.[11]

The persuasive tongue of one of the 'Saints', the wife of Admiral Sir Charles Middleton, steered William Wilberforce towards tabling the first of his series of anti-slave-trade motions in the House of Commons. But why should Wilberforce have been singled out? Since winning his York seat he had proved himself eloquent and passionate in his brand of independent politics. In February 1782 he had made a memorable speech critical of the Fox–North coalition administration and this had not only helped to see Lord North consigned to the opposition benches in December 1783, but also labelled Wilberforce as a good public orator. In addition he had recently undergone some form of personal religious renaissance. During the summer of 1785 he took an extended holiday in Switzerland and, while staying there, arrived at the understanding that his own lifestyle was less than truly Christian. Self-recrimination for sinful conduct abounding, he engaged earnestly in prayer and, in the autumn, returned home a changed man, or so his biographers claimed. In the mind of Lady Middleton, this moral fervour, coupled with powers of speech-making and his standing as an independent MP, made Wilberforce the ideal recruit to become the parliamentary champion of slave-trade abolition.

Wilberforce, however, was torn between taking on this mantle of working to end a specific moral evil thousands of miles distant, and spearheading the drive to improve morals and behaviour in a more general way at home. This personal dilemma was plain for others to see, to the extent that he was occasionally satirised wearing the two coats intimated in the *Edinburgh Quarterly Review*. A cartoon of 1797 shows him wielding a Common Prayer Book in one hand, a paper marked 'Slave Trade' in his pocket, a pistol held behind him and a Negro in livery.[12] When approached on behalf of Lady Middleton, he seems to have considered his vocation to be attendance on matters closer to home, and by the spring of 1787, after a year back in the cut-and-thrust of parliament, he concluded that as a self-styled standard-bearer for Christian morality, he should take as his prime target the reform of public manners. He shared Hannah More's view that the vice and licentiousness seen to be rampant in British society, or at least in its lower orders, were to be rooted out and quashed. He regarded the lack of any proper Church accommodation for the vast horde of spiritually unwashed congregating in the new manufacturing centres as a disgrace, one to be rectified with vigour. Furthermore the convulsions erupting across the Channel ought to serve as a timely warning of the consequences of ignoring the seamier side of life at home.[13]

Thus, in 1787, Wilberforce declined the requested promotion of an anti-slave-trade debate in the Commons, not least perhaps because his friend William Pitt was still the darling of the dominant West Indian contingent of MPs. By way of reply to Charles Middleton's overture, he merely penned a convenient opt-out: 'I feel the great importance of the subject and think myself unequal to the task allotted to me.' This reluctance to take an early stand against the slave trade belies the popular myth that he rushed to spearhead the objectives of the London Committee for the Abolition of the Slave Trade. Sir Charles Middleton for his part, impressed by the recently published English translation of Thomas Clarkson's award-winning university dissertation, eventually became more closely involved with the committee. It was an association that would prove valuable, since he not only counted among much-sought-after friendly faces at Westminster but also, as Comptroller of the Royal Navy, was able to provide inside information from official records and journals of ships of war stationed off the West African coast.

It was only with reluctance, and when no one else better suited to the job could be prevailed upon, that Wilberforce eventually agreed to represent the slave-trade abolitionists. He resolutely shared the reticence of the London Committee, however, to bring emancipation into the debating chamber and when discussion of emancipation was launched in earnest in 1823, Wilberforce became a virtual bystander both in the Commons and in the newly formed Anti-Slavery Society. In the meantime the liberation of slaves was a separate issue, as was slave ownership, and he knew very well that to introduce either of these aspects was almost certain to jeopardise any chance of seeing trade abolition through to royal assent. Wilberforce thus became the acknowledged spokesman for the anti-slave-trade lobby, even though it would be two years before he would rise to make his first parliamentary speech on the subject. Initially his response was limited to a vague promise that he would introduce the matter to parliament 'when the proper time arrived'.[14]

During the twenty-year period after 1787 that the trade abolition argument swung one way then finally another, Wilberforce's passions were often fired more by the deplorable lack of Christian evangelism in the dark recesses of the less-civilised world, rather than the suffering of human sardines aboard British slave ships. Wearing the coat of Wilberforce the missionary, he had set his sights on what he perceived as a lamentable failure to disseminate the Christian gospel into foreign and heathen lands. His tendency was to promote the trade-abolition issue with this in mind, and too frequently his rhetoric from the backbenches focused on the abominations that he perceived to be the blight not only of Africa but other Godless backwaters. It was one of his cardinal weaknesses that he did not recognise how poorly the philanthropic and evangelical arguments washed with many of his fellow parliamentarians. But his approach never changed and he remained resolutely committed to this style of moral persuasion. In a Commons speech delivered as late as 30 May 1804 he observed of the West African heathen, 'Even their superstition, in order to be consistent in our wickedness, we attempt to encourage and notwithstanding our professions of Christianity, endeavour to confirm and even increase their absurd ideas of witchcraft, and other prejudices, which we find subservient to the purposes of our avarice.'[15]

Wilberforce was not without his detractors. The writer James Boswell, no strong admirer of the abolitionists, did not mince his words when he scathingly described Wilberforce as 'a dwarf with a big resounding name'.[16] Less enviable traits included a love affair with the sound of his own voice, but the undoubted eloquence of his oratory was unfortunately matched on too few occasions by its substance. His Commons speeches tended to be interminable and rambling, often extending into the small hours. Levelling a clearly directed sideswipe in his direction, the waggish member for Plympton Erle in Devon, Henry Lawes Luttrell, Lord Carhampton, once noted that 'gentlemen may talk of inhumanity but what right has anyone do so inhumane a thing as to inflict a speech of four hours long on a set of innocent, worthy and respectable men? Gentlemen have continued this abuse day after day some of which would be equally proper for a pulpit. If there had not been a back door behind the speaker's chair for infirm gentlemen to escape, I do believe they would have died on the spot.'[17] Carhampton's colleagues considered him to be both comical and profligate, but occasionally his remarks were apt to hit the mark, as when he observed that Wilberforce and his fellow philanthropists 'undertake the care and protection of all the world, but not without squinting a little at the world to come'.

Sentiments expressed by Wilberforce on the subject of slavery probably amounted to the norm among a circle of liberal intellectuals in the closing decade of the eighteenth century, but they also undermine portrayals of him as the great political architect of black African liberation. Sanctimonious hectoring did little to rouse the passions of MPs and probably did indeed hasten more jaded members into late-night catnaps on the back benches. At the close of Wilberforce's marathon speech of 30 May, the Sussex MP John Fuller, a slave-owner who would always remain implacably opposed to abolition, rose and observed that the situation of the Negroes in the West Indian colonies was 'equal, nay superior' to the condition of the labouring poor of this country. They were better fed and more comfortably accommodated. This was the kind of objective comment to which some MPs tended more readily to open their ears, and attention was drawn more than once to the disparity between Wilberforce's focus on the plight of Africans en route to the West Indies and his apparent lack of interest in the welfare of the poor and needy in Britain.

Occasionally MPs were prepared to be fairly scathing about Wilberforce's style of rhetoric. On one occasion a member named Captain Herbert observed with a degree of scarcely veiled censure that his 'expressions of justice and humanity though generally delivered with much eloquence, are commonplace'. Wilberforce had also been found out over economies with the truth. In a debate of 13 June 1804, an member named Dent brought the attention of the House to misrepresentations of atrocities with which Wilberforce had attempted to carry an argument. Dent cited the trial in 1792 of one Captain Kimber, whose cruelty had been trumpeted by Wilberforce and other abolitionists. He pointed out that Kimber had actually earned an acquittal at the Old Bailey, after it was established that the main witness, the ship's surgeon, had been guilty of wilful and corrupt perjury when giving evidence.

Nor were Wilberforce and Pitt quite the close allies that some writers have painted. Whether Wilberforce sensed the true state of Pitt's mind is not clearly revealed in his diaries but my conclusion is that he knew where Pitt stood, if not immediately, then certainly by the turn of the 1790s. More than once Wilberforce alludes to Pitt's apathy. Aside from the vexed diary entry of April 1792, made after Pitt had withdrawn his support on account of the St Domingue issue, one can discover a scattering of other criticisms. As early as 4 June 1789, Wilberforce describes a meeting with Pitt to discuss the progress of the abolition debate as 'a sad waste of time'. A month later he writes an irritable comment, 'Called up Pitt at eleven. Wasted morning sadly.' More than two years later, his resentment again manifests itself in an entry dated 16 December 1790. He expresses frustration that Pitt and John Fenton Cawthorne, an MP for Lincoln who was an inflexible opponent of abolition or regulation of the trade and who is believed to have had slaving interests in Lancaster (then a slaving port), 'have put off the slave business till after Christmas'.[18]

Pitt is also alleged to have dubbed members of the London Committee, including Clarkson and William Dickson, a former colonial official in Barbados, somewhat acidly as Wilberforce's 'white Negroes'. The scarcely veiled complaints about Pitt continue. In the summer of 1799 Wilberforce indicates that Pitt had originally promised cooperation on securing an early abolition date but had been persuaded by Dundas to retract this pledge. On 6 June 1800 Wilberforce's pen is busy on the subject again: 'I have suffered great chagrin on the subject of the slave trade. Pitt listened too easily to the assurance of several West Indian proprietors who declared themselves willing to support a suspension for 5 years . . . this shook the resolution of our timid converts. Dundas will not, I fear, consent to support us now. Negroes have risen in price from £76 to £120 per head yet have been bought in greater numbers than ever. Pitt declares that he will, by order of Council, stop importation of Negroes into new settlements into which three-quarters more or less of the whole importation have been brought.'

Pitt stayed away from debates when it suited. On 31 May 1802 he wrote to Wilberforce from Walmer Castle, presumably in response to a plea for support, saying, 'I must not think of returning for your motion. Indeed though I should most eagerly support it, I see no chance in the present state of the session of your carrying it, unless Addington can be brought really to see the propriety of it.'[19] As late as 23 June 1804 Wilberforce wrote in his memoirs that he had 'never been so dissatisfied with Pitt'. This particular bout of irritation may have stemmed from Pitt's failure to attend the House when Wilberforce moved the order of the day in favour of an abolition debate on 20 June. Hansard notes that there were so few MPs in the Commons chamber that 'further disagreeable delay occurred by there not being a sufficient number of members present to proceed with the business'. The chamber seems to have been staffed largely by pro-slavery members including Gascoyne and Stephen Fuller.

In a written sketch found among his private papers, Wilberforce at first made polite noises about Pitt before more candid sentiments percolated through. Pitt, he complained rather viciously, 'was defective in his knowledge of human nature, or from some cause or other was less sagacious than might have been expected from his superior talents in his estimation of the future. In considering the practical influence of his character and qualities on the fortunes of this country, I have sometimes been almost ready to believe that powers far inferior to his, under the direction of a mind equally sincere and equally warm in its zeal for the public good, might have been the instrument of conferring far greater benefits on his country.'[20]

The world tended to bestow flattering compliments on Wilberforce and, indeed, Sir Samuel Romilly, the Solicitor General, paid a long and emotional tribute to him in the final 1807 debate. It was a eulogy that, unusually, according to the report in the *Morning Chronicle*, merited 'three distinct and universal cheers'. But although from time to time political colleagues were willing to applaud Wilberforce, his influence remained limited. For his part, Pitt needed to keep strong allies with him and Wilberforce did not fall into this category. Pitt had, for example, backed Dundas rather than abstaining in the 1792 debate, because Dundas held the key to the support of the Scottish parliamentary vote, and keeping his acquiescence was essential for the security of Pitt's fragile hold on government.

Ever the wily politician, Pitt seems to have quickly detected advantage in Wilberforce's passion and piety, qualities that would allow him to remain on the sidelines of a debate that would have cost parliamentary support if he had been seen to lean one way or the other. His position only changed gradually when it became clear, after 1800, that the slave trade held no further advantage for Britain and when he could discern that enough parliamentarians were coming around to similar conclusions. In the meantime he anticipated correctly that Wilberforce had neither the wit nor the wherewithal to turn many Commons heads beyond the committed few in favour of abolition. Pitt probably reckoned that Wilberforce's unforced errors, his blinkered view of the world stage and his lack of appeal in the House would serve a purpose in facilitating that which Pitt truly wished: to delay trade abolition until making the U-turn was politically desirable.

These portraits go some way towards accounting for the fact that the abolitionists did not achieve more leverage in the Commons for such a long time. Wilberforce failed to persuade a majority of MPs to switch support away from preserving the slave trade and he was certainly no match for Pitt. By focusing so rigidly on humanitarian and moral aspects, by not incorporating sufficient economic and strategic arguments, he and his supporters at Westminster missed the opportunity to exploit the far stronger abolition case that presented itself from 1799. In short, Wilberforce's influence on the abolition debate has been grossly overstated. He must be credited for his dogged persistence and for keeping his subject before parliament, but as for winning over hardbitten MPs he was perennially unconvincing. Significantly the keynote speech before the all-important division that spelled the demise of the trade, or at least its authorised activity, had come not from Wilberforce but Lord Howick, who chose to concentrate attention on that which actually concerned the government and the majority of parliamentarians. This was not the plight of the suffering African, but the effect that banning or continuing the trade would now have on the British economy.

Mine is not an intention to trash the memory of William Wilberforce, but to paint him as he really was and to refrain from eulogising him as so many others have set out to do. There is no question about his genuine sense of purpose in raising moral values and his advocacy of social reform, but his principles were robustly old-fashioned and often reactionary. To recall another comment posted in the *Edinburgh Review* he was 'a Tory by predilection, in action a Whig'. In the language of the eighteenth and nineteenth centuries, this meant that at heart he was strongly conservative (even if in his conduct he appeared to be in sympathy with the nonconformist dissenters), as well as being opposed to political intervention by the monarch and, loosely, what might be termed a liberal. The terms Tory and Whig did not identify ideological divisions in the sense that they exist in political parties today. The distinction, or rather lack of it, between the Tory and Whig parties was splendidly drawn by one of the great literary critics of the day, William Hazlitt. The two parties were, he remarked, 'like rival stage coaches which splash each other with mud, but go by the same road to the same place'.[21] Much of the evidence about Wilberforce points to a well-heeled, sanctimonious and arrogant Yorkshireman, full of what in his day would have been labelled 'humbug', who believed he understood the side on which his political bread was buttered and often relied on pious hypocrisy in attempts to exploit the mood of an equally hypocritical audience. It reveals him as a product of his time, but his political self-interest and craft, such as it was, is almost timeless, finding many echoes in the corridors of government today.

In his book *Capitalism and Slavery* published in 1944 – some have said written a little ahead of its time – the West Indian historian Eric Williams is also critical of Wilberforce, describing him as effeminate and exuding a certain smugness in his life and his religion. Sir George Stephen, one of the leaders of the emancipation campaign and highly critical of the government's past record on anti-slavery action, had him down as inept, addicted to moderation, compromise and delay, relying for success on aristocratic patronage, parliamentary diplomacy and private influence with men in office.[22]

Eric Williams opened up a large hole in conventional opinion about the chief players and their respective influences on events. The popular argument had always been that Britain had led the way in abolition because the Protestant nature of its Christian faith made it peculiarly sensitive to the moral issues. It allowed the British to flatter themselves over their uniquely civilised status. Williams dispensed with this cosy, erroneous notion and instead looked for other factors contributing to the abolition. Chief among these was the economic downside that became progressively attached to slave-trading and slavery.

Williams challenged the more traditional view of the slave trade by presenting good arguments that it did not make sound economic sense. He also highlighted the strategic issues between Great Britain and France, most notably that of St Domingue, though I wonder if he did not place quite enough emphasis on Pitt's drive to claim the island, and the implication for British empire-building. Williams was not, of course, the first writer to question the commercial value of slave-trading. That accolade goes to Adam Smith. It was when he delivered a series of Glasgow lectures on economics and their morality in the 1770s that he rendered the simple, uncluttered truth that mercantilism was a weak and outmoded system and that it was an economic error of governments to impose tariff restrictions on industry and commerce in order to underpin mercantile trade. Commerce and the individuals who ran industry, Smith argued, should be left unimpeded to make their own profits in what was to become known as *laissez-faire*, the free market. In a series of pamphlets, Smith's contemporary Josiah Tucker, the Dean of Gloucester, had put forward similar arguments, though his name remains less familiar. Both men pointed to slavery as one of the negatives of mercantilism that could never succeed in the long term, because it lost out every time against the recruitment of hired labour. Published as *The Wealth of Nations*, Smith's predictions had been available for at least a decade before the abolition movement was founded, and not only William Pitt but also his predecessors as First Lords of the Treasury, Lord North and Lord Shelburne, all recognised the wisdom of Smith's arguments. As early as 1782, Shelburne, leading a brief period of administration, had proposed a raft of revised legislation to free up trade. With an independent America offering unlimited potential for export, the only justifiable government involvement in a more liberal system of commerce was to secure the Atlantic trade routes from piracy and aggression and to oversee good credit facilities. By the late 1790s the Smith doctrine had become widely accepted, and in 1797 the MP Sir James Murray-Pulteney observed shrewdly that *The Wealth of Nations* 'would persuade the present generation and govern the next'.[23] In the meantime, however, neither North nor Shelburne had the stomach to translate Smith's logic into cancellation of the slave trade and, for most of his term of office, Pitt could not do so on account of St Domingue.

By the beginning of the nineteenth century the climate was changing. Not only had many industrialists and politicians accepted that the mercantile system, so heavily dependent on slave muscle, was outmoded, but the move towards *laissez-faire* was also resulting in a marked reduction in the benefit of slave-trading to Britain. In 1807, when Howick delivered his keynote speech in favour of banning the trade, he barely touched on humanitarian issues but presented a simple and effective raft of figures which showed that if an abolition law were passed straight away, the effect on the British economy would be minimal. What Howick did not reveal, however, but which one suspects that the majority of the better-informed MPs already knew, was that the West Indian slave-owners, still locked into dependence on slaves, were already developing other sources of supply. This aspect is not widely recorded and actual figures are hard to come by, but a black-market slave business was poised to replace at least some of the official trade. It may have had the effect of distorting the figures offered by Howick, since slaves illegally introduced into the islands were not recorded as imports. The illicit introduction allowed manipulation of the apparent ratio of births over deaths and may also explain a substantial reduction in the legal slave trade.

Years later, in February 1831, some of the details of the contraband traffic were exposed through a bundle of correspondence addressed to Thomas Pringle, the Secretary of the Anti-Slavery Society, which eventually came to replace the London Committee for the Abolition of the Slave Trade. Posted from Brighton by retired naval officer Commander A. Dickson, the letters included facsimile extracts of correspondence from Dickson's brother in Trinidad. Fifteen years earlier, after the close of hostilities with France, he had been disbanded from the colonial armed forces and had been asked by the Trinidad governor, Sir Ralph Woodford, to superintend the establishment of a free settlement of African soldiers. The letters include first-hand evidence of covert operations designed to continue providing slaves to Trinidad after the trade had been rendered illegal.

In 1807 the slave trade was forbidden in the West Indies, but as all the West Indians were inoculated with the virus of slavery and nobody [was] living in the colonies but those holding the slaves or dependent on slavery, this law was [ignored] and the slave trade still carried on up to 1819 from the French islands to our colonies. The slaves were introduced here by the French planters *poco a poco*, imperceptibly and fraudulently. They also came from the Danish and Swedish islands. In 1815 the Colombian Emigration began and freed slaves fled here, but the latter through ignorance remained with their owners though not registered as slaves and were eventually sold and resold, nobody inquiring or taking the trouble to inquire if the slaves were free or not. Many slaves did tell their new owners that they were 'brought here contraband' and that they had better not run the risk of buying them. What was the answer? This. Before those in Martinique know that you are here a slave, you will be rotten in your grave.[24]

Dickson refers to the indifference of public officers to the hardships of such duped immigrants and a conviction that nobody would deliver justice or disclose to free friends and family in French possessions such as Martinique and St Domingue, whence many came, that they had been taken back into slavery. As he observed, 'these slaves increased, of course, and their children also'. The figures he provides suggest that in the British possession of Trinidad alone, perhaps more than 10,000 people, including children, were introduced clandestinely from Colombia and the French-held islands during a period of twelve years from 1807 onwards. On the assumption that the exploitation was taking place equally in other parts of the British West Indies, the level of contraband traffic must have been considerable. Furthermore there is no reason to suppose it was not happening *prior* to 1807. As early as 1789 Pitt had expressed concern about the extent of clandestine trading in slaves. From 1791 onwards, with the onset of the French Revolution and prospects of wholesale emancipation for French-owned slaves, French planters had been desperate either to see their islands transferred to the sovereignty of Great Britain or to minimise losses. If this included selling off black Africans to British planters as contraband, so be it. Moreover the turbulent happenings in St Domingue, where years of fruitless assault by British forces had resulted in almost total destruction of the sugar plantations, resulted in many of the freed slaves seeking work elsewhere. It all added up to a convenient conduit through which the planters could actually sidestep abolition while shedding crocodile tears over the prospects of colonial ruination.

Britain was not the first European nation to impose a ban. Denmark had already done so. French options to take up where Britain left off were reduced massively through naval blockades (although there are questions over the effectiveness of policing the ban), as were those of Holland. The United States appeared ready to pass its own legislation against the trade. The only elements that had not been anticipated in making the legal ban international were Brazil's declaration of independence from Portugal and continuation of the trade, and the rapid growth of Cuban slave-imports and sugar exports. As the historian P.J. Marshall notes, 'British abolition was not merely cynical and self-interested, but neither did its authors believe that they were making a significant economic sacrifice.'[25] Alas, the observing of legal niceties was not foremost in the minds of all colonists. Their enterprise would thwart the interests of slaves and abolitionists alike.

Chapter 9

SUBTERFUGE AND DECEIT

Modern commentators such as Coupland and Hurwitz who support the philanthropic argument have labelled abolition of the slave trade an issue of public conscience largely winning the moral battle over greed and self-interest. Other authors make the case for a counterclaim that the outcome resulted from economic pressure. For a period of time Eric Williams's *Capitalism and Slavery* was hailed as having successfully challenged outmoded thinking, before a succession of academic critics began to pour cold water on his arguments about cause and effect. One suspects, however, that a degree of truth lies in both proposals and, scanning the parliamentary debates by means of which the trade abolition inched its way forward from 1788 to 1807, it is clear that humanitarians were not unhappy to throw in economic statistics when it suited. Likewise the pro-slavery lobby was occasionally prepared to argue on grounds of humanity, if this was likely to score points. In the parliamentary debate of April 1792, Benjamin Vaughan, the strongly pro-slavery son of a Jamaica merchant and planter, suggested that Negroes should be taken from cruel masters and put into trust, proposed elimination of all instruments of punishment, 'excepting the whip to which might be added confinement', and advocated the institution of medical societies to investigate diseases incurred by Negroes. Sir James Johnstone, a no-less-committed abolitionist who also owned a plantation in the West Indies, asserted that once the plough had been introduced, his grounds produced more sugar than when cultivated by Negroes.[1]

The truth is that economic and humanitarian interests were to some extent linked, but as far as the British government was concerned, both were affected by the wider strategic considerations. As the historian Howard Temperley suggests, the irony is that without the slave system, European nations would not have achieved the economic prosperity that opened people's eyes to the potentials inherent in a new world order. 'This shift in the well-being of the metropolitan powers created an ideology in terms of which neither the slave trade nor slavery could be regarded as either necessary [and by this I assume that Temperley means necessary in the economic sense] or morally acceptable.'[2]

Whatever the nature of the arguments, abolition of the trade was all-important. The American historian Edith Hurwitz claims that 'the Emancipation Act was a far more radical piece of legislation than the abolition of the slave trade'.[3] In this bare statement she appears not to accept, however, that closing down the trade amounted to the essential move, without which freeing slaves would remain a distant dream. Unless there was prior cessation of the traffic from West Africa, the way to emancipation would add up to an infinitely more difficult and high hill to climb.

In one respect Hurwitz's argument is correct, though not necessarily in the way she may have intended. Even when it became law, the British trade ban was far from being a 'done deal'. The Abolition of the Slave Trade Act of 1807 was hailed as a triumph of humanitarianism, the sweeping-away of a cruel and unjust practice. Commemorative medals were struck depicting joyful Africans, the nation either rejoiced or lamented according to where allegiances lay, and the abolitionists, to a man, patted themselves smugly on the back. But this was the public face of a situation that, in reality, was far less attractive and conducted with considerable duplicity on the part of the British government. Modern authors argue with degrees of passion about *why* Britain abolished the trade, while generally skirting around the more sensitive issue of the extent to which the government was willing to abuse its own legislation. For several years the Slave Trade Abolition Act amounted to a seriously leaky vessel, wherein the Crown and its government ministers were engaged in a thoroughly underhand exercise. Their more laudable object was to further British strategic interests in the Caribbean, but what transpired amounts to a shabby chapter in the history of nineteenth-century British colonial politics. In 1812, it almost certainly drove the Governor General of Jamaica, Sir Edward Morrison, to tender his resignation.

From the outset, the Act was unenforceable for several reasons. Contraband operations largely took over where legitimate trade had left off. The geographical situation of the West Indies positively begged for smuggling, and so it was. Surprisingly only one significant author in modern times, J.E. Inikori, has argued for a high level of 'hidden trade' and he focused on the limited period between 1800 and 1807.[4] The majority of writers have claimed, with blithe optimism, that the British trade was 'virtually annihilated by the Act of 1807'. Yet the positioning of almost all the sugar colonies made the clandestine carriage and delivery of slaves a little too easy. With assistance from nature in the shape of benign trade winds, the smugglers enjoyed minimal-risk business for twelve months of the year, and their boats could enter a host of small, sheltered bays and inlets around many of the Caribbean islands without danger of discovery or of capsizing in the treacherous surf.[5]

The British government had known of the potential for undercover operations and the impossibility of policing against them effectively for many years. One of the more consistent historical arguments of the plantation owners and slave-traders was that if legitimate trade were banned, smuggling would take over. As early as 1790 there had been clear warnings to this effect when Jamaican colonialists petitioned the House of Commons. When one of their representatives, an eminent sugar planter whose name was Wedderburn, was called before the slave-trade committee, he was asked, 'If a law were to pass in this kingdom to prohibit the importation of Negroes into Jamaica, do you think Negroes would be clandestinely introduced?' His response was emphatic: 'As far as possible I have not a doubt that they would and that the generality of the whole planters in the island would encourage it.' Wedderburn was not alone in his opinion. Another planter, James Baillie, told the Commons committee that 'it would be impossible or extremely difficult to prevent slaves being run in from neighbouring islands . . . no laws could be formed that could prevent their importation'. The Jamaica Attorney General, Sir Ashton Warner Byam, again a prominent planter and merchant, stated unequivocally, 'So long as new slaves can be had, at almost any price, they will be introduced into British lands clandestinely, in spite of every regulation that is likely to be adopted.'[6]

The practical difficulties in policing the Caribbean effectively were further highlighted in 1792 by the Assembly of Jamaica. When parliamentary questions were raised of how best to intercept the flow of supplies to Victor Hugues on the two French-held islands of Guadeloupe in the eastern Caribbean, the assembly was obliged to concede that 'in order to prevent smuggling, a very considerable naval force must be sustained'. Two years later, in 1794, it was revealed that thirty-four British warships had been committed to the policing of Guadeloupe alone, yet according to another report, 'could not in any useful degree accomplish the object'.[7]

It was, in some respects, far easier to deliver a batch of contraband slaves to a remote shore than to unload quantities of arms and other goods. It was also an enterprise against which the abolitionists had no effective ammunition because there was no proof of malpractice. As the planters smugly pointed out, the charge that Negroes were being unlawfully imported into any of the Caribbean islands fell flat because 'it was a corollary drawn from an untenable position'.[8] After 1807, rather predictably, the planters of the West Indian lobby in the British parliament also chose hotly to deny that which, a priori, they had warned was fast approaching if abolition laws were passed.

The British government might have been partly excused if the abuse of the Slave Trade Abolition Act was limited to contraband slaves smuggled to plantation owners by illegal suppliers. It could truthfully have made its defence that the total policing of the Caribbean was impossible. But matters also took another form, going to the very heart of Westminster. Documentary evidence reveals that government ministers deliberately manipulated the terms of the Act in an exercise that included no humanitarian elements, unless for the benefit of plantation owners, and was largely responding to strategic concerns over British troop levels. At the time of the passing of the Act in 1807, when the French forces in the Caribbean still posed a considerable threat, troop numbers in several British colonial regiments had reached dangerously low levels. This was particularly true among white non-commissioned officers and private infantrymen. A large proportion of soldiers had died as a result of an assortment of diseases, including smallpox, yellow fever and dysentery, and as casualties of war. They had not been effectively replaced from the mother country, and a number of West Indian infantry units were in desperate need of replenishment. To rectify this shortfall, the government embarked on a flagrant exploitation of the Act, which had also, perversely, provided them with the means. Under the terms of the legislation Africans were now regularly being forfeited as contraband cargoes and captured as escapees. The able-bodied among these were being forced into unpaid military service so as to provide the ranks of the armed forces with a source of manpower and at the same time to place troublemakers, conveniently, under strict military discipline.[9]

The authorisation whereby the military obtained supplies of slaves and was also able to cast a blind eye on the terms of the Slave Trade Abolition Act is to be found in a little-known set of Orders in Council dated 16 March 1808. Addressed 'To the Admirals commanding His Majesty's squadrons and touching the entering on board His Majesty's ships as seamen or mariners such condemned Negroes natives of Africa as shall be fit for this in His Majesty's service', the orders were sanctioned by a secret committee of the Privy Council. The instructions were that:

All slaves and all natives of Africa treated, kept, carried, dealt with or detained as slaves which shall be seized or taken as prize of war or liable to forfeiture under any Act of Parliament made for restraining or prohibiting the slave trade shall and may for the purposes only of seizure, prosecution and condemnation as prize or as forfeitures, be considered treated, taken and adjudged as slaves and property in the same manner as Negro slaves have been heretofore considered treated, taken and adjudged when seized as prize of war or as forfeited for any offence against the Laws of Trade and Navigation. The same nevertheless shall in no case be liable to be sold, disposed of, treated and dealt with as slaves by or on the part of His Majesty, his heirs or his successors . . . it shall be lawful for His Majesty, his heirs or his successors and such officers, civil or military, as shall by any general or special order of the King in Council be from time to time appointed and empowered to receive, protect and provide for such natives of Africa as shall be so condemned either to enter and enlist the same or any of them into His Majesty's land or sea service as soldiers, seamen or mariners or to bind the same or any of them, whether of full age or not, as apprentices or indentures for any term not exceeding fourteen years.[10]

Among the key words in these directives are 'apprentices' and 'indentures'. Recruitment under the category of apprenticeship meant that generally no wages were paid, and indenture amounted to a binding contract from which the apprentice could not escape. The directives were also crafted in such a tortuous and confusing manner that they amounted to little more than a shameful piece of duplicity that almost begged misinterpretation. In one breath the senior ranks at the Admiralty were instructed that any confiscated Negroes were to be 'considered treated, taken and adjudged as slaves and property', in other words to be treated no differently from before. Almost immediately, however, the advice was that the Negroes were *not* 'to be sold, disposed of, treated and dealt with as slaves'.

The Privy Council might have offered the defence that in the detail of the orders it was safeguarding the armed forces against accusations of misappropriation of runaway slaves. The procedure laid down was to hand over any confiscated Negroes found illegally on board intercepted vessels to the customs authorities in whichever British possession was nearest or most convenient and test them before a judiciary panel known as the Court of the Vice Admiralty. The majority of those arraigned had come from other parts of the Caribbean or the Spanish Main, not via the middle passage. Any hidden aboard vessels sailing illegally from West Africa were generally seized by navy ships operating close to the African coast and, so as to avoid the tribulations of the Atlantic crossing for crews and captives alike, they were processed through a special Vice Admiralty Court set up to deal with such 'forfeitures' at Sierra Leone.

The Orders in Council were also addressed 'To the officers of the customs in His Majesty's Islands Settlements and Colonies abroad in respect to the provisions of the Act and for their guidance in the discharge of their duties . . . to receive, protect and provide for such natives of Africa as have been and shall be condemned, either as prize of war or forfeitures to His Majesty's use.' Nowhere, however, did the Privy Council orders cover payment of wages, choice, liberation or return of captives to their countries of origin. Furthermore the term 'receive, protect and provide' was sufficiently vague that it could be liberally interpreted.[11]

Slaves captured by the military could not officially be bought or sold, since this would have been too blatant a contravention, but the Orders in Council eased around the restriction through an exercise in semantics. His Majesty's serving officers were to be entitled to the payment of a bounty euphemistically described as 'head money'. This amounted to £40 for handing over an able-bodied male and £30 in the case of a woman, child or other dependant. The orders noted that such payments would 'benefit the welfare of serving officers in His Majesty's army and navy', but they actually served as a crude means of allowing trade in slaves to continue. Anyone with a vague claim to legitimate authority could produce West Africans, assert they had been captured from illegal traders and thus earn 'head money'. In practice those condemned Africans seized and handed to customs officers were locked up, recorded and detailed until such time as they could be disposed of to the benefit of the British Crown. Healthy males were enlisted as military pioneers or labourers, while females, children and the infirm were apprenticed or indentured to masters and mistresses as domestic servants. They could not be employed in agriculture, but the only security they were given was that 'the master or mistress shall covenant to provide the apprentice (and dependent children) with sufficient and comfortable food, clothing and other necessaries during the stipulated term of service'. It appears from military correspondence that the customs officers were generally responsible for making the payments, but in the surviving military and civil records of the period there is no clear indication about where the 'head money' came from. In the islands' accounts a sum amounting to about £4,000 a year for each Vice Admiralty Court was set aside under a broad heading of 'condemnation of slaves', but this appears to have been exclusively to cover the costs of court appearances and incarceration.

Specific information about the abuse of the Slave Trade Abolition Act is not readily come by. However, unpublished military correspondence that passed between the colonial authority in the Jamaican capital, Kingston, and successive British government ministers is preserved in the National Archives and this provides undisguised evidence of contravention.

On 11 April 1808, Lord Castlereagh, who was serving at the time as British Secretary for War and the Colonies, wrote to Lieutenant-General Villettes, the officer commanding troops stationed in Jamaica, 'I am to desire you will take the necessary measures and give the necessary orders for receiving and enlisting into His Majesty's service all such Negroes as often as any shall be reported to be condemned or forfeited and shall be found after such inspection as you shall direct fit for His Majesty's service.'[12] It is interesting that the choice of words used by Castlereagh is drawn from the 16 March Orders in Council, yet I can discover no documents either among the military correspondence to and from Kingston or in the session papers of the Jamaica Assembly indicating that these orders were transmitted to the West Indies at any time before 1811.

Around the middle of May 1808, General Villettes fired off a complaint to Castlereagh, though not in response to his April letter, which would not have been received by that date. Piecing together the sequence of correspondence between London and the colonies can be confusing because letters took about six weeks to cross the Atlantic via the mail packet and the time-frame of sending and responding tended to be a drawn-out affair. Villettes's letter focused on the poor quality of defences and the very unhealthy state of many of the island's barracks, which had contributed not a little to the high mortality rate among troops in certain quarters.[13] The policy of forcibly enlisting black Africans into army units had already raised fears among the colonial white population and the atrocious levels of accommodation were only aggravating the possibility of mutiny. On 27 May 1808 these fears were to materialise. A localised but vicious uprising took place among black recruits of the 2nd West India Regiment at the Fort Augusta barracks in Jamaica, during which the commanding officer and his adjutant were slain. According to military correspondence, twenty-eight recruits, 'the last who had been purchased for the regiment and all of the same nation', rushed out of the fort with fixed bayonets intent on slaughtering Europeans. The mutiny was quickly put down but it left an even deeper sense of foreboding.[14]

On 17 June 1808 Villettes responded specifically to Castlereagh's instruction about enlisting Africans and his letter closes with the comment, 'As no directions are conveyed respecting the price or payment for such Negroes, I conceive this will rest with the Chief Officer of the Customs who will probably have received the necessary authority for the same.'[15] This 1808 correspondence, openly discussing the buying and selling of slaves in the aftermath of the 1807 Act, might be explained by the delay that was unavoidable when transmitting information to the colonies. Between the summer of 1811 and the late autumn of 1812, however, a more extensive exchange of letters evidences continued slave-dealing on behalf of the British government up to five years after the Act of Parliament that, in theory, abolished the slave trade throughout the British Empire. Some of this later correspondence passed between the commanding officer of a British regiment stationed in the Bahamas, the office of the Governor General in Kingston, Sir Edward Morrison, and the British Prime Minister and his Secretary of State in London.

In June 1811 Morrison wrote to the new British Secretary for War and the Colonies, the second Earl of Liverpool, Robert Banks Jenkinson, returning to the subject of serious depletions in the ranks and singling out the 5th West Indian Regiment.[16] Morrison's letter was composed in the context of more-extensive military correspondence being fired off regularly from Kingston during that year. These letters reiterate many of the issues first raised by Villettes in 1808; in particular they complain about the deplorable state of barrack facilities for senior ranks. Some of these buildings had been thrown together with wood and shingle in the 1790s, planned only to serve as temporary accommodation and not intended to last more than seven years. The most dilapidated were now partially open to the elements, rife with disease and fit only for demolition. If the correspondence fairly indicates the conditions being endured by commissioned officers, it is not hard to imagine the parlous state of housing for lower ranks.

On 3 August 1811 Morrison's deputy administrator in Jamaica, George Horsford, passed on an official instruction to Major Maclean, the commanding officer of the 2nd West India Regiment. Following the Fort Augusta incident in May 1808 and after desperate petitions had been received from Jamaican planters, a large number of potentially troublesome West African troops had been shipped a safe distance away from Jamaica to a station in the Bahamas. Maclean, however, was being ordered to take responsibility for obtaining recruits on a broader scale: 'I am commanded by the Commander of the Forces to direct that you will go on purchasing Negroes for the Kings Service after you have completed your own regiment. The men so purchased are only to receive rations and slop clothing, no pay is to be issued to them until they are further disposed of.'[17]

In a subsequent letter, dated 14 August, Edward Morrison wrote to Lord Liverpool confirming that remedial measures were being taken to boost troop numbers in several West Indian units, including the 2nd, 5th and 7th infantry regiments, and it leaves little room for doubt that the measures were compliant with official British government directives:

The officer commanding at the Bahamas having reported to me the arrival there of certain vessels with prize and forfeited Negroes, I have authorised him, conformably to the said Order in Council [16 March 1808], to purchase as many as will complete the 2nd West India Regiment, but [also] as many of them as are young and able bodied as he can procure in order that they may be disposed of as may be hereafter ordered. Should he procure more than sufficient for the completion of the 2nd West Indian Regiment, I propose furnishing the 5th and 7th West Indian Regiments. By the enclosed copy of a letter to the officer commanding at the Bahamas, Your Lordship will perceive that the Negroes when purchased are not to receive pay until further disposed of, so that they may be applied to the purpose of pioneers, or any other that may be deemed most expedient for His Majesty's service.[18]

Increasingly acrimonious exchanges were set to develop between Morrison, Liverpool and the Admiralty. Morrison had complied with Lord Liverpool's instruction about forcible enlistment of Africans captured from smugglers, but he had other problems to deal with. He had been complaining, since the autumn of

1811, about the growing number of illegal immigrants arriving in Jamaica from Cuba and Haiti. These people were coming into the island either as contraband that had avoided naval detection, or as revolutionaries and illicit escapees. A comment in the session papers of the Assembly of Jamaica indicates that ninety-nine out of a hundred were ordinary fugitives seeking a way out of servitude. From the beginning of 1812, a crisis was fast developing, with fears that these uninvited arrivals would foment insurrection; and on 11 February tensions were heightened still further when an affidavit was sworn by one John Cunningham in Montego Bay on behalf of a Spanish-Haitian planter, Don Francisco Conrado. It was reported that a week earlier, black slaves at the plantations of Barracas and Oigene had mounted a short-lived insurrection in which between eight and ten whites were allegedly killed in the initial assault. This brought immediate echoes of the Fort Augusta incident. The insurgents demanded liberty, having been informed that the King of Spain had sent out orders to give them their freedom. As many as fifty of the revolutionaries were captured and the Haitian prisons were now full. Twelve were sent to Port au Prince, where they were hanged, thirty were sent to sea to be drowned, but many others had escaped in boats and canoes and it was not known where they were gone.[19] It was concluded, however, that a fair proportion had been smuggled through Cuba and had turned up in Jamaica, where clearly they were not welcome. Something needed to be done urgently.

As an immediate response, preventative measures were put in place to deter fresh arrivals. On 21 February 1812 Morrison wrote to Lord Liverpool indicating that he was attempting to close the door on new arrivals: 'I have adopted the necessary measures to prevent the introduction into this island of any persons of colour or Negroes from the coast of Cuba.' The letter went on specifically to discuss the arrest of a Haitian armed ship, L'Amethyst, 'after an action of some continuance and attended with great slaughter on the part of the captured ship'. Arms were seized and the affair was described by Morrison as one 'of such difficulty and embarrassment', given that the vessel was flying a Spanish flag and Spain was now an ally of Britain.[20]

The exercise was only partly successful and the illegal immigrants kept coming. The combination of local black felons and fugitive arrivals all being placed in detention was causing the limited Jamaican prison system to stretch at the seams, and those languishing in its gaols had to be dispersed. The obvious route for the detainees was into the black regiments, but many remained the legitimate property of white colonials and if they were to be handed over as cannon fodder, the transactions had to be paid for. The correspondence leaves very little doubt that the continued trading in slaves extended well beyond payment of 'head money' to His Majesty's military officers following the capture of contraband cargoes. The original, civilian owners may have found the arrangement agreeable whereby they were relieved of troublemakers, but they still required compensation. On 12 February 1812 a colonial correspondent, identified as Edward P. Lyon and giving his address as Devonshire Place, had written to Lord Liverpool, informing him that the Assembly of Jamaica had raised a sum not exceeding £5,000 for the purposes of buying slaves confined in its gaols from their owners. The money was earmarked for obtaining titles 'in the name and for the use of His Majesty and being extremely anxious that they should be removed from the island without delay'.[21]

Morrison's February letter crossed with another inbound from England, in which the Secretary of State referred to those imprisoned on suspicion of treasonable practices or intentions. He recommended that the policy of deporting them to serve in army units stationed on other British West Indian islands should continue:

It appears advisable in order to remove any reasonable grounds of apprehension from the employment of those Negroes on the Island of Jamaica that no part of them should be enlisted in the Black Regiments now serving in that island but that the whole number should be sent to Barbadoes and that it should be left to Sir George Beckwith [the senior Barbadian representative of the Crown] to distribute them in such proportions as he may think proper among the remaining Black Regiments in His Majesty's Service . . . your making an application to the Admiral in Command on the Jamaica station he will be enabled to allot a vessel out of the force under his command for the conveyance of the Negroes.[22]

On 5 March 1812 Liverpool wrote again, confirming his instruction that Negroes in the Kingston gaol should not be enlisted into black regiments stationed in Jamaica, nor allowed to return there from elsewhere: 'I am bound to direct that if it should be found expedient hereafter to station these in any other black regiment than that now serving in the island in which a part of these Negroes may have been enlisted that they should not be allowed to accompany the detachment when sent to Jamaica, but should be transferred to another corps in order that there may be no ground of apprehension from the possibility of the return of the Negroes in question.'[23]

It seems that, at the time, the colonial authorities were only able to follow casually delivered directives about enlistment of West Africans in the military and payment of 'head money', and that most if not all had never received copies of the Orders in Council, first ratified in 1808. There is no evidence to the contrary either in the Jamaica Assembly Session Papers or in official correspondence between 1808 and 1811. At some time during the spring of 1812, however, Morrison received a letter from Downing Street dated 30 November 1811, enclosing full copies of the 1807 Slave Trade Abolition Act and the Orders in Council.[24] Original purchase requisitions, dated June and July 1808 and addressed by His Majesty's government to Alexander Atkinson, the senior partner of Messrs Atkinson, Bogle and Company, the Jamaican public agents, include a request for the printing of fifty copies of a letter of the Secretary of State plus sundry Orders in Council, each copy consisting of three sheets, at a cost of £36; and the specific Orders in Council relating to the slave trade at a further cost of £12, the total estimate coming to £48. However, the same file reveals that Atkinson, Bogle and Co. did not submit their invoice for these goods until 8 June 1811. Addressed to His Majesty's government, the surviving document includes a signature of approval by Edward Morrison, Governor General of Jamaica, suggesting that the colonial assembly was to shoulder at least part of the cost.[25] It raises a key question of whether the firm was simply inefficient, or mislaid the original documents, or were requested to delay printing copies of the orders and relevant letters, in order to postpone publication in the colonies for as long as possible.

In his letter accompanying the copies of the Act and Orders in Council, the Secretary of State leaves no doubt about knowing that Africans were being purchased for the depleted West Indian regiments. He also makes no suggestion that the instructions should be amended, but he is obliquely critical of Morrison about the use of terms like 'purchase': 'I therefore think it right to transmit to you copies of the Abolition Act and of the Orders in Council and circular letters grounded thereupon, in order to prevent any misapprehension as to the manner in which Negroes of the above description are to be enrolled in the West Indian Regiments.'[26]

Having digested the small print of the Orders in Council, specifically identifying that condemned Negroes were to be bought and sold under the euphemism of 'head money' transactions, Morrison reacted. As far as he was concerned, prior to receipt of the November 1811 letter from London, the term 'purchase' had accurately described the transactions. Clearly disturbed by the receipt of such belated information and uncomfortable with the game of semantics that the Orders in Council appeared to sanction, he set out to defend his position in a reply of 10 March 1812: 'In order to prevent any misapprehension on my part of the manner in which Negroes should be enrolled in the West India Regiments . . . I have the honour to acquaint your Lordship that the Negroes mentioned in my letter have been and are to be procured in the manner directed. The word "purchased" was used without due consideration in allusion to the head money granted to the captors.'[27]

Relations between Kingston and London deteriorated as Edward Morrison became increasingly troubled by the questionable standards of the British government with which he was expected to comply. Deciding to send a clear signal of his irritation to Lord Liverpool, he adopted a strategy that risked major confrontation with the Secretary of State. Morrison proposed to ship the next batch of unwanted black troublemakers, not to the military elsewhere in the Caribbean but to England, dispatching them to the British naval base of Spithead. In a separate letter to Liverpool dated 10 March he enclosed a list of twenty West African men, with the uncompromising declaration that they had been purchased from their owners by a committee appointed by House of Assembly for that purpose and were being conveyed to His Majesty to be employed in His Majesty's service. 'These Negroes', Morrison wrote, 'will be sent to England by His Majesty's ship *Dauntless* which sails on the 31st March, and I trust that as they are of a description which may be extremely useful, if distributed on board His Majesty's Ships of War not destined for this station, your Lordship will be of the opinion that I have adopted the least objectionable mode that presented itself of disposing of them for the present, and thereby putting an end to the discontent and embarrassment which their longer continuance in confinement would have kept alive between the Council and the Assembly.'[28]

The *Dauntless* actually left Port Royal, Jamaica, two days early, on 29 March, under the command of Captain Barber.[29] On receipt of the news, Lord Liverpool was incandescent, understanding that Morrison had deliberately placed him in a position where the law would probably determine that twenty rebellious slaves arriving on English shores were free. A trio of eminent Lincoln's Inn barristers was promptly instructed to report back to Downing Street on the exact legal position and, predictably, the advice they gave was not encouraging. Messrs C. Robinson, V. Gibbs and Thos Plummer expressed the view that the arrivals aboard the *Dauntless* could not, based on the principles already established in the Somerset case, be enlisted in His Majesty's naval or military service in England, nor could they be sent from England to Barbados for the purpose of being enlisted or otherwise employed there, without their own consent. The barristers also noted, in sympathy with Liverpool's predicament, that the course 'which Edward Morrison determined to adopt in sending the Negroes to England was highly objectionable'.[30]

The only recourse was to persuade the twenty that it was in their own interest to 'volunteer' their services to His Majesty's forces. By the time they arrived on British soil in late May, Spencer Perceval had been assassinated and Liverpool had become the head of government. The Admiralty wrote to Robert Peel, a rising Tory star who was appointed Secretary for Ireland in the Liverpool administration, indicating that they would accept a number into the navy, and early in June, correspondence from the Horse Guards accepted a balance of nine into the infantry. They were sent to the army depot on the Isle of Wight with the view to their being attached to the West Indian regiments serving in the Windward Islands.[31]

Morrison had delivered the twenty to Lord Liverpool as a snub over the duplicity that was taking place. It is clear that he felt an onus was being placed on him, in effect, to disregard the substance of the Slave Trade Abolition Act. From then on, however, he dispatched three further consignments, totalling 451 men, women and children, to Major Maclean, commanding the 2nd West Indian Regiment in the Bahamas. Ninety-two of these were found fit enough to join the services and were taken into army and navy units as unpaid labourers. The balance consisted of women and children, the aged and the infirm. On 30 August 1812 Morrison fired off what was to be a penultimate message to Liverpool, demanding to know how he was expected to record the purchase of these people in the official colonial accounts. The letter is angry and laced with sarcasm: 'I request the favour of your Lordship to inform me whether "Head Money" is to be paid for them [those not disposed of to the armed forces from the Collector of Customs at the Bahamas] in the same manner as if they had not been apprenticed out or whether any variation on the account is to be made.'[32]

In October Morrison tendered his resignation as Governor General of Jamaica claiming a deterioration of his health, the standard excuse for anyone wanting to get out of the colonial service. Less than two weeks later, 'a most severe earthquake' struck the island, causing major damage and loss of life. Some must no doubt have viewed this as evidence of divine displeasure.[33] To what extent the existence of the Orders in Council and their implications was known to ordinary parliamentarians and abolitionists, however, is unclear. The successive cabinets of Addington, Perceval and Liverpool were not ignorant of the smuggling and the abuse was common, if largely unspoken, knowledge in Jamaica, and presumably therefore in the other West Indian colonies too.

Among the more valuable testimonies is that of Wilberforce's brother-in-law, James Stephen, one of the few people who not only supported the abolition but also possessed first-hand experience of the situation in the Caribbean and an intimate knowledge of conditions in Jamaica. Few authors on the subject of the slavery abolition, aside from Eric Williams, mention that there were two men of the same name, father and son.[34] In later years the son went on to become a permanent under-secretary to the Colonial Office and thus earned a watchdog brief for the African slaves. The father, who served as a lawyer in Jamaica, was Wilberforce's correspondent. In 1816 he sent Wilberforce two extensive reports that he had compiled, entitled 'A Defence of the Bill for the Registration of Slaves'. These largely concern smuggling and carry no overt reference to illegal purchase of West Africans for forcible military service. It seems improbable that Stephen would have kept silent had he been acquainted with the situation.[35] To one of the reports, he adds a seemingly obtuse remark: 'If it proves a conspiracy to produce insurrections and general massacres in the sugar colonies, the planters are in a perilous plight; for among our fellow conspirators are Lords Liverpool and Castlereagh and others of His Majesty's cabinet ministers.' This, however, is only a reference to the fact that Liverpool and Castlereagh were members of the Bible Society, which had recently been accused in some sections of the press of inciting revolt.

The colonialists were, in a sense, hamstrung. Covertly they aided and abetted the contraband traffic because it kept the plantations stocked but, if their position was not to be wholly discredited, they needed to defend against any and all accusations of improper conduct. Their reaction to claims that they were supporting the smuggling was one of feigned outrage, contained in the 1815 Committee Report to the Jamaica Assembly. The accusations coming out of the mother country amounted, they cried, to a slur that fellow subjects in the West Indies were engaging in 'so foul and incredible offence as a contraband importation of slaves'. The planters of Jamaica were particularly incensed, her advocates protesting that 'the moral character of the white colonists is thus cruelly arraigned'.

With the British government discreetly backing the continuance of slave-trading, the colonists rejecting its existence and the colonial administrations caught in the middle, one of the most pressing problems for any black people arrested and gaoled, often on tenuous charges, was a lack of legal machinery to assist in their defence. Throughout the pages of the 1808 Orders in Council there is a significant reliance on the term 'condemned', suggesting that captured Negroes were considered guilty or blameworthy unless they could prove otherwise. This, however, was likely to prove extremely difficult, if not impossible, particularly when it came to questions about their status, free or enslaved.

James Stephen refers to a report on the legal rights of slaves drawn up by a special committee of the Jamaica Assembly, included among its session papers dated 20 December 1815 and now filed in the British colonial archives.[36] The report is extensive and reads as a robust defence against charges delivered by abolition organisations such as the African Institution concerning trade sanction-busting and cruelty to slaves. It states unequivocally that 'there are laws to protect Negroes, mulattoes and mestees in the enjoyment of their freedom and to assist them in its recovery, adequate to these important objects. Such laws are fairly and impartially administered.'[37] Stephen points out, however, that this defence does not stand up to scrutiny, since if it is the case that Negroes are well protected in law against criminal activity, what possible chance does the purchaser of the contraband have to profit from his crime? He could not, if the report was accurate, place any hope on getting away with his enterprise for want of evidence or because of the inability of his victim to prosecute. Notwithstanding, the document goes on to declare, 'expense of litigation seldom, if in any instance, proves an obstacle to the prosecution of the right to freedom'.[38] It cites the specific case of Watson versus Allen, 'which was instituted by the direction and at the expense of the justices and vestry of the Parish of St Elizabeth'.[39] The authors of the report flatly reject charges of slave-smuggling and other findings contained in Stephen's paper calling for registration: 'The Committee presume that they have completely disproved the allegations that an illicit and clandestine importation of slaves has taken place into this colony. The next allegation that Negroes, mulattoes and mestees, lawfully entitled to their freedom are held in slavery seems to assume that we must prove a negative.'[40]

In its defence of the integrity of the Assembly, the committee called upon the opinion of John Hinchcliffe, the judge of the Jamaica Vice Admiralty Court. His somewhat unconvincing evidence includes a declaration that neither in his official position nor in any other manner had he known of any illicit importation of slaves 'made or attempted to be made into this island, from the coast of Africa or any other place or places whatever, but with scrupulous accuracy he thought proper to mention a report he had heard of two boys having been brought to Kingston from St Domingo and attempted to be sold . . . they were sent back by order of the magistrates'. His denial, however, strongly conflicts with abundant evidence, including that presented by Edward Morrison, that regular boatloads of illegal immigrants had long been coming into Jamaica from Cuba and Haiti.[41]

Perversely the 1815 report also reveals something of the difficulties faced by a slave wishing to establish his right to freedom before a court, since the evidence of a slave was universally rejected where any free man was to be criminally or civilly affected by it.[42] Other island assemblies laid down similar rules. Section 14 of the Meliorating Act passed by the Leeward islands in 1798, and published by the House of Commons in 1804, states that 'The slave is not permitted to give evidence or to be heard even as a complainant; but the master may complain on his behalf to a justice of the Peace against any white or free person who has robbed him of his flock, vegetables, provisions, or any other article he may have by the master's consent lawfully possessed.' Though it is not specified under Section 14, this prosecution by proxy presumably included consideration of his status.[43]

By way of tenuous defence, colonists argued that if a free man were to be apprehended in the colonies where he resided, he would have no difficulty in proving his freedom because the testimony of his brother free men could be obtained. What they omitted to mention was that in a large number of cases the black man who had been caught, shackled and was facing the prospect of resale to a new owner had no recourse to friends or family to provide evidence, since he had been forcibly imported from some foreign island. Claims from colonists that 'passports' were regularly issued confirming a man's free status were, according to James Stephen, unsubstantiated and, from direct experience, he claimed that they proved, not freedom, but the nationality of 'any unknown person of colour' arriving in Jamaica.[44]

The Jamaica Assembly claimed that disqualification of nine-tenths of the population of the island to give testimony was 'scarcely any impediment to the course of justice'. In 1815, in a separate paper submitted to the House of Commons, Sir William Young admitted that this rule of evidence made all laws for the protection of slaves 'perfectly nugatory'; in other words it was futile![45] History records William Young as a staunch apologist for the slave system, but the problems for any African claiming manumission had been known for years. As early as 1789 the Assembly of Grenada had volunteered information to this effect to the Board of Trade Committee of the Privy Council.[46] In 1791 Chief Justice Ottley of the Assembly of St Vincent had testified in much the same effect before a Commons slave-trade committee.

In his second report to Wilberforce, Stephen refers to a note he had seen at Lloyd's Coffee House in London, dated 31 December 1814, in which the sale of ten Negroes was advertised following the failure of any owner to come forward and claim them. A terse comment was made of one of those held: 'He says he is free, but has no documents thereof.'[47] Stephen also made mention of the Jamaica *Gazettes* as proof that Negroes claiming freedom were often sold as slaves. Hundreds of these illegal transactions must have occurred, yet from 1808 onwards there appears to be no recorded case of a legal process known as *homine replegiando*, nor of any other proceeding for freedom taking place on the island. *Homine replegiando* required a judicial inquiry to be instigated into the true condition of a person asserting himself to be free before being sold into slavery.

The 1815 report of the special committee of the Jamaica Assembly includes several notable cases, including that of *Higgins* v. *Rutherford, Nancy and others* v. *Rutherford*. The plaintiff in the first action, Ann Higgins, was born free, her mother having been a freed slave. Ann Higgins gave birth to three children, Nancy, Alba and Oliver. Rutherford, the Jamaican plantation owner named in the case, had forcibly abducted Higgins, separated her from her children and shipped her to Honduras for sale, while holding the children in servitude to himself. Higgins had subsequently managed to persuade her Honduran master that she was legally a free person and he had provided an affidavit, allowing her to leave. Sometime prior to April 1807 she returned to Jamaica, where she obtained a judgment against Rutherford worth about £250. The case, however, was not settled on the basis of *homine replegiando*, since Higgins had obtained a sworn statement from a European master, but on a charge of trespass against her person and false imprisonment. Rutherford, nonetheless, still retained the children in slavery for six years before their mother was able to extract them from bondage.[48]

Many abolitionists, including Stephen, now believed that the only way, if not to snuff out the smuggling, then at least to curb its worst excesses and monitor what was taking place more accurately, was to establish a registration procedure for all West Indian slaves. The underlying thrust of Stephen's message to Wilberforce was that he should urge moves towards establishing a registration act. Stephen drew on records for the years between 1808 and 1811 to support the assertion that smuggling presented a major problem in the Caribbean after the passing of the Slave Trade Abolition Act. He asserted that prior to 1807 the annual loss of slaves in Jamaica through mortality was not less than 2.25 per cent. Based on the known rate of attrition, there should therefore have been a decrease of about 14,000 between 1808 and 1811. Yet at the end of March 1811, there were above 3,000 more slaves in Jamaica than at the termination of lawful trade three years earlier. Stephen showed that, even allowing for a slightly more conservative annual loss of 11,000, unless there had been a massive turnaround in birth and adult survival rates, the increase of 3,000 could only be accounted for if there had been an illicit importation of some 14,000. Many of these are likely to have come from Cuba and the Spanish-owned mainland, and there appears to have been no effective check on whether the Spanish government was aiding illicit movements, flouting British abolition laws.

The assembly session papers covering the period in question corroborate Stephen's claim about the increase in numbers. On 28 March 1808 official documents record 323,827 Negro slaves present on the island. For the same date in 1811 the number rises to 326,830, an upward movement of almost exactly 3,000.[49] Stephen, it has to be said, was extracting figures that best supported his case, because he omits to mention that the 1811 statistic is unusually high compared with those of the bracketing years 1810 and 1812, which yielded figures of 313,683 and 319,912 respectively. On the other hand, the underlying reason for the 1811 figure, which he also fails to mention, may actually provide support for his claim. Official slave totals, recorded for each of the years, are subdivided into parishes. The 1811 surge is almost entirely attributable to the parish of Vere, where the numbers jumped from 10,700 in 1808 to 14,855 in 1811, a substantial increase of over 4,000. The reason is probably to be found in an adjacent column of the tables entered in the session papers, showing that the amount of land under cultivation in Vere rose during the same period from 99,448 to 124,294 acres. This could not have been accounted for by natural increase, and no other parish on the island revealed a decline in slave numbers that would otherwise account for Vere. Clearly, black people had been imported from somewhere outside Jamaica in order to provide the additional labour.

Stephen claimed that his estimate of 14,000 illegal immigrants could be supported with first-hand observations. Between 1805 and 1807 he had been employed on one of His Majesty's ships on the Jamaica station and he reports having seen as many as twenty Spanish trading vessels lying in the Kingston Roads at any one time. When cruising between the north-eastern end of Jamaica and Cuba he had also regularly encountered seven or eight during a single day, travelling between the two islands on a round trip that took approximately three weeks. He estimated that there were probably as many as sixty 'false traders' operating this circuit. On the assumption that each of these ships might make seventeen trips a year carrying ten contraband slaves each time, as many as 10,200 could be imported. Stephen reckoned on another thirty vessels trading between Jamaica and the Spanish Main, taking about five weeks to perform a round trip. Ten voyages a year smuggling approximately ten slaves could increase the total by another 3,000. In theory it was not difficult, therefore, to account for the numbers, although Stephen's figures cannot readily be corroborated.

The situation was destined to worsen. It was exacerbated in 1814 when the prospect arose of a French resumption of slave-trading for the second time since 1800. France had already restored slavery in 1802, after the brief period of emancipation under the revolutionary Jacobin government, and she reopened the trade in 1814 under the Anglo-French treaty signed at the Vienna Congress. A year later Napoleon suspended the trade for a third time, largely as a gesture of appeasement to the British, but the ban was short-lived and France did not finally abandon slave-trading until the mid-century. In the meantime, one of the other principal players in the region, Brazil, now free of Portuguese control, was pursuing a thriving and legitimate slave trade of her own. Brazil would not pass laws prohibiting the African traffic until 1851, and against the trading of 'free birth' Negroes for twenty years after that, under the Rio Branco Law of 1871. Cuba would continue to buy and sell slaves until the 1860s. In the meantime, the abolitionists accepted that Britain's Act for the Abolition of the Slave Trade had not been entirely successful in its execution, and that registration must be their next objective.

Chapter 10

DAMAGE LIMITATION EXERCISES

In a keynote speech to his York constituents in 1807 William Wilberforce prided himself on having been 'foremost in wiping away the foulest blot that ever stained our national character'. Not one to fight shy of self-esteem, he must have relished the acclaim that would fall on him after the passing of the Slave Trade Abolition Act. Yet Wilberforce's confident assertion rings hollowly. He had long been aware that the potential for contraband trade could undermine the Act, since for several years the smuggling issue had not infrequently been aired in the Lower Chamber. Furthermore, from March 1808, unless he was excessively lax in his attention to parliamentary matters, he would be acquainted with the Orders in Council authorising purchase of slaves for the military through payment of 'head money'. Wilberforce enjoyed close association with several members of the government, and not infrequently communicated with the chief architect of the scandal, Lord Liverpool, and with his successor, Viscount Castlereagh. In short, he cannot have claimed ignorance that the British government was complicit in abuses of the Slave Trade Abolition Act after the spring of 1808.

As with so much that took place during the course of the abolition saga, considerations of propriety had little bearing on action at Westminster, either with Wilberforce or anyone else. The authors of the parliamentary abolition (as distinct from the members of the abolitionist movement) were not only hard, self-interested men who cared little about whether their government had been playing it straight, they did not even consider that they were making a significant economic sacrifice.[1] After the collapse of Napoleon's military ambitions, the need to maintain large numbers of troops in the West Indies diminished sharply and stocking the slave regiments became far less important. Economically, however, the issue went far deeper. The abolition of the British trade, followed after more than ten years by slave registration, looked to be more laudable than it really was, because the British government was no longer overly concerned about keeping up a supply of labour to the Caribbean. In 1807 the British West Indian sugar industry was already dying and nothing was about to turn the clock back. Eric

Williams paints a stark picture of the situation. In Jamaica alone, 65 plantations had been abandoned since 1788, with bankruptcy suits pending against 115 others. Furthermore, a specially convened parliamentary committee came up with the depressing conclusion that the sugar plantations were now operating at a loss. One of the factors that, perversely, had encouraged quiet support for the trade abolition among owners of older established plantations was that it would ease the pressure on them by limiting progress in more recently acquired colonies.

On 12 March 1807 George Hibbert, the MP for Seaford and parliamentary agent for Jamaica, tabled a detailed petition on behalf of a deeply gloomy interest group of West Indies planters. Various circumstances had led to their state of crisis, although the developing *laissez-faire* was not necessarily foremost among them. The protracted hostilities with France had brought a need for the government to raise taxes at home in order to reverse the drain on its war chest. One effect had been virtually to double the cost of every article imported to the colonies from the mother country. The Caribbean had thus become an expensive place to live and run a business. A second problem had arisen out of the number of sugar-producing islands that had fallen into British hands during the war. Though there had been an initial shortage of sugar after the destruction of St Domingue, there soon developed a glut of colonial produce that, because of monopolistic restrictions, could only be sold to the home market.

Although George Hibbert had never been to the West Indies, he possessed a strong financial interest in the health of the island economies. His uncle, Thomas Hibbert, had emigrated in 1734 and by his death in 1780 had become one of the leading merchants and plantation owners. George Hibbert claimed that he imported up to £250,000 of produce annually from the plantations and that he had invested a large amount of capital in Jamaica in the form of cash loans to planters. A committed anti-abolitionist, he had come before the 1790 Privy Council committee and argued a forceful case that blocking the import of slaves would ruin West Indian interests.[2] Now, he was complaining that the mercantile system underpinned by slavery was imposing restrictions on the direct disposal of surplus sugar into the wider European market. This, in turn, was offering a powerful stimulus to the cultivation of foreign colonies. Cuba had smartly stepped in to do for the world market in cane sugar what had been undone by years of strife in the former jewel of the Caribbean, St Domingue. Furthermore, the British navy had not made any serious attempt to impede the transit of enemy colonial produce to Europe. The manufacture of sugar for the European market had also been encouraged and promoted in dependencies of the British Empire not subject to colonial regulations and, as Hibbert remarked, a progressive taxation on West Indian sugar was impeding the natural progress of its consumption in a prosperous and luxurious nation. With heavy sarcasm he referred to the claims among some abolitionists that recent hurricanes in the West Indies amounted to divine retribution and wondered at the fact that no similar calamities had befallen British legislators in parliament.[3]

One additional and somewhat unexpected element added to the general feeling of malaise among the planters. When Napoleon Bonaparte conceded that he could not reconquer St Domingue, he had looked to other means of smashing British economic power. One of his cleverer weapons was an innocuous and rather unpalatable-looking vegetable, *Beta vulgaris*, which grew well under cultivation in temperate European soils and whose large roots were known to be rich in sugar. Thus began the commercial contest between the two natural sources, sugar cane and sugar beet.

Government taxation was steadily killing the West Indian sugar economy and yet for decades its ministers, steeped in the principles of mercantilism and blind to the advice of such analysts as Adam Smith, ignored warnings. Documents submitted by the island petitioners showed that the average price of sugar at the British market had for some time been barely equal to, and often beneath, its positive cost to the planter. They urged a revision of the sugar taxation system and a reduction in the levy. Hibbert provided figures that starkly reveal a change in fortunes that had peaked in 1802. In 1781 export of sugar from the British West Indies was equal to about 111,095 cwt. It then rose steadily. By 1791 it had more than doubled to 267,213 cwt and then risen again sharply so that by 1798 it stood at about 783,698 cwt. The biggest increase took place during the following four years and in 1802 it stood at a massive 1,744,263 cwt. The colonies had thus accomplished the object that the British public demanded and had not only amply supplied Britain's own consumption, but furnished Britain with a large surplus for her foreign trade, assuming that she could sell it at a competitive price. Unfortunately, she could not, and during the next four years output slumped to 960,296 cwt.[4]

The effect of punitive taxation and a product that was no longer competitive on the world market was felt in the bank balances of the West Indian owners. In 1786 a Jamaican planter enjoyed a profit margin of about 19s 6d on a hundredweight of sugar. Rising production costs and tax levels meant that by 1780 this had been trimmed to about 10s 9d. The only respite came in the wake of the St Domingue revolution. The destruction of the island's economy resulted in a short-term shortage of West Indian sugar and a corresponding rise in demand. It brought a public clamour among British consumers for a new and cheaper source. The abolitionists, scenting success, urged a British public boycott of slave-grown sugar with the launch of the so-called Anti-Saccharite Movement. According to Thomas Clarkson, up to 300,000 families 'signed the pledge' not to buy. But the campaign was never destined to achieve more than marginal success, because of soaring demand on the continent. When British consumer interest waned, the British government merely thumbed its nose at the abolitionists and increased the rate of re-export while the going was good. Attention increasingly turned to the East Indies as a potential source of sugar, neither considered to be colonies nor subject to rigid British mercantile control. But the monopolists, determined to protect West Indian interests at any cost, would have none of it. In 1803, margins had improved again for the West Indian planters and were briefly back up to 18s 6d. This, however, was the end of the boom. Still further increases in taxation brought margins down to 12s 6d. By 1805 they had slid back to 12s, and by 1806 had been reduced to zero. The greater part of the crop of 1806 was sold for about 35s 6d per hundredweight before duty, when it had been proved that this was virtually the same as the cost of producing it.[5]

Influential elements of the British government remained locked into a belief in the mercantile system, wholly underpinned by slavery in the Caribbean, and after 1807 there followed a notable silence over the progress of the Slave Trade Abolition Act. Westminster cast a blind eye to circumvention and for a considerable time it was as if the subject became taboo. An important question, however, is why William Wilberforce was so slow to respond and why the British anti-slavery movement outside parliament did not address the problem of their government's disregard for its own legislation. Is it that the Society for the Abolition of the Slave Trade did not know what was going on? The remnants of the London Committee came together once in April and twice towards the end of May that year, but nothing of consequence emerged from their meetings. Granville Sharp, now 73 years of age and in declining health, took no part in proceedings. Here was a propaganda coup waiting to be exploited, yet the only interest seems to have been in letting fly with smug condemnations against foreign governments for their reprehensible behaviour. As Roger Anstey declares, 'for sixteen years after 1807 the British anti-slavery movement was dominated by a concern to end the continued participation of foreigners in the slave trade, as this was confidently expected to lead to the speedy amelioration of slave conditions'.[6]

For some time, little concerning slavery transpired. On 17 March 1807 Lord Percy, the Duke of Northumberland, moved for leave to bring in a bill for its gradual abolition in the West Indies, proposing that children born after a certain time, a period to be legally determined, should be considered free. Percy's suggestion, however, was swamped by a wave of protesters, *including Wilberforce*, who claimed that emancipation was a measure that would be injurious to the Negroes and ruinous to the colonies, if enacted at that time. The same year saw the foundation of a new organisation, the African Institution, under the presidency of the Duke of Gloucester, with the purpose of 'maintaining guard' over the situation.[7]

The first serious rumblings about the ineffectiveness of the Slave Trade Abolition Act appear to have surfaced in the House of Lords when a period of more than three years had elapsed since the legislation had come into force. On 12 March 1810 Lord Holland, concerned that the Act was not being properly enforced, noted that during the intervening span, 'scarcely anything had been heard of what progress had been made, or was being made, towards the accomplishment of that desirable end'. Holland clearly believed it was high time to alert fellow peers about the possibility that not all was well. He stood up to level a scarcely veiled criticism about the government's record. 'What will be thought of this country – in what light will the decision of the British legislature be considered, if, after having adopted measures so serious and come to a decision so solemn, for the abolition of the slave trade, we should afterwards seem to forget that we had ever entered into the merits of this question, or adopted such grave resolutions?'[8]

Shortly afterwards, on 15 June 1810, Holland's accusation was echoed in the Commons by the MP for Camelford, Henry Brougham. A Whig by choice, Brougham was one of the most eloquent and persuasive opponents of Lord Liverpool's ministry, a man deeply committed to reform of the outworn mercantile system. He specifically demanded to know whether 'any and what measures could be adopted in order to watch over the execution of the sentence of condemnation which Parliament had, with singular unanimity, pronounced upon the African slave trade'. Wilberforce was not present, indisposed, and in his absence Brougham conceded that though the abolitionists had foreseen difficulties in rooting out abuses of the trade ban, they had considerably underestimated those difficulties. While on the one hand it appeared that nothing had been done to curtail the foreign slave trade, 'it was now found that this abominable commerce had not completely ceased, even in this country'. Brougham reminded the House that the trade might officially be banned in America, but that this did not prevent it being carried on illegally in American-owned ships for supply of American as well as foreign plantations. In Portuguese and Spanish colonies, slave-dealing was still sanctioned by law and even received peculiar encouragement from respective governments. The import of Negroes, especially into Cuba, 'appeared to be very great', Brougham stated. The contraband trade now being operated in American and Spanish-owned vessels was supplying anyone who cared to buy, British colonial settlers not excluded. Brougham reminded the House that Jamaica was within a night's sail of Cuba, the largest slave colony of Spain. Other British colonies lay in the path both of the Spanish and American slave ships.[9]

Brougham proceeded to outline a number of recorded smuggling incidents, including one concerning a vessel named the *Amedie*, sailing under American colours and captured as an illegal slaver in December 1807. Brougham asserted that the enslaved Africans taken from the *Amedie* had been, 'according to our Abolition Act restored to their freedom'. His comments suggest that either the forcible recruitment of slaves into black regiments had not begun prior to the issue of Orders in Council that appeared in March 1808, or he was ignorant of the situation prevailing in the summer of 1810. When the *Amedie* was found to contain a slave cargo, it had been escorted into Tortola under British armed escort and although its master claimed his destination to be the Carolinas, the naval authorities considered that he was probably headed for Cuba and thus ordered the confiscation of the West Africans aboard. Brougham did not identify the adjudicating authority, but the next parliamentary speaker, who happened to be James Stephen, referred to the Court of the Vice Admiralty in Sierra Leone, as if unaware of the activities of comparable courts established in the Caribbean. Two extensive reports being prepared by him also make no mention of Vice Admiralty Courts operating in the Caribbean. In any event the Lord Chancellor, Spencer Perceval, declined to take the bait. Instead he complimented Brougham warmly on the eloquence of his speech, and declared that he could not, regrettably, approve of the passage in the address of the learned gentleman that pledged the House to the adoption of remedial measures in the next session.[10]

Predictably the planter lobby was quick to respond to any suggestion of illegality dirtying its backyard. George Hibbert, the implacable opponent of the abolition bill, bristled with indignation. He declared that of all the West Indies islands, he was most acquainted with Jamaica and after the most diligent inquiry on his part, he was satisfied that 'into that island there had not been illegally imported one single Negro since the Abolition Act took effect'. One imagines that this brought a few wry smiles around the Commons chamber and Brougham responded pointedly that, since the Act, the price of slaves being embarked on the West African coast had fallen from 100 dollars to 20 dollars. This, he suggested, meant that, far from having dried up, supply now exceeded demand. Although Brougham probably did not know it, the cash price also meant that officers of the British navy were earning a healthy premium, since 'head money' was set at £40 for an adult male slave. Despite Spencer Perceval's request for an amendment, Brougham succeeded in moving 'That this House has learnt with great surprise and indignation, the attempts which have recently been made to evade the prohibitions of the Act abolishing the African Slave trade; and that this House will, early in the next session of Parliament, take into consideration such measures as may tend to prevent such daring violations of the law.'[11]

William Wilberforce was not involved in these somewhat tongue-in-cheek 1810 Commons exchanges. Allegedly prevented from attending the House through indisposition, he may have been fearful of the effect on his personal reputation if serious investigations were to begin into abuses of the Slave Trade Abolition Act. If sidestepping of the regulations and the level at which it was being condoned had been more generally advertised, it would have eroded his credibility as the man who brought about the end of the slave trade. But this was not the entire reason for Wilberforce's lack of enthusiasm. His interest had waned. Immediately after the passing of the Act, his attention had switched to an issue that was probably always nearer to his heart than thwarting contraband trade in slaves. It was his personal evangelistic dream to bring Christianity to India, a crusade that he described quaintly as 'the civilisation of the Hindoos'. On 23 November 1807 he had written to a friend, the Revd Francis Wrangham, declaring that there was a pressing need to correct 'the most depraved and cruel system of superstition which ever an enslaved people is under . . . the greatest by far, now that the slave trade has ceased, of all the national crimes by which we are provoking the vengeance and suffering the chastisement of Heaven'.[12]

Claims about the abuse of the Act persisted. On 5 March 1811 the House renewed its discussion and, once again, Henry Brougham opened the debate, this time with the object of making slave-trading an indictable felony for British subjects. He was forthright in his approach: 'Still it appears that there are persons who, in spite of their authority, do deal in this horrid trade and do contrive to evade the penalties which they have imposed for the purpose of preventing it. Information before the House can leave no doubt whatever that a considerable traffic is still carried on in the trade in question, by subjects of this country, resident in our colonies. . . . The trade is now carried on, not by vessels supposed to be employed in such a traffic, but in the more innocent one of trading in wood and ivory.' Brougham cited several cases of British ships operating out of West Africa under false identities. These included a vessel displaying the name *Marquis Romana* that, in reality, turned out to be the English-registered *Prince William*, its owners apparently well known in London social circles, in which 109 Africans were discovered by a British naval boarding party. Captains of English ships were even giving themselves Spanish-sounding names in order to evade detection. Hence George Woodbine, the master of a contraband slaver arrested with an illegal cargo, identified himself as 'Georgio Mandesilva'.[13]

William Wilberforce was in his Commons seat for this debate, but did no more than thank Brougham. Such was his apparent disenchantment with the politics of slavery that in the summer of 1811, at the same time that the correspondence was taking place between Edward Morrison and Lord Liverpool about purchasing slaves for the West Indian regiments, he began to broadcast hints about retiring from politics. A number of factors seem to have influenced him. In 1807 he had nearly lost his York seat, scraping home by a narrow margin of just over 600 votes when only one out of twenty-four dissenting clergy voted for him. His election campaign had been viewed by many of those sufficiently interested as little short of a nationwide referendum on the abolition issue, and the narrow result proved that his message had not been well received in the country. He was also clearly disgruntled about the realisation that he was not popular with the British press. By and large, journalists regarded him as long on rhetoric and short on substance. On 29 July 1811 he wrote peevishly to a friend named Roberts, complaining that newspaper treatment of him was unfair and did not reflect the share he took in public debates. 'I am often left out and more frequently dismissed with a much shorter account of what I have said than is given of what comes from other speakers.' The man dubbed, not without a hint of callous mirth, the 'nightingale of Westminster' began to question whether he should stand down from the Yorkshire seat and even talked of leaving the country for good.[14]

By January 1812, however, Wilberforce seems to have changed his mind about immediate retirement. Towards the end of 1811, he had received news that Methodist ministers were being persecuted in Trinidad and Demerara and he anticipated that if nonconformists stole a march in pressing for further abolition reforms, the effect would be to dampen 'establishment' support for the cause. In February 1812 he wrote to a friend, a Mr Butterworth, 'I fear that if the Dissenters and Methodists come into action before our force from the Establishment has stirred, a great part of the latter will either desert our ranks, or be cold and reluctant followers.'[15] He and James Stephen were concerned about lack of control on illicit slave imports and, among sympathetic politicians, were circulating the idea of moving for a registry bill. Discussions took place with Sir Samuel Romilly and Henry Brougham. A decision was then reached to apply through Spencer Perceval to the Privy Council for a pilot scheme to be launched by way of immediate registration in Trinidad. A select committee sitting in closed session handled the issue and its inquiry exposed what Wilberforce described obliquely in his diary as 'a fearful extent and degree of disaffection'. In the course of time the Trinidad scheme would take off, but the initial approach to the Privy Council failed. In spite of a continued drain on the British treasury to what seemed a perpetual war situation, virtually all of the West Indies, with the exception of Haiti, was now in the hands of the British or a friendly Spanish administration and parliament felt it was not the time to put another dent into shaky mercantile confidence. Furthermore, on 11 May 1812

John Bellingham, a London broker said to be both bankrupt and mentally unhinged, chose the Commons lobby as a suitable venue to shoot Spencer Perceval dead, resulting in the formation of a new administration.

Who among ordinary MPs knew the extent of government complicity in sidestepping the legislation? How many were familiar with the details of the 1808 Orders in Council concerning forcible recruitment of slaves on payment of 'head money' to the military? I can discover no trace of publication among Hansard references, and the general response during the 1810 debate indicates that the details were not widely discussed outside the cabinet office of Lord Liverpool, the Secretary of State for War and the Colonies. The first reference to the recruitment scandal does not emerge from the transcripts of parliamentary debates until the end of 1812, and if abolitionist MPs such as Wilberforce knew of the true situation, they chose not to advertise the fact. Wilberforce presented an address to the Commons on 7 December. This, however, was in order to demand copies of communications from the governor of the Cape of Good Hope, and from the governor of the islands of Bourbon (Réunion) and Ile de France (Mauritius), so far as they related to the continuance of slave-trading in those settlements or in any of the neighbouring islands, most of which were far distant from the west coast traffic.

The whistle-blower on the machinations taking place behind closed doors was Anthony Browne, an otherwise obscure MP who sat for Hedon in East Yorkshire. Facing Wilberforce across the floor of the Commons, he prompted an embarrassing confrontation:

> If an excuse is wanting for that sort of evasion of the Abolition Bill, of which the honourable member [Wilberforce] complains, it is to be found in that system of recruiting in Africa that has been lately established under the authority of government for the purpose of filling up the ranks of the black regiments in the West Indies; a system which while perpetuating all the evils of the trade, has, at the same time, the effect of inducing in the eyes of Europe, a doubt of the sincerity and good faith of our intentions on the great question of the abolition of that trade . . . it is no answer to say that the object of this recruiting establishment is to procure free persons only.[16]

Browne admitted that he was 'at a loss to know where persons were to be found in Africa to exercise any discretion on the question of enlistment' and I interpret his remark to mean that he did not know who actually issued the orders. But Browne was in no doubt over the practice of forcible enlistment. Wilberforce might have seized on a golden opportunity to challenge government behaviour, but only responded with the lame opinion that accusations 'ought to be looked into'. He claimed to have known the original intention of the scheme but thought it accompanied by sufficient safeguards to prevent abuse. 'With respect to the conduct of our navy on the African station,' he declared strenuously, 'it has been such as reflects upon it the highest credit. Even the common sailors have refused to share the wages of iniquity and slaves that are discovered have been released.' Wilberforce was either woefully ignorant or blatantly lying. Castlereagh, having risen to the sensitive post of Foreign Secretary, opined that whatever foundation there might be for Browne's apprehensions, it would be a subject better fitted for discussion on some future day. But the subject was never reopened in Westminster debate and one is drawn to the conclusion that parliamentarians, including Anthony Browne, were politely advised against enquiring further into such awkward matters.

Other than his passing admission in the House, Wilberforce seems to have simply shut his ears, reluctant to expose the connivance of the British government either through letters to the press or in his constituency speeches. On 14 July 1813 he was on his feet again in the Commons, not to press for an investigation into homespun complicity but to take the high moral ground and deliver a priggish criticism of Portugal, whose slave trade had greatly increased since Britain officially relinquished hers: 'Under fresh circumstances of aggravation and oppression, the Portuguese have taken the ground which we have abandoned in Africa and by doing so have disappointed the fair hopes we have entertained of redressing the wrongs of injured Africa. . . . It is time to institute some inquiry in order to know what measures the Portuguese Government have taken to fulfil the treaty of 19th February, 1810, in Rio de Janeiro, for gradual abolition of the slave trade.'[17] Castlereagh nodded his approval at this line and any further delving into British involvement in slave-trading, thanks partly to William Wilberforce, was effectively postponed. Four days earlier Granville Sharp, the grand old man of the trade abolition, had died aged 79.

The level of government underhandedness is exposed in a Commons debate of 28 April 1814, when a move was made to introduce a bill allowing ships seized in the slave trade and condemned, to be registered under British colours.[18] A few days later, on 2 May, Wilberforce launched into another of his interminable bouts of parliamentary rhetoric, which largely went over old ground and conveyed nothing new. He patted Britain on the back for her impeccable conduct and implored other nations to follow suit, declaring a very serious duty on the British government to procure a general abolition.[19] ·Not everyone in the Lower House that day, however, was entirely convinced about this. Among the sceptics was Sir Samuel Whitbread: 'Those are deceived who imagine that every man in England wishes for the abolition of the Slave trade . . . there are persons in this country base enough to wish for the return of peace [with France] on account of the facilities it will afford for carrying on this detestable traffic under another flag.'[20]

The termination of hostilities with the French might well have put an effective seal on the abolition, permitting Britain to apply her military clout in order to enforce an inclusive European ban; but it was not to be so. In the summer of 1814 Britain may have basked in the accolade of victor over Napoleon Bonaparte but the glory was somewhat mired in the detail. During horse-trading with the French at the Congress of Vienna, which underpinned the peace, Castlereagh agreed at least one less-than-desirable concession, namely that France under the Bourbon restoration should be permitted to resume slave-trading in order to restock her colonies. Although the year had seen the effective end of the Dutch slave trade (the treaty with Holland agreeing immediate cessation was formally signed on 4 May 1818), the Vienna peace treaty delivered a sop to the French in the form of sanction to reopen business for five more years and there appeared to be no effective machinery in place to force cessation at the end of that period.[21] It amounted to a thoroughly devious gesture on the part of a British government, knowing that the concession opened the way for French traffickers to continue supplying slaves discreetly to the British West Indian plantations. Among abolitionists, the reaction to Castlereagh's deal was one of outrage and on this occasion Wilberforce was not slow in coming forward. On 27 June 1814 he and Lord Grenville each delivered impassioned addresses, to the Commons and the Lords respectively, railing at the disgrace of the British compromise. Both men agreed that this was the time for the nation to exercise its new-found European dominance by insisting on total abolition. Demands for continuance or resumption among several European nations, most notably France, would not do! As Grenville put it,

> We receive a partial contract at the Congress of Vienna by which the British Crown has sanctioned and guaranteed the slave trade. We find our own sovereign made an accomplice, our free and happy country the instrument of its revival and extension. By our own act we consign to misery, by our own hands we deliver up again to slavery and death, thousands, millions, to whom our protection was already pledged. On this Government, with shame I say it, on this Government, and on that of France alone this dishonour has fallen . . . France has proposed, England has consented. Do we expect to obtain, five years hence, by the spontaneous concession of France, that renunciation of felonious profit which neither peace nor commerce, nor augmented territory have purchased from her?

Grenville's motion included a request for the Prince Regent to order that copies of representations made by His Majesty's ministers in the peace negotiations should be laid before the House, together with the responses. This was rejected by a majority of thirty-five. The planter lobby was still an effective force in the House and had, once again, achieved the aim of holding open a door to allow continuance of slave-trading.[22]

A full year passed before Wilberforce was stung into any further action. On 13 June 1815 he moved for 'a Bill for better preventing the illicit importation of slaves into the British colonies'. In practice he was asking for the establishment of a qualified registry of slaves, a matter that had recently been detailed in a report prepared by the committee of the African Institution. Wilberforce insisted that supplementary measures were now needed to counter the practices that undoubtedly existed in the West Indies and the object of the exercise was to check the various means by which the abolition laws were evaded or violated. Wilberforce revealed that he had intelligence information from various sources to support the allegations of contraband trafficking. Illicit introduction of slaves into the West Indian islands was being carried on to 'a very great extent' and a strong pointer by way of confirmation was that there had been little increase in the price of slaves since the passing of the Act. It had taken Wilberforce, the spokesman for the abolitionists, five years to act on information that had been provided to the Commons by Henry Brougham in 1810. He was careful, even at this juncture, to exclude Jamaica from his general criticism, her interests still too strongly represented in the Commons, but by the end of the summer of 1815 registration was under way as a trial measure in Trinidad and, Wilberforce claimed, was proving highly beneficial. In theory, if the government kept a proper account of the number of slaves in each plantation, a curb could be exerted on harsh treatment. Wilberforce argued for expansion of the scheme because although a slave register was kept in every island, it was often not sufficiently detailed or exact to provide a sound means by which the identity of a slave could be confirmed. Duplicates of the registers, he insisted, should be transferred to Britain for inspection and retained here as evidence.[23]

Wilberforce received support among a minority of MPs, including Sir Samuel Romilly, but his motion immediately raised fierce criticism among many others concerned about constitutional principles. Britain, it was being murmured, had no right to legislate for the internal and domestic business of the colonies. The government condemned the proposal, and opposition parties that had first been thought sympathetic to registration, broke ranks. A dismayed James Stephen wrote to Wilberforce, 'I once was fool enough to think Whigs and Jacobins our sure friends . . . that we should have zealous support from the opposition when they found the Government against us over the Registry Bill.' One of those who voted against registration was the future government head, George Canning. Ordinary members of the Commons, including Anthony Browne, also opposed it. In spite of having voiced objection to the policy of forcible military recruitment, he regarded any move to prevent illicit importation of slaves to the West Indies as a 'questionable and hazardous interference in the internal conduct of the colonies'. Wilberforce, he said, had used almost his whole speech in reprobation of the general system of the colonies. Browne was thus sticking firmly to the planter-interest line and denying that clandestine slave importation had taken place in any of the islands. Instead he wanted a parliamentary inquiry to establish if such allegations had any material basis.[24]

Browne eventually withdrew his demand, but in the face of wider opposition, Wilberforce found himself with little alternative but to agree postponement of further debate until the next session. Many of the anti-abolitionists still occupied influential places at Westminster despite changes in administration. Not least among the elite circle of conservative, pro-slavery men was the Duke of Wellington, shortly to serve in Lord Liverpool's government. Such people now felt confident to act in their own interests, having led Britain to such a comprehensive victory against Napoleon. They argued that the Registration Bill was being presented in a fanatical, uncharitable and revolutionary spirit, and with insidious and mischievous designs. 'It is unnecessary,' they clamoured indignantly. 'It is unconstitutional. If passed into law it will produce dangerous disaffection in our West Indian islands.' James Stephen even added his own sour comment that 'it is not very obvious how the Registration Bill, registering men as slaves tends to make them free'.[25]

It must have struck most Westminster politicians that a contraband trade had significantly replaced much of the formerly legitimate business and that the registration route was desirable if any kind of checks and balances were to be brought in. Yet Wilberforce's motion remained stalled, with the government staunchly resistant to anything likely to uncover abuses that might be traced back to His Majesty's ministers. In the face of setbacks and sensing lack of support in the country, Wilberforce laid blame squarely on the British public, which he claimed was 'utterly uninformed on this subject'. More to the point, perhaps, was the lack of personal enthusiasm. From 1813 onwards he had been increasingly preoccupied with achieving reform of the East India Company's charter, an essential step if his cherished ambition to lavish the benefits of Christian missions, cheap cotton goods and sundry trinkets on 'the Hindoos' was to succeed. According to his biographers the stirring-up of petitioning on this issue was 'the greatest object which men ever pursued'. He persisted with this ideological obsession in spite of astute warnings from a majority of Anglo-Indians in parliament that attempts to Christianise the East must infallibly cost Britain her dominion. How true! Wilberforce, however, was insensible to this inevitability. Knocking incessantly on doors in pursuit of influential backers, he may have expended far more personal energy on the East India Company charter than ever on slave-trade abolition.

Wilberforce's true vocation of Christian evangelism thus came to the fore. He was an ardent supporter of the vogue of 'Practical Christianity' advocated by the Claphamite intellectuals of John Venn. To such activists the most pressing task lay in educating the native towards better manners, monogamy and a generally more God-fearing lifestyle in place of heinous black magic. In September 1814 Wilberforce would confide a revealing sentiment to James Stephen: 'If Haiti grants to France a colonial monopoly in return for recognition of its independence, I fear that all commerce with us will be excluded and with it our best hopes of introducing true religion into the island . . . to introduce religion appears to me the greatest of all benefits . . . my principles have always been the same.' It was, according to Robert Wilberforce, 'the secret spring that led to many of his father's abolition efforts'.[26] These comments reinforce the view that William Wilberforce's chief ambition was to save the Negro (and any other heathen soul that came under British jurisdiction) from the pains of hell rather than those of enforced servitude and the overseer's lash. 'Practical Christianity' certainly influenced his resistance to early emancipation and was probably at the root of any interest that he professed over abolition of the slave trade. The permanent winning of souls was likely to be thwarted when challenged by a burgeoning supply on one side of the Atlantic and a high rate of attrition on the other.

Wilberforce spoke at great length on the subject of reform of the East India Company charter in a Commons debate of 22 June 1813. It was, he declared, an opportunity for:

the friends of Christianity to be the instruments of wiping away what I have long thought of, next to the slave trade, the foulest blot on the moral character of our country – the suffering of our fellow subjects in the East Indies to remain, without any effort on our part to enlighten and reform them, under the grossest, the darkest and more depraving system of idolatrous superstition that almost ever existed on earth. By enlightening the minds of the natives, we should root out their errors, without provoking their prejudices; and it would be impossible that men of enlarged and instructed minds could continue enslaved by such a monstrous system of follies and superstitions as that under the yoke of which the natives of Hindostan now groan. . . . There never was a subject which better deserved the attention of the British parliament.

Under Wilberforce's visionary crusade the subcontinent would, in short, become Christian and better for it. The government was eventually to agree to his ill-starred proposal for converting the Hindus, and the new East India Bill, including clauses to this effect, was passed on 12 July 1813.[27]

James Stephen delivered his two extensive reports pressing the need for registration to Wilberforce's door in 1816. Coincidentally, the Slave Law of Jamaica was passed on 19 December, providing for the subsistence, clothing, better regulation and government of slaves. It also enlarged the powers of the Jamaica Assembly for preventing their improper transfer, so matters were already in hand at colonial level. Although Stephen's reports contain much of the first-hand information about the level of smuggling, they do not mention the military trade. The reports note that 'we have not a West Indian island, Barbadoes excepted, that does not lie within eight or ten hours sail of some foreign port from which slaves may be brought. For the most part, the run which the smuggler has to make from the nearest foreign shore is not six hours, and in some cases not three hours long . . . many small bays and inlets exist where boats may enter at all times.'[28] Yet Wilberforce continued to procrastinate and parliament might well have turned its blind eye to the more pressing matter of slave trade abuse ad infinitum had it not been for a new slave revolt that coincidentally erupted in Barbados in 1816.

The insurrection took place on the night of 14 April in the parish of St Philip. Colonel Codd, the commanding officer, asleep in barracks in the neighbouring St Ann parish, was alerted at two o'clock in the morning of the 15th. At approximately ten o'clock he marched out to the trouble spot at the head of more than 650 infantrymen, and hauling three field-pieces under the command of Major Brough. At St Philip he witnessed an alarming degree of plunder and devastation, with many buildings set alight and goods scattered in the roads and fields.

The slaves surrendered fairly quickly when the military began burning their houses, thus depriving them of hiding places, and in a letter of 25 April to Sir James Leith, the Captain General in Barbados, Codd confirmed that in his view the main cause of insurrection lay in 'the general opinion which has pervaded the minds of those misguided people since the proposed introduction of the Registry Bill, that their emancipation has been desired by the British Parliament and this idea seems to have been conveyed by mischievous persons. . . . The insurgents maintained to me that the island belonged to them, and not to the white men, whom they proposed to destroy, reserving the females, whose lot in case of success is easy to conceive.' Cobb also revealed that passions had been heightened by the sight of a flag used by the insurgents, on which was drawn a crude depiction of the sexual union of a black man with a white female.[29]

The reaction of the white population was predictable. The uprising had caught the planters badly off guard and it resulted in a vicious mauling of slaves at the hands of plantation owners and local militia. As James Leith reported, 'Some of the militia of the parishes in insurrection were induced to use their arms rather too indiscriminately in pursuit of the fugitives.' On 30 April 1816 he mailed a report to Lord Bathurst, the Colonial Secretary, with a stark message:

It was not probable that the discussions which have so generally taken place of late on the question of slavery, attended by the misconception, heat and exaggeration of many individual opinions, and followed by the mischievous delusions of those who have availed themselves of every circumstance to influence the minds of the slaves, should have occurred to such an extent without producing dangerous effects . . . from the confusion which the late unfortunate revolt occasioned and in consequence of many of the slaves who were implicated being unaccounted for on the estates to which they belong, it is at present impossible with any certainty to state the numbers who have fallen; about fifty however are at present conjectured to be the amount.[30]

On 26 April Leith issued a public notice to the slave population of Barbados, confirming that he was not in possession of manumissions that would have put them in possession of their freedom. It contained a blithe exhortation that they should 'return cheerfully to servitude while His Majesty's government would do all it practically could for their well-being, progressive posterity and happiness . . . do not, however, allow me, in expressing the benevolent feelings which I shall ever entertain towards you, to mislead you into a belief that I could for a moment permit you to resist with impunity the just exercise of that authority which the law has placed over you'.[31]

The shock of the assault and the subsequent losses suffered by the Barbadian black population probably served to move an increasing number of MPs in favour of a registration bill, even though it was the mistaken prospect of such intervention leading to early emancipation that had allegedly triggered the uprising. Perversely it also armed the West Indian planters with a new propaganda weapon of their own. On 7 June Wilberforce noted ruefully in his diary, 'From the very first Abolition efforts they had kept clamouring, *It is emancipation you mean, you mean to make our slaves free*; we all the time denying it. In short the artillery they had loaded so high against us bursts among themselves, and they impute to us the loading and pointing of it.'

Wilberforce was now worried that talk of registration would weaken the prospect of Spanish cooperation on ending their trade and for this reason he agreed to delay efforts for internal regulation of British colonies. He expressed his fears to James Stephen that a 'loud cry could be depended on that we were fomenting insurrections and that this would operate powerfully against us in the Spanish cabinet'. He also reported that Castlereagh was of the opinion that Spain would probably abolish entirely and that there was no urgent reason for pressing the registry bill. 'It will be better', he confided, 'to find some other motion to which the Government will agree and which will yet produce discussion.' That other motion would involve agreement in theory to establish an international system of mutual search in order to enforce the abolition law. In practice the scheme rarely worked, since governments of all description tended to be squeamish about the idea of foreign navies boarding their vessels in search of contraband flesh. Spain, in the meanwhile, had little intention of putting the brakes on a lucrative business in which it now enjoyed virtually a joint monopoly with the Portuguese.

Had it gone ahead the registration scheme was unlikely to have been applauded by the British public at large. It was being promoted at a time when large masses of people would have been astonished, and certainly not a little aggrieved, at the measure of attention being directed onto the plight of West Indian slaves. The overwhelming majority of the British public had little political support of its own and no means of stating a hardship case other than through the unwieldy process of petitioning parliament. The peace after the Napoleonic Wars had brought prolonged and intense economic depression and, with it, an unprecedented level of social deprivation. In the early part of the nineteenth century, housing for many of the working-class urban and rural communities was appalling, diet often amounted to a monotonous fare of bread and cheese, disease was rife and medical care virtually non-existent. The term 'social welfare' had not been invented. It was only in 1815 that the elder Sir Robert Peel opened a bid that the Commons should agree a reduction of working hours for children aged 9 or 10 to eleven hours a day in the foul air of the cotton mills. Elsewhere, children were not so lucky.[32] In the less-immediate term, all of this malaise contributed to the final chapter of mercantilism and the swifter rise of *laissez-faire*, the free market economy, which in turn would negate any remaining excuses for maintaining the slave system.

In a speech to the Commons on 13 March 1817, Henry Brougham was scathing towards the conservative opponents of *laissez-faire*: 'The old mercantile system has long been exploded, but these wise personages, having been born and bred up in it, seem to have caught hold of its last plank, to which they still cling with all their might, perpetually conning over its grand motto, "All trade and no barter; all selling and no buying; all for money and nothing for the goods". To support the remnants of a doctrine, universally abandoned in every enlightened country, all means are resorted to, fair and foul.' His address also summarised the more recent commercial problems of the sugar industry. During the three years between 1803 and 1806 the duty on West Indian sugar had been increased by about 50 per cent, in part because the St Domingue source had been eliminated, largely to fund the British war chest. The average revenue raised through sugar duty in the three years before the increase had been £2,778,000. In 1804, when the level of duty had been raised 20 per cent, revenue was not the £3,330,000 that it should have been had consumption remained the same, but only £2,537,000. The average revenue in 1806 and 1807, after the whole 50 per cent duty increase had been added, was only £3,133,000 instead of £4,167,000. Thus both trade and revenue actually suffered. But after the ending of hostilities, the taxation burden had not been reduced and Brougham reminded the House that rigid adherence to monopolistic ideals and the resultant lack of competitiveness meant that Britain was now shut out from most parts of continental Europe 'as if war was still waged against our commerce'.[33]

Brougham was equally blunt about the consequences. 'There exists in the country a great and universal distress, a distress wholly without parallel in any former period of its history.' He outlined the serious deprivation to which British workers in many industries were now subject. In the Lancashire cotton mills the average weekly wage for a weaver in 1802 was 13s 10d. By 1806 it had fallen to 10s 6d. In 1808, largely because of government duty interference, it was down to 6s 7d; in 1812 it was 6s 4d and in 1816, the third year of peace when matters should have been improving, it hit a trough of 5s 2d, marking a reduction of 50 per cent in ten years.

Brougham highlighted the way in which customs statistics about the 'health' of British trade could be deceptive. On the face of it, Britain was exporting massive quantities and importing very little, the core of the mercantile dream. But customs returns did not expose the proportions of export cargoes that actually found a market, or what parts had been sold under their prime production cost, or what parts remained unmarketable at any price. As Brougham put it, many millions of goods were sent abroad for which no returns were received and which 'never produced six pence for the exporter'. The real evidence of the unhealthy state of the British economy was better revealed in the fact that, between 1815 and 1816 alone, there was a decrease of 826,000 tons in the amount of British shipping being employed, a statistic equal to nearly 5,000 vessels having been laid up or scrapped. The mercantilism that had underpinned the West Indian sugar industry was experiencing its death throes, and on 17 March 1817 Henry Brougham introduced a resolution to the Commons, calling for immediate revision of the present system of commercial rules and regulations.

In the Commons debate that took place on 9 July 1817, an abolitionist sympathiser, James Maryatt, raised once again the sensitive subject of payments to naval officers involved in the capture of slave ships. He disclosed information that can hardly have been welcomed by Castlereagh. When judgment against a contraband slaver was delivered by the Court of the Vice Admiralty at Sierra Leone, the captors continued to receive between £30 and £40 for each slave. However, it was the legal right of the indicted party to appeal to the Court of the Admiralty in London against the decision of the colonial court. According to statistics produced by Maryatt, the higher court had declined to overturn a mere three judgments of condemnation, and when restitution was decreed the appellant was entitled to receive not less than £75. Given that the current cost of a slave had come down to about £5 10s, or twenty dollars, Maryatt may have been justified in asking, 'was it possible to conceive a more powerful stimulus to the continuance and extension of the trade?'[34]

Slave registration was fudged by being placed in the hands of colonial authorities. By the beginning of 1819 the colonial assemblies had passed or were passing registration bills, but mostly these proved ineffective since many of the returns were either never submitted or were incomplete. The bill to register slaves more thoroughly was eventually introduced to the Commons on 8 June 1819, not by Wilberforce but the Under-Secretary for War and the Colonies, Henry Goulburn. His motion had been prompted by reports that during the previous two-year period, 5,700 slaves had been imported into Trinidad, while Barbados was alleged to have gained an additional 9,836. Not less than 50,000 had been imported into Cuba, where much of the smuggling operation took place. Leave was thus given to bring in the bill.

Wilberforce had been right in his anxiety over Spanish ambitions. Both Spain and Portugal paid lip-service to trade abolition. Each made formal agreements and each ignored them. A treaty with the Portuguese for immediate cessation had been completed in February 1818, and another with Spain, to terminate all of her slave trade in May 1820, was signed in Madrid on 23 September 1817. Spain had demanded £600,000 in compensation from Britain and actually received £400,000 of British tax payers' money, while she, on the other hand, exerted total prohibition on the import of many British-manufactured goods, including cotton, woollens and linens.[35] As Lord Lansdowne noted in a speech of 19 February 1819, the Spanish slave trade on the African coast north of the Cape Verde islands showed no signs of abating and was being carried on with the greatest activity.[36] On the same day in the Commons, it was reported that a naval squadron was ready to sail for the West African coast in order to enforce compliance, but that commissioners had not yet been appointed to adjudicate on captured prizes. One MP, William Ellice, observed that at no period had the slave trade prevailed with such disgusting eagerness than at present. Not only were the Spanish, Portuguese and Americans involved, but also British merchants. Wilberforce displayed a rare glimpse of sarcasm when he noted that less alacrity had been shown in filling the situations than there would have been if they had been of a more desirable nature. In his diary he also referred to a refusal by both the French and the Americans to support a plan whereby the right of trying slave ships' masters and owners was placed in the hands of a commissioner from each nation, unless they gained some concession of British maritime rights.[37]

Chapter 11

FREEDOM MOVES

O ne of the more telling indictments of the British government's casual attitude towards enforcement of the abolition of slave-trading came in a Commons debate of 6 February 1821, a full fourteen years after a ban on the trade in British-owned shipping. Seven years had elapsed since the Treaty of Vienna, after which Britain had possessed the muscle and the influence to implement the abolition effectively across Europe had she so wished. Two years had passed since, in theory, France was obliged to cease buying and selling West Africans. Yet when the MP William Smith rose at Westminster and spoke of France, Spain and Portugal continuing in a manner more disgraceful than had been witnessed even in the worst times of British involvement, Lord Castlereagh revealed the extent of concern on the part of His Majesty's ministers. 'It is satisfactory', he responded in a true spirit of *laissez-faire*, 'that Parliament should, from time to time take up the consideration of this most important question'; whereupon he sat down.[1]

The abolitionists now accepted that no trade ban or registration would ever be wholly effective. Britain was making a semblance of effort to track down and seize illegal slave ships, but in the meantime massive slave imports continued to Brazil and Cuba and, until the onset of the Civil War in 1861, the United States would obstruct surveillance of ships flying the American flag. On 31 January 1823 a small, eclectic group assembled in the King's Head Tavern, Poultry, in the City of London. Chairing the meeting was an old hand in the abolition saga, William Smith. Joining him were Thomas Clarkson, Zachary Macaulay and Thomas Fowell Buxton, in company with a few others. Their purpose was to found the London Committee on Slavery, a successor to the old London Committee for the Abolition of the Slave Trade and the precursor to a new anti-slavery society. At the close of their discussion the group resolved that 'The individuals composing the present meeting and deeply impressed with the magnitude and number of evils attached to the system of slavery which prevails in many of the colonies of Great Britain have long indulged a hope that the great measure of the abolition of the slave trade would have tended rapidly to the mitigation and gradual extinction of Negro bondage in the British colonies. But in this hope they have been painfully disappointed and after a lapse of sixteen years they have still to deplore the almost undiminished prevalence of the very evils which it was one great object of the abolition to remedy.'[2] Thus began the first tentative moves towards outright emancipation of Afro-Caribbean slaves.

Wilberforce had not been involved in the inauguration of the new committee, although his name was included among its other founding members in company with James Stephen, George Harrison and Samuel Hoare, who continued as treasurer. For some time, Wilberforce had been reluctant to expose himself to further criticism and during 1822 had actually contrived delaying tactics to avoid bringing an emancipation motion before the House, ostensibly because the timing was wrong but, more to the point, because he did not see it as the right answer. He favoured the line taken by the Church of England that what really mattered was civilising and Christianising. It was far easier and healthier to do this in places where the Negro was under proper control than if he was running around free and, even worse, if he was returned to the spiritual hellhole of Africa as some were now proposing.

The attitude of the Anglican Church is to no small extent summed up by the sentiments of the nineteenth-century American divine and witch-hunter Cotton Mather in his essays on good works. He saw little distinction between the discipline of a loving father towards his children and that of the master with his slaves:

How can we pretend to Christianity if we do no more to Christianise our servants. . . . If any servant of God may be so honoured by him, as to be made the successful instrument of obtaining from a British parliament, an act for the Christianising of the slaves in the plantations; then it may be hoped, something more may be done than has yet been done, that the blood of souls may not be found in the skirts of our nation, a controversy of heaven with our colonies may be removed, and prosperity may be restored. . . . I would always remember, that my servants are, in some sense, my children; and by taking care that they want nothing which may be good for them; and, as far as the methods of instilling piety into them, which I use with my children, may be properly and prudently used with my servants, they shall be partakers in them.[3]

Wilberforce regularly echoed Cotton Mather's view in his speeches, but he had also come to a timely admission concerning his lack of popularity, although, as always, this was to be blamed on others. In the spring of 1818, on 22 April, after delivering one of his interminable and rambling addresses to the House pressing for a registration bill, he was stung by an unusually savage attack in *The Courier*. He wrote in his diary that he had spoken long but not well: his speech had suffered from 'too much matter imperfectly explained and without due method. But the mercenary feelings of some and the prejudices of others, with the cry against me, make the reporters so inattentive to me that they do not affect to report what I say. . . . I used to fear that I was too popular.'[4]

On 18 March 1823, however, some six weeks after the first meeting of the committee, Wilberforce was persuaded to table a more radical petition in the House of Commons. It was made on behalf of the Society of Friends, praying for the abolition of slavery throughout British dominions. In making his presentation he defended that fact that he and others, including Thurlow, Sheridan and Percy, Duke of Northumberland, had not pursued the matter earlier out of fear that pressing it might prove counterproductive.[5] His biographers deliver a characteristic excuse about his tardiness: 'It was not to spare himself that he consented to postpone until another year his great attempt for the West Indian Negroes.' But Wilberforce probably had no intention of acting as the London Committee's spokesman in another round of anti-slavery debate, as his diary again indicates: 'I wish that Buxton or Whitmore should take chief management of the slave trade concerns and let me give occasional assistance as my indifferent health and infirmities will allow.' He also declared, somewhat unconvincingly in light of earlier declarations, 'Not I only, but all the chief advocates of the Abolition declared from the first, that our object was by ameliorating regulations, and by stopping the influx of uninstructed savages, to advance slowly towards the period when these unhappy things might exchange their degraded state of slavery for that of free and industrious peasantry.'[6] The statement, however, stands in stark contrast to Wilberforce's more robust denial of April 1792, when he stood accused of interest in emancipation. It also conflicts with a statement put out by the London Committee at the time, namely that their only interest was in the abolition of the slave trade and that they had been misrepresented in suggestions that emancipation was their objective.

Wilberforce's Commons speeches and his personal diaries make for an interesting and rather sad aside, in that he virtually never mentions Thomas Clarkson after 1807. As late as June 1823 and at the advanced age of 64, Clarkson was to agree to embark on another sapping round-Britain tour in order to drum up support for the cause. On 26 December, having completed the first exhausting schedule, he accepted a request from the committee to visit a further fourteen counties with the intention of obtaining emancipation petitions.[7] This resulted in a level of Commons petitioning that had not been seen since 1814, when public interest was raised briefly but intensively following the reopening of the French slave trade for five more years. At that time the abolitionists obtained a list of signatures the size of which was unprecedented in the history of British public petitioning, and it had been enough to jolt Castlereagh into raising the status of international abolition to something of a priority issue. Yet it is as if, for Wilberforce, the other man had virtually ceased to exist.

Differences of view on slavery between Wilberforce and Clarkson constantly rise to the surface. They bubbled up again in 1823, on this occasion over a humanitarian move to repatriate slaves from the British West Indies to the new colony of Liberia, founded in 1822 by the American Colonisation Society as a settlement for liberated American Negroes. Clarkson supported the proposal but it was not part of Wilberforce's vision of the future. Far from being the great liberator of the black African, to the end of his life he resisted the freeing of slaves as he also opposed the parliamentary reform that he knew would facilitate their emancipation if it restricted West Indian influence at Westminster. A revealing entry appears in his diary of 1818 concerning the slave trade: 'Our grand object and our universal language was and is, to produce by its abolition a disposition to breed instead of buying. This is the great vital principle, which would work in every direction, and produce reform everywhere.' According to Robert and Samuel, this journal entry is particularly memorable as 'the first time the word emancipation occurs among his secret counsels'. Privately Wilberforce wanted to see Afro-Caribbeans stay where they were, under British administration. To educate the savage and to increase the black population of the West Indies through the institution of properly ordained marriage would more than compensate for the shortcomings of enslavement. Critical as ever of Thomas Clarkson and clearly resistant to the Liberian option, Wilberforce wrote to him in 1823, first profusely apologising for delay in responding to an earlier letter, then in a familiar patronising tone: 'But my friend, do you not use the hyperbolical language when you speak of two and a half million of slaves being sent back to Africa without cost? £7. 10 shillings is the sum for each Negro's being planted in Liberia and having thirty acres of land.'[8]

The dissident Society of Friends, on the other hand, now came out openly in favour of emancipation. Having for a long time denied the objective, it was now willing to admit that the ultimate goal was abolition of slavery and that the first step had been to abolish the trade. Wilberforce must have delivered the Commons petition with less than wholehearted enthusiasm and it appears that he was caught off guard by some of the reaction. George Canning, who had attained the post of Foreign Secretary in the Liverpool cabinet in September 1822, probably sensed Wilberforce's reluctance and chose to challenge him directly over intentions about presenting a Commons motion on slave emancipation. According to the Hansard record of the day's proceedings, Wilberforce denied any such intention and informed the House that Thomas Fowell Buxton would be taking responsibility. Appropriately, Buxton then came to his feet giving notice that on 22 April he would submit a motion that the House should take into consideration the state of slavery in the British colonies.[9]

The authors of *The Life* present a different version of the exchange and the reporting of the matter provides a striking example of how Robert and Samuel Wilberforce were willing to distort the record in order to enhance their father's image. They concur that Wilberforce was 'quite confounded' when Canning put the question to him of a motion, but they make conflicting claims about their father's further reaction and omit any mention of Fowell Buxton. According to Robert Wilberforce, 'The influence of personal attachment gave his [Canning's] powerful mind a strong but secret bias to the wishes of the planters, and hence he was most anxious to put this trying question quietly aside. But though baffled at the moment Mr Wilberforce was not of a temper to yield the interests of a great cause to such impediments; and it was speedily resolved that this skilful resistance required him at once to bring the subject forward in a definite motion.'[10] This was clearly double-talk, since the abolition committee was already aware that Wilberforce senior would not be presenting the motion and had agreed that Fowell Buxton would take over the responsibility. The London Committee member Zachary Macaulay had written to Elizabeth Clarkson on the matter four days earlier: 'Wilberforce was to have presented the Quaker petition today but Canning has begged him to put it off till Monday that he may be there. Buxton will then give notion of his intention immediately after the Easter recess to move for a committee to consider the whole question of Negro slavery.'[11] Had Robert and Samuel's version of events been correct, it would effectively have amounted to Wilberforce going against the policy of the London Committee that Buxton should now represent its interests.

Wilberforce did not get on particularly well with Canning, and once said that his speeches called forth admiration but no sympathy.[12] To an extent there is truth in this, and when he was president of the Board of Control in 1816, Canning had opposed Wilberforce's motion for regulation of slavery in the West Indies on constitutional grounds. But there is no clear evidence that Canning showed bias in favour of the planters in any speech before 1823, when he would advise caution against proceeding too rapidly. As early as February 1794, Canning had voted in principle for abolition of the trade, defending the principle again in 1797, and in April 1798 he carried a resolution to prevent the use of slave labour to cultivate new land in the West Indies.

If one accepts an element of candour in Wilberforce's assertion that the earlier timing for presenting the emancipation issue before parliament was wrong, what had materially altered? A number of interrelated considerations were responsible for a climate change at Westminster but none, at this stage, involved philanthropic protest, although the humanitarians had received some valuable ammunition in the form of reports of two outrages that came almost on top of one another in 1821, and earned a measure of publicity that the plantation owners would have preferred to avoid. The first, on 1 September, took the form of an illegally run slave trial. It was held in Clarendon parish, Jamaica, where a slave called John Poorman, a trustworthy 53-year-old father of a family, who had been an estate worker owned by Thomas Bourke Ricketts of the Thomas's River Estate, was sentenced to be transported from the island for life. His alleged crime was to have harboured a black escapee from the neighbouring Pennant Estate, but the statutory minimum of six days' notice of the trial was not given to Poorman's owner. According to Donald McLean, the senior advocate on the island, the presiding magistrates in Clarendon were not even in agreement over the offence and one of them considered the evidence too slight for the case to have been brought. The Governor General, Henry Conran, quashed the order and granted Poorman His Majesty's pardon. The outcome was satisfactory but it opened the way for criticism that the colonial judiciary did not always act correctly in slave trials.[13]

The second incident also involved an unauthorised slave trial, the outcome of which was far more serious. In December, Conran wrote to Earl Bathurst, the Secretary of War and the Colonies, reporting the execution of a slave 'through the gross and unpardonable ignorance of the magistrates'. In March of the same year, the slave, whose name was 'Neptune, alias William Dehaney', had been found guilty of horse-stealing and absenting himself from his owner. He had been sentenced to be transported for life, a punishment that generally meant removal from British colonial jurisdiction to the harsher life of slavery in Spanish- or Portuguese-held territory. One of the magistrates issuing the sentence, however, had added the words, 'and if found at large at any time hereafter in the island, to be hanged'. Although in other respects the sentence conformed to law, this addendum was illegal, since the Jamaica Slave Act of 1807 had removed the punishment of death for slaves returning voluntarily from transportation, other than for murder, rebellion, conspiracy, obeah (witchcraft) and arson. According to the official correspondence, Dehaney was sold to a Spaniard named Jose Raphael of the ketch *San Josef*, lying in the harbour of Lucca, and transported to Cuba sometime during April. But later he had returned voluntarily to Jamaica aboard His Majesty's frigate *Sybille*, with a pass in his possession purporting to be a discharge and signed 'John Williams – free man'. Having been arrested and the pass deemed a forgery, he had been summarily sentenced and hanged within the day, his jurors knowing that the proper Assize Court was sitting within twenty miles of where the 'kangaroo court' took place. The Jamaica Privy Council and Assembly, appalled by the adverse publicity that would result, immediately passed a bill declaring that no slave should in future be executed except by warrant under the hand of the governor. They also issued a public statement that they had introduced clauses into the Consolidated Slave Law of 1816, protecting the rights of freed slaves and making it incumbent on any magistrate to attend to every assertion that was made by a slave claiming title to freedom.[14] Yet the abuses continued and in March 1822, in the Jamaican parish of Manchester, a slave was savagely beaten to death in the stocks by his owner, Charles Newman.[15]

In the future, public revulsion against slavery, fuelled by such incidents, would play its part, but not for several years to come. For the time being, economics was the main focus of concern, not the unshackling of Afro-Caribbeans from their misery. In many British eyes the West Indies were looking decidedly unattractive as a national asset because, in a fast-changing world, reliance on slave labour coupled with the restrictions imposed by mercantilism were becoming outmoded and commercially unhealthy. In *The Life* one finds a rare recognition from Wilberforce that economic factors were increasingly of interest: 'It is recognised that West Indian property was currently yielding no annual return and for that reason rather than any threat of slave emancipation, was virtually unsaleable.' The authors of the biography willingly agreed that 'it was not that the present system of slave labour secured profits for the planters and that this system was endangered but that they received no returns even as it was'.[16]

Increasingly the new breed of British industrialists now viewed the propping-up of the West Indies slave system and the mercantilism with which it was linked to be a burden throttling British export opportunity. One of the chief areas of concern lay with failure to exploit the potential of the East Indies, a region that offered vast opportunities for British manufacturers in areas of enterprise that extended far beyond sugar production. India could produce sugar cheaper than her Caribbean rivals, but Indian growers were effectively kept out of the marketplace because the duty imposed on them was accountably higher than that on sugar exports from the West Indies. The West Indies benefited from a virtual monopoly of the British home market while their sugars, with preferential tariffs, were allowed to enter into direct competition with East Indian sugars in foreign markets, thus giving them an unfair advantage.[17]

The West Indian planters did not see things in the same light. They were willing to blame everything and everybody rather than face the reality that slave-grown sugar, without the trade to replenish losses, and in the overworked soils of the Caribbean islands, was no longer competitive. They could not grasp that times had changed and that the rigid dependence on restrictive trade tariffs and monopolies that had ensured their commercial existence in past years was now increasingly untenable. Adam Smith, no lover of the mercantile system, had raised an argument in 1776 that the good effects of the colony trade more than counterbalanced the bad effects of the monopoly.[18] But this claim could no longer be used as an excuse, and a week before Christmas in 1820, the Jamaica House of Assembly petitioned the king about the deplorable condition of the island's colony:

> Our staple commodities of sugar and rum have to contend with so great a depreciation at market, with duties so oppressive in their amount and in the mode of their imposition, and with so great an increase in every contingent charge of cultivation that our plantations cease to afford to their proprietors a remuneration for their capital and labour and in many instances yield scarcely an indemnity against annual and unavoidable expenditure. Peace brought a short relief in the advance of the price of sugar but sugar and rum have since been unfortunately reduced in exchangeable value in those markets to which we are restrained. The price of sugar is reduced by our being compelled to send the whole of our produce to the mother country and by a market overstocked with supplies from the conquered territories and the East Indies [including the Indian subcontinent].
>
> The sugar planters of HM colonies have to contend with the unlawful importation of slaves by Spaniards and Portuguese beyond the term permitted by treaty. Slave trade conducted in Portuguese settlements under sanction of law. Labourers are procured at comparatively cheap rates; lands unimpoverished and almost without limit are ready for their employment. Sugar cane cultivation is thus less expensive to Spanish and Portuguese settlers than to those who have complied with abolition. The quantity of sugar exported from Brazil is already equal to the export of sugar from Jamaica.[19]

This kind of talk prompted the drawing of familiar battle lines, though now between the old order of mercantile planters and traders and the new breed of *laissez-faire* industrialists beginning to make their mark in the expanding manufacturing centres of the English Midlands and North. The complaints of the planters rest in stark contrast to a petition delivered at Westminster on 4 May 1821 by Lord Stanley on behalf of the Manchester Chamber of Commerce, protesting against the additional duty imposed on East Indian sugar in order to protect West Indian growers. The MP for Berwick-upon-Tweed, Charles Bennet, was quickly on his feet, demanding to know why the English consumer should be obliged to pay more for sugar from the West than from the East Indies. He was not, he snorted, inclined to give preference to people who had vested their capital in dealing in human flesh. A few speakers queued up to describe slavery in the West Indies as a system of a cruel and atrocious nature, but the main thrust of debate was on economics. For the planters, a former Governor General of Jamaica, now the Chancellor of Exchequer, Nicholas Vansittart, set out to vindicate the policy of laying higher duty on East Indian sugar. It was only right that Britain should honour her commitments over the great investment placed in the West Indies since the time of Queen Elizabeth I. Robert Gordon declared that it was impossible for the West Indian trade to go on, unless by aid of such a protecting tariff. John Barham resorted to more emotive language. Burdens twenty times greater than on any other body had fallen on the West Indians and they were surely justified in calling for some relief to enable them to exist.[20]

These somewhat rhetorical arguments were set to run for a full decade. The islanders' situation was not helped by a severe drought in the latter part of 1821, when there was no rain for many months, resulting in famine conditions for the slave population because few of their subsistence crops could be harvested. Henry Conran was under severe pressure to get the island's ports opened to vessels belonging to foreign nations, to allow importation of vital foodstuffs in exchange for sugar and rum. Free and direct trade was also requested with the United States. Early the following year, the British parliament softened its position in view of the dire need for provisions and passed an act altering the Navigation Laws so that Jamaican ports could engage in free trade. But although this relieved the immediate crisis, it did nothing to enhance the long-term prospects for slave-grown British sugar.[21]

The planters sounded even more desperate when they petitioned parliament on 12 December 1821:

Sugar is now reduced to a price so low as to be in most instances inadequate to pay the duties to your Majesty's revenue, the charges incurred in transporting to Great Britain and the expense of cultivation. The present state of the British market will give the price of £57 for 1 ton of sugar of moderate quality; of this £27 are paid to Customs, £15 are deducted to pay for the freight and other British charges and the small proportion of £15 remains to the colonist. The additional duty imposed upon sugar imported from the East has been proved by experience to have been estimated upon fallacious grounds, and not to have attained the object of full protection to the produce of the W Indian colonies.[22]

The petition protested strongly against any invasion of the right of the old colonies to an exclusive trade to the mother country.

No article of European growth or manufacture could be purchased unless imported from the mother country. The whole of our produce is sent in British shipping to the market of the mother country; and net revenue of £3,500,000 of duties on sugar alone is paid to support the government. Signed David Finlayson, Speaker.[23]

At the close of 1821 the colonists were also more nervous than ever about security, with memories of the Barbados uprising still strong. Alarmed that a great number of discharged black troops were roaming their island, the Jamaica House of Assembly approached the lieutenant governor requesting that the ex-soldiers be collected together at Fort Augusta or some other garrison post and that the British government be asked to have them removed from the island. Their unease would be heightened still further by a revolt in the Demerara region of British Guyana in 1823. From the point of view of the British government, there was little to be done to protect the colonists other than the undesirable and costly measure of stationing large numbers of white troops around the Caribbean islands.

Whatever the woes of the colonists, it was the economic position that always met with greatest concern. The British government continued to demand a level of duty on West Indian sugar that had been set in a war situation. The growers found this to be punitive but it was maintained for no better reason than that the Caribbean colonies and their output constituted a major source of wealth for the British exchequer. On the other hand, the government continued to support the monopoly because a substantial element of the British aristocracy in government had invested large amounts of its capital in the Caribbean, and with royal approval had done so since the time of Elizabeth I. The argument ran that this gave a preferential, and even God-given, right to earn a healthy return from the investment. In the safety of hindsight we can view both positions and find them untenable, even nonsensical, but in the 1820s, old traditions died hard and there were many at Westminster ready to support what they blindly insisted was the best and only way for British trade and industry to continue.

When the profits of sugar harvesting in the British-owned West Indies collapsed because of progressive impoverishment of the soil and the ban on obtaining cheap sources of slave labour, the planters began to squeal at virtually everyone about unfair play. They complained that the Spanish and Portuguese were able to undercut their prices because these nations had circumvented slave-trade agreements and their colonists had more or less unlimited access to rich, hitherto uncultivated lands in Central and South America. They complained that the differential tax levy encumbering Indian sugar was not adequate to protect them. India was not viewed in the same protective light as the West Indies and for this reason its sugar exports were burdened not only with high levels of duty, but also Indian growers were restricted in the markets they could use. The subcontinent was part of the empire but did not amount to a colony as such, because it was not populated with Europeans in the way that the islands of the West Indies became stocked with a white hierarchy from the mother country, controlling an imported slave population. India already possessed its vast indigenous people with its own social and business hierarchy. The British merely intruded with a military presence and as commercial and government administrators. The West Indian entrepreneurs complained even more loudly about possible further relaxation of the Navigation Laws so that cheap East Indian sugar would be able to challenge them in the one market place where they faced no competition, that of the home country.

Meanwhile, the new *laissez-faire* British industrialists were tearing their hair in frustration because, unless the Indian producer was allowed to sell home-grown material to the British and European markets in return, they were prevented from exploiting the potential of the vast eastern market. Adam Smith had been right to warn that monopoly of the colony trade, excluding the competition of other nations, diminished the productive labour of Great Britain.[24] As many of the merchants and shipowners were keen to point out, the use of sugar as dead weight to ships returning from India was essential to the existence of trade with that country.[25] This they could not do because the British government refused to allow East Indian sugar into the country for sale to the domestic consumer and because of the continued imposition of excessive duty. Time after time the vexed issue of the tax levy imposed on East Indies sugar was brought up in parliament and each time it was stalled. Here were mercantilism and restrictive trade practice at their most self-defeating, while other slaving countries including Cuba and Brazil steadily undercut British sugar prices in continental Europe. Some people detected underhandedness in British tactics. One of the new breed of active abolitionists, James Cropper, a Liverpool Quaker who became one of the prime movers in setting up the Anti-Slavery Society, wrote to Clarkson on 12 March 1822, noting that 'on the abolition of the slave trade and the efforts of the British government to induce other governments to follow their example, there is some suspicion of a mixture of motive in the latter part, nor can we wonder at it when we see the Assembly of Jamaica petitioning the King to use his influence to induce other countries to abolish it and at the same time petitioning against the introduction of East India sugar into this country'.[26]

In another 1822 letter, on this occasion to Zachary Macaulay, the founder of the main news-sheet of the emancipation, the *Anti-Slavery Monthly Reporter*, Cropper continued to chip away at the issue: 'The Jamaica planters pray for the abolition of the slave trade and they pray for the exclusion of East India sugars. Why are East India sugars to be excluded? The reason is plain enough. They are not cultivated by slaves and can be sold cheaper. They [the West Indian planters] know their free introduction will destroy their system of cultivation. Why have the sugars of Sierra Leone been refused? For the same reason. The West Indian planters know that if the cultivation of sugars on the African coast were duly encouraged, it would be as likely that they should sell sugars to the West Indies as they do rice!'[27]

Fowell Buxton's promised debut speech in the Commons on the subject of gradual emancipation was a little delayed and he presented his motion on 15 May 1823. A different breed of political orator from Wilberforce, he was concise, gritty and influential, with little of the flowery humbug that had characterised so many of his predecessor's offerings in the Commons. Buxton did not feel it necessary to send his audience into a state of slumber by spending an hour delivering rhetoric so familiar that they could almost recite it by rote. In short order, Buxton went through the motions of paying homage to Wilberforce, declaring that the state of slavery was repugnant to the principles of the British constitution and of the Christian religion, and then got down to business. No motion, he declared, had ever been made in the House on the subject of Negro slavery, which had not been met with the same predictions and almost the same language. The perennial cry of the West Indians that all moves would result in insurrection of blacks and murder of all whites was the same cry that they had raised in 1787. Fowell Buxton made no bones that his object was the extinction of slavery in the whole of the British dominions, but in doing so he threw out an essential caveat to prevent the process stopping dead in its tracks with a mass reaction of West Indian and conservative interest. 'We are', he said, 'far from meaning to attempt to cut down slavery in the full maturity of its vigour. We shall rather leave it to decay – slowly, silently, almost imperceptibly, to die away and to be forgotten.' He quoted figures indicating that at present there were about 1 million slaves in the West Indies. In ten years time he expected that number to be visibly diminished, but in the meanwhile he demanded a number of specific improvements:

that the slave be attached to the island and to the soil, without forcible moving particularly if the result is to split families;
that slaves cease to be chattels in the eye of the law;
that all obstructions to manumission are removed;
no governor, judge or attorney-general shall be a slave owner;
effectual provision must be provided for religious instruction;
marriage must be enforced and sanctioned;
Sunday must be devoted to the slave for his repose and religious instruction;
measures must be taken to restrain the authority of the master in punishing his untried slave;
children to be stripped of servitude.[28]

In the first demand, to restrict the movement of slaves, Fowell Buxton was looking to close a loophole in the Slave Trade Abolition Act of 1807 that allowed for continued buying and selling within the Caribbean community. This was still a regular practice when convicted slaves were sold for transportation, but it also occurred legally even when no offence had been committed. The evidence is not hard to find. The front page of the *Barbados Mercury* dated 30 April 1816 includes advertisements for two separate sales of six Negroes, lodged between notices for the cleaning and lighting of the Bridgetown lamps and details of a forthcoming cockfight. Such sale notices were commonplace and by 1823 the situation was scarcely different.

In response to Fowell Buxton, George Canning urged caution and delay, much as Pitt had done in years gone by over trade abolition, because Canning was a pragmatist and knew that governments could be brought down by such risqué overtures. He found no objection in the measures of detail but was concerned that the subject had been treated 'more with powerful declamation than with sober statement'. The slave system could not be undone at a stroke and required patience and impartiality. Canning aired the sensitive point that Christianity was being put forward to serve a political purpose and suggested that Buxton ought to agree that the proposition that slavery and Christianity could not exist together was historically false.[29]

Canning exposed a major sticking point when he reminded the House that emancipation would mean the discharging of slaves from any and all obligations to obey their masters. This was indisputably unlawful under the British constitution. 'Property must be approached as a creature of law and when that law has sanctioned any species of property, we cannot legislate as if we were legislating for a new world with surface totally clear from obstruction of antecedent claims and obligations.' His words were sweet in the ears of the colonialists. Playing to both sides of the House, Canning proposed key amendments to Buxton's motion, including the adoption of effective and decisive measures for ameliorating the conditions of the slave population. Through judicious and temperate enforcement he anticipated progressive improvement in the character of the slave population to prepare them for participation in civil rights and privileges. On the other hand, compatible with the well-being of slaves and safety of colonies, he recognised the need for fair and equitable consideration of the interests of private property.[30] Canning was opening an issue that the colonialists had been muttering darkly about for some years. If they were to be forced to relinquish their investments, they wanted financial compensation and Westminster talk of deals was the kind of language that they could respond to. By 1823 many of the more prudent West Indian planters had ceased to anticipate a long-term future protected by the British government. They recognised that, however colourful their warnings of disaster and however loud their protest, the economic momentum was running against them. More than a whiff of parliamentary reform hung in the air and they could anticipate the eroding away of their interest by a fresh breed of politicians representing the new order of industrialists and free trade. Increasing hardship was the only reward to be gained from hanging on and they were now looking for ways to extricate themselves without being impoverished. Their best hope was to stave off the inevitable for as long as possible and in the meantime to press for a just settlement in the shape of cash compensation for loss of property.

For their part the abolitionists believed that if they adhered to pressing the economic argument and kept religious and humanitarian issues in the background, they could also achieve success. James Cropper was to play a major role in keeping his fellow activists 'focused' on this strategy. He had recently received a paper from an American abolitionist, Philip Thomas of Baltimore, including 'incontrovertible proof' of the effects of the slave system on the relative price of land where slavery did and did not exist, and Cropper wasted no time in contacting Macaulay to gauge his opinion on whether the salient details should best be published before or after Wilberforce's Commons address. Cropper was also keen to expand the London Committee into a full-blown abolition society and urged Macaulay to form an association in London 'if ever so small'.[31] Its strategy first and foremost would be to obtain information on the state of slavery in British and foreign colonies in the West Indies and in North and South America, in order to prove the argument that free labour was cheaper than slave labour but that the expense of cultivation would also be lessened by the amelioration of the hard treatment of slaves.[32]

None of this is to maintain that sentiments were entirely static on the humanitarian question. In an unpublished letter to Fowell Buxton in 1823, Wilberforce noted, 'To find two Houses of Parliament each full of members to the brim consulting about the interests and comforts of those who not long ago when you speak of bodies of beings, were scarcely rated above the level of oran outings [sic], would itself be a mark of gratifying and encouraging spectacle.'[33] But for the time being there was little enthusiasm for renewed public petitioning and the emancipation debate went into a seven-year period that amounted to political limbo.

The lethargy applied as much to the abolitionist effort as to the response of the British government. On 13 March 1828 a frustrated Ipswich correspondent, Douglas Alexander, wrote to the Anti-Slavery Society secretary, Thomas Pringle: 'Is any specific scheme arranged for the present session of parliament towards which the friends of the cause in the country could lend their aid and may we be informed what is the present aspect of affairs in the view of the committee who have a much better opportunity of forming an opinion from a frequent interview with members of parliament than the most zealous friends at a distance from the metropolis have (such as our friend Clarkson for instance)?'[34]

The eventual loss to the abolitionists of the physical energies and sheer determination of Thomas Clarkson, now frail and in his twilight years, must have been a severe blow. No longer was he able to drum up support around the provinces, by travelling on horseback or riding the mail coach through the long hours of the night. Far more reliance now had to be placed on the newspapers, and the press was not always sympathetic. At the beginning of 1831 a correspondent, J. Allen, wrote to Pringle, noting that the *Christian Record*, one of the sheets favoured by abolitionist intellectuals, 'has not said much against slavery for a long period'.[35] In August another abolition sympathiser, John Chandler, wrote from Chelmsford outlining a general tenor of complaint: 'The unwillingness of the London press to take up the anti-slavery cause is very evident and we should be glad to see it take a right direction. Many cannot take on the expense of a daily paper or take the trouble to go to a reading room.' Against this limitation, the writer noted, 'The West Indian lobby are circulating most atrocious falsehoods and endeavour to run us down by private scandal.'[36] Buying a newspaper in the nineteenth century was a luxury for many people and other letters addressed to the society's offices highlighted the problems of countrywide communication. A correspondent from Cork wrote that, admirable as press coverage in the London papers might sometimes be, it did not assist those in the provinces. 'There is not in our committee – and I believe I might add in this city – a single individual who takes, or would be likely to go to the expense of taking, a London daily paper.'[37]

The reality of the situation for the Committee on Slavery in 1831, just two years before the Emancipation Act was to enter the statute books, was that its communication strategy was ineffectual and its finances were in an even worse mess. It was hardly acting as the great positive driving force that some have claimed. When the voice of public protest was belatedly mobilised, the incentive did not stem from radical dissidents in London but from local campaigners in the newly industrialised Midlands and North. There, the new breed of business entrepreneurs and artisans tended to place slavery in the same basket of undesirables as the aristocratic old guard who supported it and with whom they had little in common.

Chapter 12

A QUESTIONABLE KIND OF LIBERTY

In 1740 a subscriber contributing an indignant letter to the *London Magazine*, one of the more popular periodicals in distribution around the British capital, lamented the conduct of West African despots towards their subjects. His comments underscore the curiously blinkered thinking that prevailed in Europe over matters of human rights during the eighteenth and much of the nineteenth century: 'The inhabitants of Guinea are indeed in a most deplorable state of slavery, under the arbitrary powers of their princes both as to life and property. In the several subordinations to them, every great man is absolute lord of his immediate dependents. And lower still; every master of a family is proprietor of his wives, children and servants; and may at his pleasure consign them to death, or a better market. No doubt such a state is contrary to nature, since every human creature hath an absolute right to liberty.'[1]

The writer omitted any suggestion that the African forced into servitude in the Americas faced a similarly deplorable situation. Generations of otherwise rationally thinking people had become conditioned to believe that slavery in Africa was morally and socially indefensible, but that the same institution when practised by Europeans was acceptable because it bettered the spiritual and material lives of the enslaved compared to anything they had known before. Afro-Caribbean servitude amounted to an environment in which the beastly savage could be made civilised and, eventually, become Christianised. Spiritual conversion and enlightenment were what mattered, and remained the true goal of many intellectuals, churchmen and liberals in the home country. This was not, however, the dream of the New World colonialists, who by and large considered such an education charged with hazards. The savage kept in a state of ignorance was a savage who could be controlled and opponents of emancipation were not slow in identifying specific risks inherent in schooling Negroes to grasp some of the finer points of life and liberty. Many of the West Africans who had been imported to the Caribbean spoke different languages, which made communication among them difficult and therefore reduced the chances between ethnic groups of orchestrating incitement to cause trouble. Teaching them to read the Bible and to speak and write English was seen to be an excellent recipe for insurrection.

Thus far I have paid very little attention to the position and influence of the Church, but it would be wrong to conclude without doing so because, to the bitter end, senior Anglican clerics played a game that was probably as devious as any engaged in among the secular members of the establishment. One might have imagined that the Church was united in opposing slavery, but this was not the case. At appropriate times the Protestant authority in England was ready to pay lip-service to the idea of emancipation but at heart it remained deeply resistant. Men of the calibre of William Wilberforce were not unusual in their attitudes and when he spoke out against the slave trade, yet supported slavery, he was only articulating the views of many Anglican intellectuals. Therein, aside from differences in social standing, lay a cause of much of the lifelong friction that existed between Wilberforce the dyed-in-the-wool Anglican and Thomas Clarkson the nonconformist dissident. Edith Hurwitz suggests that in 1833 'a political and ecclesiastical establishment, formed and operating through a consensus of well-established power relationships that had long supported not only the vested interests connected with slavery but also the values of property on which that institution was based, took the revolutionary step of doing away with them both',[2] but she does not mention that much of the mainstream Church hierarchy was dragged kicking and squealing into revolt at the eleventh hour.

The Church of England position remained significantly at odds with that of the nonconformists, who were less inclined to interpret anachronistic passages from the Bible in a way that justified enslavement and who cared little for historical precedents that gave slavery the secular nod of approval. The majority of dissidents, especially the Methodists and Quakers, rejected the Biblical claims that some are destined to master and others to serve, and thoroughly backed emancipation. In 1792 the preacher Samuel Bradburn had delivered a persuasive message to fellow Methodists in Manchester that the Negro was a fellow subject, and his view was consistently upheld:

Whatever may be the opinions of others, you, Brethren, believe that God hath made of one blood all nations of men, for to dwell on the face of the earth, and hath determined the times before appointed, and the bounds of their habitation. Who then has any right to go, or to authorise others to go across a vast ocean, to enslave a free and in relation to us, a harmless people. None but the sovereign ruler of the universe has power to grant such a right. There is nothing plainer than that the Negroes have as good a right to invade Britain and make slaves of us as we have to invade Africa and make slaves of them.[3]

The Church of England begged to differ and what it preached in the home country in support of manumission was not necessarily that which its missionary arm was practising elsewhere. Frequently, Anglican conduct in the colonies left much to be desired. In the 1930s the California-based social historian Frank Klingberg visited the London offices of the Anglican Church's missionary arm, the Society for the Propagation of the Gospel in Foreign Parts, or SPG. From plantation documents discovered in the archives, he gathered together a remarkable dossier about the conduct of the society. The papers, covering activities between 1710 and 1838 on two Barbadian sugar plantations known as the Codrington estates, owned by the SPG, are of considerable historical importance in establishing the particular attitude of the religious establishment. A hierarchy of archbishops and bishops in the Church of England effectively controlled the society, and so its conduct at Codrington stands as a good example of its more general policy towards slaves in the West Indies. The documents also provide a rare detailed insight into the way British plantations were managed.[4]

The two adjacent estates were bequeathed to the SPG in April 1710 after the death of Christopher Codrington, on the understanding that they should continue unchanged with 300 or so slaves kept as before, but that a convenient number of professors and scholars be sent out and maintained there in order to educate the slaves and convert them to Christianity. The society was quick to accept the bequest of Codrington, but less keen to honour the expectation of maintaining a regular clergy on the estates. Within a short space of time, the society had employed absentee management and put in place an overseer to run, hire and fire. Concerned to practise what it had often preached in reprimanding the Caribbean planters for not taking proper steps to Christianise their chattels, and savouring a lucrative enterprise through which to fund its aims, the society invested in construction of an elaborate college building. In 1718, however, the money supply began to dry up after a sharp reduction in sugar and rum output from Codrington, and in 1725, with construction almost finished, work was halted and the building boarded up, in which forlorn state it remained for the next twenty years.[5]

For the colonialists, the time had come to shake their heads and mutter sagely. As one Barbadian wrote, somewhat tongue-in-cheek, 'The eyes of all are on Codrington College as they are inquisitive of what steps are taken there for the conversion of the slaves.' The inquisitive discovered that the number of steps was few. Stung by early criticism of its failure to set an example, the SPG next sent out a so-called 'specialist missionary'. The Revd Joseph Holt, a man of limited zeal with a susceptibility for the bottle, arrived in Barbados armed with orders for the manager, John Smallridge, that he release the slaves from plantation labour on Saturday afternoons in order that they could give up their free Sundays for religious instruction. Smallridge flatly refused to countenance this wasteful loss of working hours in the fields, whereupon the Revd Holt went absent on an extended vacation and was promptly dismissed by the society for desertion. It was also taken into account that he was, according to certain anonymous Barbadian observers, immoral, heterodox, idle and regularly drunk. His replacement, the Revd William Brown, was only the first of many. Such was the measure of achievement at Codrington that by 1745 not a single African had been baptised there and as late as 1826 there had been no marriages performed on the two estates. It has to be said, in fairness, that marriage was a particularly sensitive issue among plantation owners throughout the West Indies, since it limited the movement of the male labour force. The SPG might have considered wedlock a laudable humanitarian objective from its safe vantage point in Britain, but the Codrington chaplain, John Pinder, saw the matter from a less rosy, West Indian perspective, wherein evangelical ministers promoting family life for the slave could readily be persecuted by planters for 'bucking the system'.[6]

Not surprisingly, British abolitionists lambasted Codrington with the accusation that its overseers were protecting their own backs by aligning with planter interests, and demanded an honest admission that Christian management of slave plantations was a contradiction in terms. Here was an example, they cried, of Anglican hypocrisy, an official missionary enterprise holding slaves of its own, arguing that they could be made Christian, yet not treating them any better than those on other plantations. The Codrington College could be seen to have failed miserably in its original purpose as a ministry for educating Africans because, when it did eventually open, it was run as a cheap classical grammar school for the sons of the gentry, with not a black child in sight.

In 1827, a full four years after Fowell Buxton's recommendations for amelioration of plantation conditions had been approved at Westminster, Codrington overseers continued to use the whip, women were still being flogged for trifling offences, no punishment records were maintained and manumission was only granted occasionally and in extraordinary circumstances. This was strong meat for the abolitionists, who were quick to point out that the estates, promoted as the outposts of humanitarianism in the West Indies had done little other than give their solid support to the opposition. How could Christians countenance a vicious labour system that permitted generations of Africans to suffer a miserable and brutalised existence and then to die in ignorance of Christ? In May 1827 the abolitionist monthly publication, the *Christian Observer*, did not hold back in its comments: 'In ranging from North America to Southern India, the Friends of the Society omitted to mention [in their reports on missionary activity] their own slaves, whose labours on their plantations augment their funds . . . let the friends of the unhappy slave never relax their efforts till the Society can fairly expurgate itself from the guilt of being slave-holders, and from watering the tree of life planted in India or America, with the tears and blood of unhappy Africa.' Far from justifying itself, the SPG continued to publish accounts of their great success in making the Codrington estates models of Christian slavery at work.[7]

Eventually the SPG was forced to respond to the Anti-Slavery Society with a lengthy communication in which it made an apology devoid of any suggestion that it was prepared to implement even gradual emancipation: 'The Society do not consider they would consult the advantage of the Negro by facilitating his emancipation without regard to the use which he is likely to make of it – the consideration is not altogether one of property and if the whole value of the slaves could be tendered for their emancipation it would still remain doubtful whether looking solely to the benefit of a certain number of human beings they would be justified in acceding to the point.'

It was not until 21 January 1831 that the Society for the Propagation of the Gospel met to put into effect the 1823 parliamentary recommendations. Under mounting pressure and realising that mandatory emancipation was in sight, they acquiesced to two additional demands. These included the allocation of task labour, a device intended to place some limit on the amount of work that slaves were obliged to do; and partial manumission through an instalment plan wherein slaves could buy one free day a week in which to earn money to buy further days of release. Both measures proved singularly ineffective and amounted to little more than lip-service. The managers at Codrington knew very well that task allocation was virtually impossible under the Barbadian system, wherein slaves not only grew sugar cane but also raised food crops for the estates. If a system of fair allotment of work was ever seriously considered, it did not get off the ground. Manumission was also largely evaded. Prior to the enactment of government legislation that made emancipation obligatory, freedom was granted to only 4 Codrington slaves out of more than 400 on the estates because most found it impossible to save enough to purchase the initial free day for their own enterprise. Even in 1832, when there was no alternative but to move for 'safe and orderly emancipation', no plans were put into effect until the last moment before the Slave Emancipation Act came into operation, on 1 August 1834. On 28 July the slaves at Codrington were counted up and found to number 411. One of the few successes involved a breeding programme that had expanded the population since 1807. Under the terms of the Act the SPG would collect compensation to the value of £8,823 8s 9d.[8]

The American churches demonstrated no better track record in their attitude towards slavery. In March 1841, several years after British enactment of emancipation, the octogenarian Thomas Clarkson would write to Fowell Buxton about the plight of 3 million slaves still languishing in the United States. His resolve sounded as strong as ever. 'It is shameful that the clergy there, of the various denominations, are the great bulwarks and supporting of it [slavery]. They have not only the audacity to defend it in conversation but to declare, even from the pulpit, that there is no sin in slavery, that genuine piety is compatible with slavery and that the Scriptures born of the Old and New Testament sanctioned it. I have been urged by several gentlemen in America to make a direct contradiction of such statements and have this work circulated in America.'[9]

The Codrington experience amounts to a microcosm, reflecting the general situation across the West Indies. Between 1817 and 1830, records of manumission in Jamaica reveal that the number of slaves voluntarily granted freedom, even at a price, was very small. In many of those years it totalled less than 500, and only in the first year did it exceed 700. About half of those emancipated bought themselves out for considerations ranging from £100 to £200.[10] Codrington also brings into sharp focus a certainty that the West Indian colonial assemblies could not be relied on to support the gradual amelioration of conditions on the plantations. Progress at Codrington had remained in a state of near stagnation not least because its Bahamian overseers did not wish to fall foul of the island's council.

If the Anglican Church did little to further the drive towards emancipation, what became of the predominantly nonconformist British Anti-Slavery Society and its branches during the final years leading up to 1833? Seymour Drescher calculates that in 1814 there were over 200 local anti-slavery groups in Britain, some 800 in the mid-1820s and 1,300 at the climax of emancipation fever. I have no reason to dispute these figures but I would have to take issue with his assertion that 'after 1806 the abolitionist network lay in reserve, ready to apply discreet or highly visible pressure on the legislature'.[11] For much of the time the society's correspondence and minute books suggest that the network was disorganised and exercising little or no pressure on the legislature. It was not until 1833 that the Commons even bothered officially to record synopses of petitions and, as Drescher notes, the campaigns to drum up public support for emancipation in 1830 and 1831 failed to obtain any significant response.

In the years following the foundation, in 1823, of the Anti-Slavery Society, its membership was neither especially energetic nor effective in its purpose. For much of the time the organisation hovered close to insolvency and was perennially short of sponsors, while the number of anti-slavery petitions began to rise but only very slowly. The society received something of a moral boost in 1824, when the Duke of Gloucester took the chair at a meeting held on 25 June, but for the most part it contented itself with printing and circulating reports. An approach to George Canning in March 1825 earned an evasive response about progress on the 1823 resolutions of parliament. The matter was, Canning explained, with the Colonial Office and he was not prepared to state what, if any, future measures would be taken. On 2 May the society's minute books record 'deep regret and disappointment' among committee members that 'so little progress should hitherto have been made in carrying to effect the benevolent intentions of His Majesty's government, the unanimous resolutions of Parliament and the wishes and prayers of the nation at large, for the mitigation and eventual extinction of colonial slavery'.[12] Canning actually had his hands tied because, perversely, the 1820s saw fewer committed abolitionists in the Commons and stronger West Indian representation than there had ever been prior to 1807. The abolitionist MP Stephen Lushington considered that the planter lobby ran to 56 Commons members in 1825. Modern research suggests that there were no more than 31 committed abolitionists, and perhaps as few as 15.[13]

Judging from correspondence received by the secretary of the society, Thomas Pringle, a momentum began to develop among abolitionists from 1828, although until 1831 it was barely perceptible. A measure of progress can be detected in the foundation of local anti-slavery groups, particularly those attracting women members, for whom the whole sentiment of emancipation lay close to the heart. In March 1828 the Revd Joseph Gray reported from Chelmsford that 'a Ladies Association embracing all parties and denominations has just been formed under very flattering auspices'. They had promptly ordered 100 copies of the *Anti-Slavery Reporter* for February, to be continued monthly, 25 pamphlets entitled *Pity the Negro*, plus 100 *Flogging of Women* all to be delivered on the next day's coach. They also made a request for issues 1, 3 and 25 of a periodical called *The Comfort of Being Flogged*.[14] But there was also criticism of the parent committee in London in terms of its effectiveness in passing on information and advice. In March 1828 a writer from Sunderland wanted to know whether his local association should petition parliament in the current session. A correspondent in Birmingham suggested that the quickest way to obtain petitions was for the local associations to liaise with different religious congregations in their areas. Yet neither seems to have received a reply.[15] On the other hand there were complaints about the sheer volume of copies of the *Anti-Slavery Reporter* being run off the press to some local activists. One local group secretary, Alex Monleath, advised that receiving 200 copies at a time was too much, and back issues were gathering dust in a depository. The level of unease grew that both the *Reporter* and the *Christian*

Record were over-larding the case, but the concentrated anti-slavery propaganda was set to continue.

At about this time, the aged William Wilberforce, his health failing, could still demonstrate a lifelong willingness to switch sides when it suited. He wrote to Fowell Buxton on 24 July 1828, questioning the efficacy of the current government policy of shifting the onus of responsibility away from Westminster and onto the colonial assemblies, which he felt would simply delay the outcome *ad infinitum* and entreated Buxton to resist: 'It is folly to expect the colonists to be honest executors of principles meant for a purpose they consider only another word for their utter ruin. . . . [Edmund] Burke's plan for settling the gradual progress of the slaves through the means of religion and morality to the enjoyment of civil rights goes into much detail and provides for the manumission and education of slaves. . . . Against that we should now be told to be contented with looking forward to ultimate emancipation through the long vista of centuries to come.'[16] Wilberforce was particularly scathing in this letter about the conduct of the Duke of Wellington, whose support for the planters was never far from the surface. 'He [Wellington] tells the West Indians that he is highly pleased with their progress when their motion, if it is motion at all, is so slow as to be invisible.'[17] But Wilberforce, nearing the end of his life, took no more of an active involvement. Fate would deprive him of the satisfaction of witnessing the final enactment. He passed away on 29 July 1833.

In terms of positive action or directing the endeavours of its supporters, the Anti-Slavery Society seems to have lacked decisive leadership and often fell well short of the mark. Men of the calibre of James Cropper and Zachary Macaulay were 'grey' committee men whose best endeavours tended to be channelled into firing off endless correspondence. I have on my bookshelves a volume set of the old *Nelson's Encyclopaedia*, in which Clarkson and Wilberforce earn their places. Yet Cropper is not included at all and Macaulay receives only a single-line mention in an entry for his more famous son, the historian Thomas Macaulay. Too much reliance was placed on wordy publications, too little on personal drive. In August 1831 Thomas Graham, the local abolitionist chairman from Coalbrookdale, warned Thomas Pringle that 'several of the friends of the cause think the subject is rather overdone by *The Recorder* – they come so fast upon us that I fear they are in many instances thrown by as waste paper. I know several who say they cannot spare time to read them.'[18] These publications contained a surfeit of well-meaning rhetoric and very little practical advice or information. As Joseph Gray noted shrewdly, 'One of the most oft-asked questions is, what are you grasping? What positive good may reasonably be hoped to result from your exertions? Can you in any way ameliorate the conditions of male and female Negroes? What is the amount of actual good that can be secured for them if the legislature does not interfere on their behalf? I wish your Society had an ably written tract of four pages bearing fully and directly on these points.'[19] Gray had homed in on the weakness of the abolitionists, because the only practical advice that Pringle could have given him by way of reply was to generate more petitions and churn out more pamphlets. The Anti-Slavery Society was powerless, and knew it, until the parliamentary make-up became altered in its favour at Westminster.

At the beginning of 1832, the year before the Slave Emancipation Act was passed, the Anti-Slavery Society was, perversely, facing a major crisis of its own. It had made some progress in obtaining press support and members were engaging in the lecture circuits to drum up further backing, but the organisation was virtually insolvent and facing collapse. James Cropper wrote to Pringle on 15 February in sombre mood: 'It seemed to be the general opinion of the Agency Committee [one of the subcommittees of the society] that unless some other means than have yet been adopted, are taken to raise funds, the operations of the Society cannot go on.'[20]

Against the general run of lethargy and gloom, however, women became moderately successful in raising the public profile of the campaign. They began to petition en masse against slavery from 1830 onwards, and the enterprise reached its climax in 1833, when a single petition of 187,000 'Ladies of England' was literally dragged into parliament by four burly male attendants.[21] This kind of political adventuring, however, long retained a somewhat risqué flavour. As late as February 1831 Pringle received a letter from Brighton, advising that a local ladies' association was about to be formed, and asking whether he could provide any information and advice on the propriety of such a move. Pringle responded with a list of twenty-five ladies' associations already established, coupled with six 'Ladies Rules'.[22]

Some authors have paraded large-scale petitioning as the key to Westminster's eventual shift in favour of emancipation, but their argument that the social force of public opinion eventually prevailed in the abolition struggle is impossible to substantiate. Petitioning existed in 1830 and 1831 but it produced no significant response from the government. The real moves were achieved only after the second of two fundamental changes had gone through the parliamentary process. The first of these was the Catholic Emancipation Act, approved by both Houses in April 1829, but destined to split the Tory party, many of whom had stood bitterly opposed. Catholic emancipation had set in motion a machinery of social reform, but the more significant legislation was the great parliamentary Reform Act of 1832. In a twist, disaffected Tories rallied behind parliamentary reform, muttering darkly that if the Commons had been more representative, it would never have approved Catholic emancipation. The latest revolution in France, bringing about the fall of Charles X in 1830, also worked up some fresh enthusiasm for a reform of parliament sooner rather than later, on the compelling argument that if the French could eject their reactionary government with such apparent ease, the British could emulate them.

After Lord Liverpool's long stay in office, there had been brief reigns at the head of the government in 1827, by George Canning immediately prior to his death in August, and then by Viscount Goderich. With both political parties in a state of turmoil, the Duke of Wellington had attained power in January 1828 but singularly failed to push for reforms. He had shrewdly assessed that the British public would never follow their French counterparts into open revolt and ignored the mood of discontent. His intransigence, however, led to the formation in 1830 of the ultra-right-wing Whig government of Earl Grey, who had 'done a deal' promising reforms, but only on condition that he was allowed to form a ministry. Grey's government was said to have been the most aristocratic and reactionary of any that people could remember and during the autumn of 1830, popular disturbances arose, egged on by radical speakers, including William Cobbett and Richard Carlile, rabble-rousing activity that earned Carlile a hefty fine and a prison sentence. Observing these rumblings of irritation the lofty Whigs decided to make concessions and they drew up the first Reform Bill, which was tabled in the Commons on 1 March 1831.

The bill condemned many of the rotten boroughs, including sixty with less than 2,000 inhabitants, and allowed in new members representing the modern industrial centres of Manchester and Birmingham. But the construction of the bill still favoured the old parliamentary balance of power. Grey's Whig cabinet was hence seen to be out of touch and its arrogance generated still more dissent, so that the bill scraped through its second reading by only a single vote. This was enough to give the Tories the whiff of victory and they triggered a general election shortly afterwards by defeating the government in committee. A somewhat chastened Grey managed to find his way back into control, but the reformers increased their majority and the second Reform Bill passed the Commons vote more easily. It was, however, rejected in the Lords and, when the news reached Birmingham, the tolling of muffled bells could be heard across the city. The British public was not happy. More riots broke out, this time in Bristol, and mass public meetings took place up and down the country. When the third version of the bill was presented, more political agitation followed and the barometer of opinion encouraged Earl Grey to resign again from office, albeit temporarily. The outcome was then inevitable, and on 4 June 1832, the Reform Bill was finally accepted in the Lords. William IV, smarting over the erosion of aristocratic privilege and unwilling to attend the House in person, gave his royal assent *in absentia*.[23]

The passage of the bill swept away much of the influence of the colonialists in the Upper and Lower Houses. Yet it is worth keeping in mind that parliamentary reform was achieved *before* slavery abolition and with far fewer public petitions. Parliament was no more interested in mass protest in the 1820s and '30s than it is today, probably rather less so. The real shift of influence and power occurred *inside* parliament, as new members arrived representing, for the first time, a mobilised working class in cities like Manchester, in the industrial heartland. Not all workers in the country displayed outright enthusiasm for abolition, and some were positively hostile, seeing emancipation for black Africans as little more than a distraction from the plight of wage slaves at home. In Blackburn, the working men's political union condemned the abolitionists as misleading the people. In Oldham, a mere thirty miles away, such was the level of enthusiasm for abolition that the old warhorse of civil rights at home, William Cobbett, was obliged to give his backing, albeit with some reluctance. But frequently, factory workers found support among abolitionists, who recognised the sense of a public relations exercise that applied some of their anti-slavery ideology on the home front. Many of the first-time parliamentarians thus took their seats equipped with a blend of commercial realism and abolitionist sympathies.

Parliamentary reform is only part of the story. A more distant factor was also destined to influence the way that events finally unfolded in 1833. In Jamaica, a major slave uprising took place at the close of 1831 that shook not only the planters and the colonial assemblies scattered around the Caribbean, but also the British government. It alerted the various authorities to a timely recognition that the emancipation question could not be perennially put to one side. Trouble had been brewing in several parishes in Jamaica since the early part of the year, precisely because of persistent rumours about a change in slave status, and the Privy Council in London was sufficiently alarmed that it took the step of issuing a royal proclamation on 3 June:

> Whereas it has been represented to Us that the slaves in some of our West Indian colonies and our possessions on the continent of South America have been erroneously led to believe that orders had been sent out by Us for their emancipation, and whereas such belief has produced acts of insubordination, which have excited Our highest displeasure . . . We do hereby declare and make known that the slave population of Our said colonies and possessions will forfeit all claim on Our protection if they shall fail to render entire submission to the laws, as well as dutiful observance to their masters.[24]

Unfortunately the notice was not received throughout the colonies until late December, by which time rumours had been stoked sufficiently that many of the slaves in Jamaica believed they had been granted emancipation and that it was their owners who were withholding freedom. Violence erupted at Christmas in an orchestrated uprising that inflicted widespread damage on plantation property in the western part of the island, mainly in the form of arson. Losses in the parish of St James alone amounted to more than £600,000 (about £23 million in 2005 values). When slave trials began in February 1832, judicial response was swift and savage, its particularly brutal nature an indication of the increased vulnerability felt by the islanders. By December 1832, in St James, of 81 individuals brought before the slave courts, 1 had been pardoned; 43 received either punishments of 150–200 lashes (probably fatal for many) or, in a minority of cases, transportation; and 37 were executed. The hanging was carried out ad hoc on the estates, so it must have been regularly improvised and frequently gruesome in application.[25]

Blame was laid quickly on the British government and on the loose tongues of dissident missionaries, particularly Baptists. During the trial hearings, Thomas Stewart, the Anglican Rector of Westmoreland parish, claimed that the causes of the revolt had been 'from the unceasing interference of Parliament with the legislature here on slave government and from influence of passages of the Scriptures misunderstood by or misinterpreted to the slaves, most of whom were Baptists'.[26] The revolt brought the dangers home to all concerned and increased the general sense of nervousness. On 6 January 1832 the Lieutenant-General of Jamaica, Constantine Henry, Earl of Mulgrave, wrote to Viscount Goderich in London detailing the extensive and destructive nature of the insurrection and advising that he had proclaimed martial law. Almost immediately there were demands for fresh troops to be stationed on the island in order to quell further unrest.

It was the 1831 uprising in Jamaica and warnings about the potential for further disruption reaching British shores in 1832, as much as any public petitioning, that determined, not the outcome, because emancipation would have happened eventually, but rather the timing. The King's Speech at the opening of the 1833 parliamentary session had not even mentioned slavery, but as early as May the government was throwing its weight behind the emancipation bill, knowing that it had become inevitable. It is difficult to imagine that the rush at Westminster was not spurred by the threat of more violence in the Caribbean, while the unprecedented volume of signatures arriving through its doors at home merely added to the sense of urgency. Even so, the outcome was subject to protracted wrangling in both Houses, which served to maintain tensions in a heightened state.

Edward Stanley, the Secretary for War and the Colonies, led the opening gambit in the Commons on 14 May 1833, by which time petitions were beginning to flow in. His motion included a number of immediate and effectual measures for the entire abolition of slavery throughout the British colonies. All children born after the passing of the Act, or any under 6 years of age, should be declared free, subject to any temporary restrictions deemed necessary. All slaves should be entitled to registration as apprenticed labourers, thus acquiring the rights and privileges of freedom, subject to restriction of labouring under conditions and for a time to be fixed by parliament, for their present owners. Stanley knew that he could not sidestep the compensation issue, since there could be no denial that plantation owners would sustain losses through the abolition of slavery and the stripping of their property. His proposal included a loan, not exceeding £15 million in total, to be repaid in a manner and at an appropriate rate of interest to be fixed by parliament. In the meantime the British taxpayer would shoulder the interest charges.

Two weeks later, the debate passed to committee stage and it was here that parliamentary reforms began to tell, with the new influx of MPs showing their mettle. Sir Richard Vyvyan observed astutely that the shift in influence brought about by the reforms 'more seriously affected the interests of the colonies than any other portion of the British dominions'. One of the most immediate effects was the rejection of a proposal to give direct representation to the colonies in the debate. Colonel Leith Hay, for the planters, did what he could, protesting that the apprenticeship proposal would be acted upon by able-bodied slaves only, leaving children, the aged and the infirm, as much as two-thirds of the overall black population, a burden on the estates. But such objections no longer carried the same weight as under the old system, wherein the planters enjoyed substantial influence at Westminster. Until 1832 it would have been inconceivable to dismiss their views. Now most of their rights were dissipated, stolen by the inhabitants of Manchester, Birmingham and the other great manufacturing towns. Power, it was said, had moved from £10,000 West Indian property owners into the hands of modest £10 householders (the minimum asset required for the electoral right to vote). Even the Duke of Wellington, presenting petitions from the planters demanding that parliament proceeded in concert with the colonial legislatures, could not command the authority that he had enjoyed in past times.

Noting the way things were going, the Anglican Church weighed in with its own riposte. The Dean of Wells was on his feet in the Lords demanding that the planters should either be allowed to enjoy their property or should obtain compensation. It was this, the amount of payback to the planters, which resulted in the most heated wrangling during the coming summer months. The planters, discovering that God was on their side, rejected an initial government suggestion of £15 million and made their counterclaim of £44 million, coupled with temporary conscription of slaves to agricultural labour; otherwise, they argued, it would be impossible for the planters to continue cultivation through the agency of Negroes.

By the middle of June 1833 the planters were threatening to obstruct any and all mercantile transactions to and from the Caribbean islands unless parliament raised its offer of compensation to at least £20 million. This was reluctantly conceded, but with the proviso that no sum should be paid to the planters until all of the proposed regulations had been enacted, in other words until apprenticeship had expired. The planters were not about to swallow this kind of medicine and a stalemate appeared inevitable until Fowell Buxton proposed that 'no sum' should be replaced by 'fifty percent'. Eventually it was agreed that the Treasury could raise loans not exceeding £20 million and could grant annuities as the consideration for such sums over a twelve-year period. The rate of interest to contributors was not to exceed 5s per cent per annum above the market rate for such annuities and the monies were to be paid into a new West India Compensation account. Interest and management charges in respect of the £20 million were to be chargeable upon and made payable out of the Consolidated Fund of the United Kingdom of Great Britain and Ireland. In the Commons, James Silk, the MP for Buckingham, refused to let the compensation issue be put to rest and decided it was time to strip away the jargon. When rid of its flummery, the £20 million grant from the British nation amounted to a massive burden on the British taxpayer, who would have to stump up the interest on the loan over a twelve-year period, during which protective duties, bounties and other privileges to the planters would be continued, making at least £24 million more. The £20 million clause remained intact.

The motion inched its way into a second reading and at this juncture Fowell Buxton elected to challenge the real 'rotten apple' of the proposed Act, the concept of apprenticeship. He professed difficulty understanding how the scheme amounted to emancipation since, when stripped of the froth, it was as much about continuing slavery as granting freedom. Where, he demanded shrewdly, were the Orders in Council that explained how the new society would function? Surely the House was entitled to inspect the details? This, according to Edward Stanley, the new Secretary for War and the Colonies, was not possible since the Orders in Council would need to be framed in the context of the bill and the bill did not yet exist. Buxton then changed tack to the subject of who was going to enforce the rules. He pointed out waspishly that on 14 May Stanley had stated in the House that the colonial legislature had done nothing to gratify the wishes of parliament and were not to be trusted. Now it was discovered that no less than twenty-nine articles had been signed over to the colonial legislature and it was left to them to make the laws necessary for the establishment of the emancipation regulations. Had the colonial assemblies suddenly earned a vote of confidence? Stanley insisted less than convincingly that the colonial assemblies would carry out the wishes of parliament, while also admitting that the applicable resolutions had not yet been laid before them, since they did not meet until November.

In July, the colonists received word of the government's putative plans, which put Mulgrave into a sufficient state of alarm in Kingston that he issued a public notice urging obedience and patience until the true situation became known. He also fired off desperate pleas for the 8th West India Regiment to be shipped from Bermuda in order to quell potential violence, and wrote to Stanley warning of dire consequences if government prevarication continued:

> The excitement during the first few hours was very great . . . the language of the white inhabitants of Kingston was, I understand, violent and inflammatory and there was no project of resistance so insane as not at first to find some advocates. . . . The misconstruction among the slaves has extended to both extremes, some believing they are already free, others that all change in their direction has been postponed for twelve years. It is impossible not to feel that it is one's first duty to give every protection in one's power to the peaceable inhabitants from the possible outbreak of a half savage population who may fancy themselves suddenly relieved from all previous restraint.[27]

Still with no information about the precise terms of abolition, Mulgrave next took the unusual step of proroguing the Jamaica House of Assembly. It reconvened belatedly on 25 October after he had eventually received copies of the Slave Emancipation Act, and the assembly gave its approval on 26 November following the third reading, though not without bitter reaction. On 12 December the assembly petitioned William IV, complaining that its local institutions had been superseded, the right of property invaded, political immunities disregarded and all that is dear and sacred to man, in his social character, placed in imminent hazard. It pleaded for a sufficient military and civil force to preserve peace and for an amendment of that part of the Act dealing with compensation. The Jamaican planters believed they were being cheated in the distribution of the £20 million of compensation money, which gave unfair advantage to the newer colonies, and they demanded that all persons entitled to compensation should have a share in proportion to the number of their slaves.[28]

I suggested at the beginning of this book that the steps towards elimination of slavery involved a complicated interaction of pressures without any one of them bearing overall responsibility. Abolitionism was linked to the social and commercial changes resulting from the early stages of the British industrial revolution. There was, as Seymour Drescher argues, a putative relationship between the British abolition process and 'free labour ideology'. A generation of nineteenth-century industrial Britons was discovering a new kind of economic reality. Some were becoming factory owners themselves, while many found an appeal in religious nonconformism. They had freed themselves from the drudgery of factory labour, in which they saw unmistakable elements of enslavement to the loom or the pick and shovel, and had become part of the wider enlargement of civil and social rights. With this came a new social awareness, a desire to cast off the ways of the eighteenth century. Increasing numbers viewed the slave system and the restrictive trade practices that went with it as being anachronistic and having a retarding effect on British industrial prospects. It also gave them the opportunity to attack the position of the aristocracy, whose interests were historically with the planters and the colonial estates. With these combined elements in their experience it was they who became strong candidates for support of abolition, rather than the radical intellectuals living in London and the Home Counties.

The task of the evangelicals was to give a final push in the right direction. Activists around the country captured the imaginations and interest of the growing numbers of skilled workers and craftsmen in the manufacturing and mining areas, especially in Lancashire, the West Riding of Yorkshire, the Midlands, southern Scotland and Cornwall. The post-1830 wish for parliamentary reform had already fired up the passions of large numbers of working class, who felt excluded from the political process in Britain. The abolitionists recognised an advantage in this and a sufficient number offered to transfer the anti-slavery ideology to the factory movement in return for its support over emancipation for black Africans. It was not, however, evangelism per se that brought emancipation of the African, nor was it the emotive knee-jerk eruption of humanitarian sentiment. Philanthropic protest, or whatever the public actually thought they were protesting about, eventually well orchestrated in 1833 by the abolitionists, merely dictated when the end came.

Convoluted arguments about the part that economics played in the overall result have been put forward by a number of authors, beginning with Eric Williams, who promoted the theory of economic decline in the West Indies, based on British overseas trade data compiled by Charles Whitworth and published in 1776. Whitworth's figures do not lend convincingly to Williams's argument even in respect of the abolition of the trade, nor do they seem particularly relevant to the outcome of emancipation in 1834. Most of the more exhaustive economic claims, it seems to me, are based on the extrapolation of statistics that can be modified selectively to press home a range of conflicting arguments, and this is one of the perennial weaknesses in placing too much reliance on data.

It was a conjunction between the demise of mercantilism and social reform, between economic and political change, that drove the process forward. The planters themselves provided a large part of the answer when they pleaded that a preferential treatment, so extreme as to be pie in the sky, was the only way that they could survive economically after 1807. It was also clear that a continuing slave-based economy in the West Indies was throttling any potential for a more expansive and prosperous business with the East Indies.

The House of Lords accepted the Slave Emancipation Act at its third reading on 20 August and it received the royal assent on 28 August 1833. Slavery was to be replaced by apprenticeship, the conditions of which were hardly generous. Under the terms of the Act, which did not come into effect until 1 August 1834, most 'liberated' slaves were obliged to serve out a term of apprenticeship for another six years, labouring for their old owners during a maximum of forty-five hours a week. Provided that they behaved themselves they would then be granted 10 per cent of that time to work for themselves. An apprentice could, if he was able to save enough money, buy his freedom during the six-year period, but if he attempted to leave without his employer's permission, the penalties were severe. Female apprentices were spared a beating, but a man could be sentenced to fifty strokes of the lash and hard labour for a period of up to six months. He would then be required to make up the loss to his employer on his release at up to fifteen hours a week.[29]

Mulgrave retired as Lieutenant-General of Jamaica on 15 March 1834 and the vacant position was taken by Howe Peter, Marquis of Sligo. It was he who oversaw the final transition from slavery to apprenticeship in Jamaica and its situation reflected that of the rest of the British Caribbean. If the British people comforted themselves that in 1833 they did the decent thing and banished enslavement from the British Empire, they were sadly mistaken. It was merely continued under a different name. One form of obligatory servitude replaced another and British society, led from the top down, conveniently failed either to notice or perhaps to care too much about this new mode of degradation. William Cobbett, that erstwhile scourge of the abolitionists who felt that the entire process drew a smokescreen over social deprivation at home and who only supported emancipation at the eleventh hour to comply with the wishes of his Oldham supporters, probably never uttered truer words than when he labelled abolitionism of his day as 'negrophile hypocrisy'. Sligo's proclamation to the black population of the island in May 1834 is in some respects the most appropriate ending that I can give to this account. It sums up much of the shabbiness and duplicity of Britain in dealing with the phenomenon of Afro-Caribbean slavery between 1788 and 1840:

On August the first you will be apprenticed to your former owners for a few years in order to fit you all for freedom. It will therefore depend entirely on your own conduct whether your apprenticeship be short or long, for should you run away you will be brought back by the maroons and by the police and have to remain in apprenticeship longer than those who behave well. You will only be required to work four and a half days each week (ten hours a day), the remaining day and a half will be your own time and you may employ it for your own benefit.

I trust you will all be obedient and diligent subjects of our good King, so that he may never have cause to be sorry for all the good he has done for you.

'Sligo'[30]

NOTES

Place of publication is London unless otherwise stated.

Chapter 1

1. *Code of Hammurabi* ##226–7.
2. N.E. Cantor, *The Civilisation of the Middle Ages*, HarperCollins, 1963, p. 2.
3. Plato, *Republic*, tr. P. Shorey, Harvard University Press, Cambridge, MA, 1930, VIII. (iii).
4. Aristotle, *Politics* 1, iv.
5. Cato, *Agriculture*, V. 56–9.
6. P. Salway, 'Roman Britain' in *The Oxford History of England*, Oxford University Press, Oxford, 1981, p. 533.
7. Strabo, *Geography*, tr. H.L. Jones, 8 vols, Harvard University Press, Cambridge, MA, 1967, vol. IV, pp. v, 2.
8. Tacitus, *Germania*, tr. M. Hutton, Harvard University Press, Cambridge, MA, 1970, p. 20 ff.
9. T.G.E. Powell, *The Celts*, Thames & Hudson, 1980, p. 120.
10. Vetus Testamentum, King James trans., Genesis 21: 12.
11. *Ibid.*, Nehemiah 5: 5.
12. Josephus, *Antiquities* IV, 273; *Against Apion* II, Harvard University Press, 215.
13. Philo, *De Vita Contemplativa*, tr. C.D. Yonge Hendrickson, 1993, 70.
14. Philo, *Hypothetica*, tr. C.D. Yonge Hendrickson, 1993, 11.4.
15. A. Smith, *An Inquiry into the Nature and Causes of the Wealth of Nations*, Modern Library, New York, 1994, p. 92.
16. Bede, *A History of the English Church and People*, Penguin Classics, 1968, II. (i).
17. Jaffé, *Regesta Pontificum Romanorum*.
18. Bede, *History*, XXII.
19. Plato, *Republic*, lib. ix.
20. R. Fletcher, *The Barbarian Conversion – from Paganism to Christianity*, University of California Press, CA, 1997, p. 6 ff.
21. H.H. Ben-Sasson (ed.), *A History of the Jewish People*, Weidenfeld & Nicolson, 1976, p. 397.
22. P. Fabre and L. Duchesne (eds), *Les Registres de Grégoire IX*, 4 vols, 1890–1955.
23. W. Shakespeare, *The Tempest*, Act I, Scene ii.
24. P. Colquhoun, *A Treatise on the Wealth, Power and Resources of the British Empire*, 1814.

Chapter 2

1. E. Donnan, *Documents Illustrative of the History of the Slave Trade to America*, New York, 1965. vol. 1.
2. N. Davies, *A History of Europe*, Oxford University Press, Oxford, 1996, p. 452.
3. C.H. Haring, *The Spanish Empire in America*, New York, 1947, pp. 55–6.
4. D.B. Davis, *The Problem of Slavery in Western Culture*, Cornell University Press, Oxford, 1966, p. 165 ff.
5. A.T. Buxton, 'Cherokee Slave Revolt of 1842', www.freerepublic.com, posted 1996.
6. Davis, *Problem of Slavery*, from du Tertre, *Histoire Générale*, vol. II, p. 490.
7. E. Williams, *Capitalism and Slavery*, University of North Carolina Press, Williamsburg, NC, 1944, p. 9 ff.
8. J. Horn, 'The Origins of Empire' in *The Oxford History of the British Empire*, Oxford University Press, Oxford, 1998, p. 176 ff.
9. J.A. Williamson, *John Hawkins*.
10. N. Canny (ed.), *The Oxford History of the British Empire*, Oxford University Press, Oxford, 1998, p. 1.
11. A.E. Smith, *Colonists in Bondage: White Servitude and Convict Labour in America*, North Carolina, 1947.
12. N. Tattersfield, *The Forgotten Trade*, Jonathan Cape, 1991.
13. C. Davenant, *Reflections on the Constitution and Management of the Trade to Africa*.
14. *Ibid.*
15. Smith, *Wealth of Nations*.

Chapter 3

1. F. Jennings, *The Invasion of America*, University of North Carolina Press, 1976, p. 45.
2. N. Canny, 'Origins of Empire' in *The Oxford History of the British Empire*, Oxford University Press, Oxford, 1998.
3. *Ibid.*
4. P.J. Marshall, 'The Eighteenth Century' in *The Oxford History of the British Empire*, Oxford University Press, Oxford, 1998.
5. *Ibid.*
6. R.M. Bliss, *Revolution and Empire: English Politics and the American Colonies in the Seventeenth Century*, Manchester, 1990.
7. Canny, 'Origins of Empire'.
8. J.S. Watson, 'The Reign of George III' in *The Oxford History of England*, Oxford University Press, Oxford, 1960.
9. W. Cobbett (ed.), *The Parliamentary History of England from the earliest period to the year 1803*, British Library, 1788–1803.
10. Marshall, 'The Eighteenth Century'.
11. Davenant, *Reflections*.
12. L.S. Sutherland, 'The Accounts of an Eighteenth Century Merchant: The Portuguese Ventures of William Braund', *Economic History Review*, 1931–2, vol. I, no. iii.
13. Davenant, *Reflections*.
14. Vetus Testamentum, King James trans., Genesis 9: 25.
15. J. Locke, *Treatise on Civil Government*, 1783.

16. J. Locke, *An Essay concerning the True Original, Extent and End of Civil Government*, 1783.
17. Cantor, *Civilisation of the Middle Ages*.
18. Smith, *Wealth of Nations*.
19. J. Hanway, *Letters on Importance of Rising Generation*, 1767.
20. B. Williams, 'The Whig Supremacy' in *The Oxford History of England*.
21. B. Franklin, to the *Public Advertiser*, 2 January 1766.
22. B. Franklin, to the *Gentleman's Magazine*, January 1768.

Chapter 4

1. T. Clarkson, *The History of the Rise, Progress and Accomplishment of the Abolition of the African Slave Trade by the British Parliament*, 1808.
2. T. Taylor, *A Biographical Sketch of Thomas Clarkson*, Joseph Rickerby, 1839.
3. From a facsimile printed by Girard Bank in cooperation with the Wyck Association, Philadelphia, PA, 1983.
4. S.J. Buck, *The Planting of Civilisation in Western Pennsylvania*, University of Pittsburg Press, PA, 1939.
5. Williams, *Capitalism and Slavery*.
6. W.C. Braithwaite, *The Beginnings of Quakerism*, 1912.
7. R. Hubberthorn, *Works*.
8. Williams, *Capitalism and Slavery*.
9. G. Clark, 'The Later Stuarts' in *The Oxford History of England*.
10. W.C. Braithwaite, *The Second Period of Quakerism*, 1919.
11. Drake, *Quakers and Slavery*.
12. A. Benezet, *A Caution and Warning to Great Britain and her Colonies*, Philadelphia, PA, 1766.
13. A. Benezet, *Some Historical Account of Guinea*, Frank Cass, 1968.
14. A. Benezet, *A Caution*.
15. E. Grubb, *Quaker Thought and History*, New York, 1925.
16. Prince Hoare, *Memoirs of Granville Sharp*, 1820.
17. *Ibid.*
18. *Ibid.*
19. Proceedings of the London Committee for the Abolition of the Slave Trade, f. 21255.

Chapter 5

1. E. Hurwitz, *Politics and the Public Conscience*, G. Allen & Unwin, 1973.
2. R.I. and S. Wilberforce, *The Life of William Wilberforce*, 5 vols, 1886.
3. *Ibid.*
4. Taylor, *A Biographical Sketch*.
5. J. Elmes, *Thomas Clarkson: a Monograph*, Blackader, 1854 (Mnemosyne, repr., 1969).
6. Proceedings of the London Committee for the Abolition of the Slave Trade, f. 21254. Minute for 16 February 1788; f. 21255. Minute for 29 July 1788.
7. *Ibid.*
8. Wilberforce and Wilberforce, *The Life*.
9. Proceedings of the London Committee for the Abolition of the Slave Trade, f. 21255.
10. Taylor, *A Biographical Sketch*.

11. R.I. and S. Wilberforce (eds), *The Correspondence of William Wilberforce*, 2 vols, 1815.
12. T. Clarkson, *Strictures on a Life of William Wilberforce*, 1838.
13. Clarkson Papers, vol. VII, f. 99.
14. H.C. Robinson, editor's notes attached to Clarkson, *Strictures*.
15. Clarkson, *Strictures*.
16. R.I. and S. Wilberforce, *The Life of William Wilberforce*, vol. 1, 1886.
17. Clarkson, *Strictures*.
18. Wilberforce and Wilberforce, *Correspondence*.
19. Clarkson, *Strictures*.
20. Proceedings of the London Committee for the Abolition of the Slave Trade, f. 21255, flyleaf.

Chapter 6

1. M. Postlethwayt, *Great Britain's Commercial Interest Explained and Improved*, 1759.
2. T.C. Hansard (ed.), *The Parliamentary Debates from the year 1803 to the present time, 1803–1900*, vol. IX, f. 168.
3. Clarkson, *Strictures*.
4. Proceedings of the London Committee for the Abolition of the Slave Trade, f. 21254.
5. *Ibid.*
6. Clarkson, *The History*.
7. Proceedings of the London Committee for the Abolition of the Slave Trade, f. 21254.
8. Benezet, *A Caution*, appendix, p. 68.
9. Proceedings of the London Committee for the Abolition of the Slave Trade, f. 21254.
10. *Ibid.*
11. Clarkson, *The History*.
12. *Parl. Hist.*, vol. XXIX, f. 250 ff.
13. J. Latimer, *Annals of Bristol in the 18th Century*, Bristol, 1893.
14. Clarkson, *The History*.
15. A.P. Wadsworth and Julia de L. Mann, *The Cotton Trade and Industrial Lancashire 1600–1780*, Manchester University Press, 1931.
16. Elmes, *Thomas Clarkson*, p. 172 ff.
17. Prince Hoare, *Memoirs of Granville Sharp*.
18. Williams, *Capitalism and Slavery*, p. 35.
19. S. Drescher, *Capitalism and Antislavery*, 1986, p. 112.
20. *Ibid.*
21. Proceedings of the London Committee for the Abolition of the Slave Trade, f. 21255.
22. *Ibid.*
23. *Ibid.*
24. E.P. Thompson, *The Making of the English Working Class*.
25. Proceedings of the London Committee for the Abolition of the Slave Trade, f. 21255.
26. *Ibid.*
27. E. Donnan, *The Slave Trade to America*.
28. Drescher, *Capitalism and Antislavery*, p. 53 ff.
29. Proceedings of the London Committee for the Abolition of the Slave Trade, f. 21255.
30. L. Namier and J. Brooke, *The History of Parliament: The House of Commons 1754–1790*, HMSO, 1964.

31. Proceedings of the London Committee for the Abolition of the Slave Trade, f. 21256.
32. *Ibid.*
33. *Ibid.*
34. Hurwitz, *Politics and the Public Conscience*, p. 22.
35. Drescher, *Capitalism and Antislavery*, p. 81

Chapter 7

1. Drescher, *Capitalism and Antislavery*.
2. The Register of the Privy Council 1788–9, PC2, f. 491 ff.
3. *Parl. Deb.*, vol. IX, f. 168.
4. Clarkson, *The History*.
5. *Parl. Hist.*, vol. XXVII, f. 396.
6. *Ibid.*, vol. XXVII, f. 497.
7. Taylor, *A Biographical Sketch*.
8. Board of Trade, MS 6, tranche 9.
9. *Ibid.*, tranche 10.
10. *Ibid.*
11. *Ibid.*
12. *Parl. Hist.*, vol. XXVII, f. 505.
13. *Ibid.*, f. 573.
14. *Ibid.*, f. 575.
15. *Ibid.*, f. 578.
16. *Ibid.*, f. 584.
17. *Ibid.*, vol. XXVIII, f. 42 ff.
18. *Ibid.*, vol. XXIX, f. 250 ff.
19. *Ibid.*, f. 1055 ff.
20. *Ibid.*, f. 1203.
21. *Ibid.*, vol. XXXII, f. 752 ff.
22. *Ibid.*, f. 737 ff.
23. *Parl. Deb.*, vol. II, f. 550.
24. A.N. Wilson, *The Victorians*, Hutchinson, 2002.
25. *Parl. Deb.*, vol. VIII, f. 946 ff.
26. *Parl. Deb.*, vol. IX, f. 168.

Chapter 8

1. Williams, *Capitalism and Slavery*.
2. Wilberforce and Wilberforce, *The Life*, vol. 2, p. 225.
3. *Ibid.*, vol. 1, p. 341.
4. Marshall, 'The Eighteenth Century'.
5. Board of Trade, MS 6, tranche 10.
6. *Parl. Hist.*, vol. XXXV, f. 1072 ff.
7. *Ibid.*, vol. XXIX, f. 1147 ff.
8. Williams, *Capitalism and Slavery*.
9. Wilberforce and Wilberforce, *Correspondence*.
10. J.S. Watson, 'The Reign of George III' in *The Oxford History of England*.

11. M.G. Jones, *Life of Hannah More*.
12. British Museum Prints and Drawings, no. 9046.
13. Wilberforce and Wilberforce, *The Life*, vol. 1.
14. Taylor, *A Biographical Sketch*.
15. *Parl. Deb.*, vol. II, f. 413.
16. W. Sypher, *Guinea's Captive Kings*.
17. *Parl. Hist.*, vol. XXIX, f. 1281.
18. R.G. Thorne, *The History of Parliament: The House of Commons 1790–1820*.
19. *The Private Papers of William Wilberforce*.
20. *Ibid.*
21. L. Woodward, 'The Age of Reform' in *The Oxford History of England*.
22. Hull Museums, George Stephen personal papers.
23. Smith, *Wealth of Nations*; Watson, 'The Reign of George III'.
24. British Empire MS s. 18, f. C1/19 and C1/19a, Rhodes House Library Oxford. Words in square brackets have been inserted by me where the original manuscript is either damaged or illegible.
25. Marshall, 'The Eighteenth Century'.

Chapter 9

1. *Parl. Hist.*, vol. XXIX, f. 1083 ff., 1265 ff.
2. H. Temperley, 'The Ideology of Antislavery' in Eltis and Walvin (eds), *The Abolition of the Atlantic Slave Trade*, University of Wisconsin Press, WI, 1981.
3. E. Hurwitz, *Politics and the Public Conscience*.
4. J.E. Inikori, 'Measuring the Atlantic Slave Trade: an Assessment of Curtin and Anstey', *Journal of African History* 17 (1976), 197–223.
5. J. Stephen, first letter to William Wilberforce in *A Defence of the Bill for the Registration of Slaves*, Butterworth & Hatchard, 1816.
6. *Ibid.*
7. *Ibid.*
8. *Ibid.*
9. CO 137/123, Colonial Office military correspondence, The National Archives, f. 17.
10. PC2/176, Orders in Council (16 March 1808), The National Archives, f. 144 ff.
11. *Ibid.*
12. CO 137/123, Colonial Office military correspondence, The National Archives, f. 17.
13. *Ibid.*, f. 25.
14. *Ibid.*, f. 33.
15. *Ibid.*, f. 41.
16. CO 137/133, Colonial Office correspondence, The National Archives, f. 3.
17. CO 137/133, Colonial Office miscellaneous letters, The National Archives, f. 48.
18. CO 137/133, Colonial Office correspondence, The National Archives, f. 46.
19. CO 137/134, Colonial Office correspondence, The National Archives, f. 48.
20. *Ibid.*, f. 46.
21. CO 137/134, Colonial Office miscellaneous letters, The National Archives, f. 272.
22. CO 137/134, Colonial Office correspondence, The National Archives, f. 58.
23. CO 137/135, Colonial Office correspondence, The National Archives, f. 46.

24. CO 137/133, Colonial Office correspondence, The National Archives, f. 50.
25. CO 137/134, Colonial Office correspondence, The National Archives, ff. 54, 55.
26. CO 137/133, Colonial Office correspondence, The National Archives, f. 50.
27. CO 137/135, Colonial Office correspondence, The National Archives, f. 55.
28. CO 137/134, Colonial Office correspondence, The National Archives, f. 60.
29. *Ibid.*, f. 68.
30. CO 137/135, Colonial Office miscellaneous letters, The National Archives, ff. 308, 309.
31. *Ibid.*, ff. 310, 323.
32. CO 137/135, Colonial Office correspondence, The National Archives, f. 99.
33. *Ibid.*, f. 113.
34. E. Williams, *Capitalism and Slavery*.
35. J. Stephen, first letter to William Wilberforce in *A Defence of the Bill*.
36. CO 140/99, Jamaica Assembly Sessional Papers, The National Archives, f. 162 ff.
37. *Ibid.*
38. J. Stephen, second letter to William Wilberforce in *A Defence of the Bill*.
39. CO 140/99, Jamaica Assembly Sessional Papers, The National Archives, f. 162 ff.
40. *Ibid.*
41. *Ibid.*
42. *Ibid.*
43. CO 137, Meliorating Act, Leeward Islands, The National Archives.
44. J. Stephen, second letter to William Wilberforce in *A Defence of the Bill*.
45. *Parl. Deb.*, vol. XXXI, f. 772 ff.
46. Board of Trade, MS 6.
47. J. Stephen, second letter to William Wilberforce in *A Defence of the Bill*.
48. CO 140/99, Jamaica Assembly Sessional Papers, The National Archives, f. 162 ff.
49. *Ibid.*, ff. 98, 414.

Chapter 10

1. J.R. Ward, *British West Indian Slavery 1750–1834*, Oxford University Press, Oxford, 1988.
2. Board of Trade, MS 6, tranche 9.
3. *Parl. Deb.*, vol. IX, Session Papers: Report on the Commercial State of the West India Colonies, f. 98 ff.
4. *Ibid.*
5. *Ibid.*
6. R. Anstey, 'Religion and British Slave Emancipation' in *The Abolition of the Atlantic Slave Trade*.
7. Wilberforce and Wilberforce, *The Life*, vol. 3.
8. *Parl. Deb.*, vol. XVI, f. 12.
9. *Parl. Deb.*, vol. XVII, f. 639 ff.
10. *Ibid.*
11. *Ibid.*, f. 658 ff.
12. Wilberforce and Wilberforce, *The Life*, vol. 3.
13. *Parl. Deb.*, vol. XIX.

14. Wilberforce and Wilberforce, *The Life*, vol. 3.
15. *Ibid.*
16. *Parl. Deb.*, vol. XXI, f. 198 ff.
17. *Ibid.*, vol. XXVI, f. 1211.
18. *Ibid.*, vol. XXVII, f. 576.
19. *Ibid.*, f. 637.
20. *Ibid.*, f. 646.
21. Drescher, *Capitalism and Antislavery*.
22. *Parl. Deb.*, vol. XXVIII, f. 268 ff.
23. *Ibid.*, vol. XXXI, f. 772 ff.
24. *Ibid.*, f. 1127.
25. Stephen, *A Defence of the Bill*.
26. Wilberforce and Wilberforce, *The Life*, vol. 3.
27. *Parl. Deb.*, vol. XXVI, f. 831 ff.
28. Stephen, *A Defence of the Bill*.
29. CO 28/85, Colonial Office correspondence, The National Archives, f. 14 ff.
30. *Ibid.*, f. 11 ff.
31. *Ibid.*, f. 21 ff.
32. *Parl. Deb.*, vol. XXXI, f. 624 ff.; Woodward, 'The Age of Reform'.
33. *Ibid.*, vol. XXXV, f. 1004 ff.
34. *Ibid.*, vol. XXXVII, f. 332.
35. *Ibid.*, vol. XXXIX, f. 511.
36. *Ibid.*, f. 542 ff.
37. Wilberforce and Wilberforce, *The Life*, vol. 4.

Chapter 11

1. *Parl. Deb.*, new series, vol. IV, f. 428.
2. British Empire MS s. 20, f. E2/1, Rhodes House Library Oxford.
3. Cotton Mather, *Essays to do Good*, Glasgow, 1825.
4. Wilberforce and Wilberforce, *The Life*, vol. 4.
5. *Parl. Deb.*, new series, vol. VIII, f. 624.
6. Wilberforce and Wilberforce, *The Life*, vol. 5.
7. British Empire MS s. 20, f. E2/1, Rhodes House Library Oxford.
8. Clarkson Papers, vol. VII, f. 142.
9. *Parl. Deb.*, new series, vol. VIII, f. 624 ff.
10. Wilberforce and Wilberforce, *The Life*, vol. 5.
11. Clarkson Papers, vol. VII, f. 132.
12. Thorne, *The Commons 1790–1820*.
13. CO 137/152, Colonial Office correspondence, The National Archives, f. 105 ff.
14. *Ibid.*, f. 168 ff.
15. CO 137/153, Colonial Office correspondence, The National Archives, f. 20.
16. Wilberforce and Wilberforce, *The Life*, vol. 5.
17. *Parl. Deb.*, new series, vol. VIII, f. 337.
18. Smith, *Wealth of Nations*, p. 657.
19. CO 137/152, Colonial Office correspondence, The National Archives, f. 225.

20. *Parl. Deb.*, new series, vol. V, f. 508 ff.
21. CO 137/153, Colonial Office correspondence, The National Archives, f. 151.
22. CO 137/152, Colonial Office correspondence, The National Archives, f. 245.
23. *Ibid.*
24. Smith, *Wealth of Nations*, p. 657.
25. *Parl. Deb.*, new series, vol. VIII, f. 337.
26. Clarkson Papers, vol. VII, f. 127.
27. *Ibid.*, f. 104.
28. *Parl. Deb.*, new series, vol. IX, f. 257 ff.
29. *Ibid.*
30. *Ibid.*
31. Clarkson Papers, vol. VII, f. 127.
32. *Ibid.*, f. 108.
33. British Empire MS s. 559, f. 1, Rhodes House Library Oxford.
34. British Empire MS s. 18, f. C1/1, Rhodes House Library Oxford.
35. *Ibid.*, f. C1/3.
36. *Ibid.*, f. C1/12.
37. *Ibid.*, f. C1/6.

Chapter 12

1. *London Magazine* 9 (1740), 493–4.
2. Hurwitz, *Politics and the Public Conscience*, p. 19.
3. S. Bradburn, *An Address to the People called Methodists: concerning the wickedness of encouraging slavery*, 1792.
4. H.J. Bennett, *Bondsmen and Bishops: Slavery and Apprenticeship on the Codrington Plantations of Barbados 1710–1838*, University of California Press, Berkeley and Los Angeles, CA, 1958.
5. *Ibid.*
6. *Ibid.*
7. *Ibid.*
8. *Ibid.*
9. British Empire MS s. 558, f. 3, Rhodes House Library Oxford.
10. CO 137/184, Colonial Office correspondence, The National Archives, Jamaica Manumission Returns.
11. S. Drescher, *From Slavery to Freedom: Comparative Studies in the Rise and Fall of Atlantic Slavery*, New York University Press, NY, 1999, p. 58.
12. British Empire MS s. 20, f. E2/2, Rhodes House Library Oxford.
13. P.F. Dixon, 'The Politics of Emancipation: the movement for the Abolition of Slavery in the British West Indies 1807–1833' (PhD thesis, University of Oxford, 1970).
14. British Empire MS s. 18, ff. C1/27, 1/43, Rhodes House Library Oxford.
15. *Ibid.*, f. C1/59.
16. British Empire MS s. 558, ff. 21, 22, Rhodes House Library Oxford.
17. *Ibid.*
18. British Empire MS s. 18, f. C1/26, Rhodes House Library Oxford.
19. *Ibid.*, f. C1/27.
20. *Ibid.*, f. C1/16.

21. G. Stephen, *Anti-Slavery Recollections*, 1859.

22. British Empire MS s. 18, f. C1/28, Rhodes House Library Oxford.

23. Woodward, 'The Age of Reform', p. 75 ff.

24. CO 137/181, Colonial Office correspondence, The National Archives, f. 81.

25. CO 137/189, Colonial Office correspondence, The National Archives, f. 87.

26. CO 137/181, Colonial Office correspondence, The National Archives, f. 68.

27. CO 137/189, Colonial Office correspondence, The National Archives, f. 23 ff.

28. *Ibid.*, f. 257 ff.

29. *Ibid.*, f. 185 ff.

30. CO 137/192, Colonial Office correspondence, The National Archives, f. 197

BIBLIOGRAPHY AND SOURCES

Place of publication is London unless otherwise stated.

Primary Sources

Bede. *A History of the English Church and People*, revised edn, Penguin Classics, 1968

Bell, K. and Morrell, W.P. *Select Documents on the British Colonial Policy: 1830–1860*, Oxford, 1928

Benezet, Anthony. *Observations on the Inslaving, Importing and Purchasing of Negroes with some Advice thereon Extracted from the Epistle of the Yearly Meeting of the People called Quakers held at London in the Year 1748*, 2nd edn, 1760

——. *A Caution and Warning to Great Britain and her Colonies*, in Grubb E., *Quaker Thought and History*, New York, 1925

——. *Historical Account of Guinea*, reprint, Frank Cass, 1968

Booth, Abraham. *Commerce of Human Species and the Enslavement of Innocent Persons Inimical to the Laws of Moses and the Gospel of Christ*, 1792

Boudin. 'Du Nègre Esclave chez les Peaux Rouges' in *Bulletin de la Société d'Anthropologie 5*, 1864

Bradburn, Samuel. *An Address to the People called Methodists: concerning the wickedness of encouraging slavery*, 4th edn, 1792

Bridges, G.W. *Annals of Jamaica*, London 1828, vol. II

Burke, E.F. *A Philosophical Enquiry into the Origin of our Ideas of the Sublime and Beautiful*, 1757

Buxton, T.F. *Memoirs of Sir Thomas Fowell Buxton*, 1849

Cary, John. *An Essay on the State of England*, 1695

Clarkson, T. *The History of the Rise, Progress and Accomplishment of the Abolition of the African Slave Trade by the British Parliament*, 1808

——. *Strictures on a Life of William Wilberforce*, 1838

Cobbett, William (ed.). *The Parliamentary History of England from the Earliest Period to the Year 1803*, British Library, 1788–1803

Colquhoun, P. *A Treatise on the Wealth, Power and Resources of the British Empire*, 1814

Cumberland, R. *The West Indian: a Comedy*, 1775

Cunningham, P. (ed.). *The Letters of Horace Walpole*, 1891

Dalby, Thomas. *An Historical Account of the Rise and Growth of the West India Colonies*, 1690

Davenant, Charles *Reflections on the Constitution and Management of the Trade to Africa*, Whitworth's edn, 1709, R. Horsfield, 1771

Ferguson, William. *A Letter to Thomas Fowell Buxton on the Character of the Liberated Africans at Sierra Leone*, 1839

Gee, Joshua. *The Trade and Navigation of Great Britain Considered*, 1729

Godwin, B. *Lectures on Slavery*, Boston 1836

Halley, R. *The Sinfulness of Colonial Slavery: Lecture 7*, 1833

Hansard, T.C. (ed.). *The Parliamentary Debates from the Year 1803 to the Present Time*, 1803–1900

Hanway, J. *Letters on Importance of Rising Generation*, 1767

Hoare, Prince. *Memoirs of Granville Sharp*, 1820

Jobson, Richard. *The Golden Trade*, 1623

Latimer, John. *Annals of Bristol in the 18th Century*, Bristol 1893

Locke, John. *An Essay concerning the True Original, Extent, and End of Civil Government*, 1783

——. *Treatise on Civil Government*, 1783

Mather, Cotton. *Essays to do Good*, Glasgow, 1825

Mun. *England's Treasure by Forraign Trade*, reprint, Basil Blackwell, 1928

Philo. *The Works*, tr. C.D. Yonge, updated edn, Hendrickson, 1993

Plato. *Republic*, tr. P. Shorey, revised edn, Harvard University Press, 1930

Postlethwayt, Malachy. *Great Britain's Commerical Interest Explained and Improved*, 1759

Ramsay, J. *Memorial on the Supplying of the Navy with Seamen*, Rhode House Library, Oxford 1787, f. 23v

Sharp, Granville. *The Just Limitation of Slavery in the Laws of God*, 1776

——. *The Law of Liberty or Royal Law by which All Mankind Will Certainly Be Judged*, 1776

Smith, Adam. *An Inquiry into the Nature and Causes of the Wealth of Nations*, reprint, New York, 1994

Stephen, George. *Anti-Slavery Recollections*, 1859

Stephen, James. *Reasons for Establishing a Registry of Slaves in the British Colonies*, 1815

——. *A Defence of the Bill for the Registration of Slaves in Letters to William Wilberforce*, Butterworth & Hatchard, 1816

——. *The Slavery in the British West Indies Delineated*, 1824/30

Stirling, James. *Letters from the Slave States*, New York, Kraus Reprint Co., 1969

Strabo. *Geography*, tr. H.L. Jones, 8 vols, Harvard University Press, 1967

Tacitus. *Germania*, tr. M. Hutton, revised edn, Harvard University Press, 1970

Watson, R. *The Works of the Reverend Richard Watson*, 12 vols, 1834–7

Wesley, J. *Thoughts on Slavery*, 1774

Whitworth, C. *The Political and Commercial Works of Charles Davenant*, 1781

——. *State of the Trade of Great Britain in its Imports and Exports, Progressively from the Year 1697–1773*, 1776

Wilberforce, A.M. (ed.). *The Private Papers of William Wilberforce*, 1897

Wilberforce R.I. & S. (eds). *The Correspondence of William Wilberforce*, 2 vols, 1815

Wilberforce W. *A Letter on the Abolition of the Slave Trade*, 1807

Wood, W. *A Survey of the Trade*, pt III, 1718

Woolman, John. *The Journal of John Woolman*, Andrew Melrose, 1898

Published Sources

Andrews, Kenneth R. *Trade, Plunder and Settlement: Maritime Enterprise and the Genesis of the British Empire*, Cambridge, 1984

Ashley, Maurice. *England in the 17th Century*, reprint, Penguin, 1963

Bean, R.N. *The British Transatlantic Slave Trade*, New York, Arno Press, 1975

Belmont, K. *Hero for Humanity: a Biography of William Wilberforce*, Navpress, 2002

Bennett, J. Harry. *Bondsmen and Bishops: Slavery and Apprenticeship on the Codrington Plantations of Barbados 1710–1838*, University of California Press, Berkeley and Los Angeles, CA, 1958

Ben-Sasson, H.H. (ed.). *A History of the Jewish People*, Weidenfeld & Nicolson, 1976

Bliss, R.M. *Revolution and Empire: English Politics and the American Colonies in the Seventeenth Century*, Manchester, 1990

Bolt, C. and Drescher, S. *Anti-slavery, Religion and Reform*, Folkestone and Hamden, 1980

Braithwaite, W.C. *The Beginnings of Quakerism*, 1912

——. *The Second Period of Quakerism*, 1919

Bready, J.W. *England before and after Wesley – the Evangelical Revival and Soc. Ref.*, 1938

Brebner, J.B. *North Atlantic Triangle: the Interplay of Canada, the United States and Great Britain*, 1945

Brown, Philip A. *The French Revolution in English History*, Frank Cass, 1965

Buck, S.J. *The Planting of Civilisation in Western Pennsylvania*, University of Pittsburg Press, 1939

Budge, E.A. Wallis. *Babylonian Life and History*, revised 2nd edn, Barnes & Noble, New York, 1993

Caird, C.B. *The Apostolic Age*, Duckworth, 1993

Canny, N. (ed.). 'The Origins of Empire' in *The Oxford History of the British Empire*, Oxford University Press, 1998

Cantor, N.E. *The Civilisation of the Middle Ages*, HarperCollins, 1963

Carrington, Selwyn H.H. *The Sugar Industry and the Abolition of the Slave Trade 1775–1810*, University of Florida Press, 2002

Coupland, Reginald. *The British Anti-Slavery Movement*, 1933

Craven, M.J. *The Effects of the American Civil War upon the People of Bolton*, Chorley Day Training College, 1964

Curtin, P. *The Atlantic Slave Trade*, University of Wisconsin Press, 1969

Davidson, B. *Black Mother*, revised edn, Boston, MA, 1961

——. *The African Slave Trade*, Boston, MA, 1980

Davies, K.G. *The Royal African Company*, Longmans, 1957

Davies, N. *A History of Europe*, Oxford University Press, 1996

Davis, David B. *The Problem of Slavery in Western Culture*, Cornell University Press, Ithaca, New York, 1966

Dixon, P.F. 'The Politics of Emancipation 1807–1833', PhD thesis, University of Oxford, 1970

Donnan, Elizabeth. *Documents Illustrative of the History of the Slave Trade to America*, reprint, New York, 1965

Drescher, Seymour. *Capitalism and Antislavery*, 1986

——. *From Slavery to Freedom: Comparative Studies in the Rise and Fall of Atlantic Slavery*, New York University Press, 1999

Edwards, D.L. *Christianity – the First Two Thousand Years*, Cassell, 1997

Elmes, J. *Thomas Clarkson: a Monograph*, Blackader (Mnemosyne reprint), 1854

Eltis, D. and Walvin, J. (eds). *The Abolition of the Atlantic Slave Trade*, University of Wisconsin Press, WI, 1981

Dunn, Richard S. *Obtain Sugar and Slaves*, University of North Carolina Press, Williamsburg, NC, 2000

Findlay, G.G. and Holdsworth, W.W. *The History of the Wesleyan Methodist Missionary Society*, 5 vols, 1921

Finlay, M. *Ancient Slavery and Modern Ideology*, 1982

Fletcher, Richard. *The Barbarian Conversion – from Paganism to Christianity*, University of California Press, Berkeley, CA, 1997

Gary, A.T. 'The Political and Economic Relations of English Quakers, 1750–1785', PhD thesis, University of Oxford, 1935

Greenidge, C.W.W. *Slavery*, 1958

Griggs, E.L. *Thomas Clarkson: the Friend of Slaves*, reprint, Greenwood, 1970

Hair, P.E.H. 'Protestants as Pirates, Slavers and Protomissionaries, Sierra Leone 1568 and 1582', *Journal of Ecclesiastical History* 21 (1970)

——. *Africa Encountered. European Contacts and Evidence 1450–1700*, Aldershot, 1997

Haring, C.H. *The Spanish Empire in America*, New York, 1947

Harlow, V.T. *A History of Barbados 1625–1685*, Oxford, 1926

Herrin, Judith. *The Formation of Christendom*, Princeton University Press, NJ, 1987

Hurwitz, Edith F. *Politics and the Public Conscience: Slave Emancipation and the Abolitionist Movement in Britain*, G. Allen & Unwin, 1973

Inikori, J.E. (ed.). *Forced Migration*, Hutchinson University Library, 1982

Johnson, M.P. and Roak, J.L. *Black Masters: A Family of Color in the Old South*, New York, Norton, 1984

Judd, Gerrit P. *Members of Parliament 1734–1832*, Yale University Press, New Haven, CT, 1955

Kelly, J.N.D. *Dictionary of Popes*, Oxford University Press, Oxford, 1986

Klingberg, Frank J. *The Anti-Slavery Movement in England: a Study in English Humanitarianism*, New Haven, CT, 1926

MacInnes, C.M. *Bristol – A Gateway of Empire*, Bristol, 1939

Mallett, M.E. *The Borgias: the Rise and Fall of a Renaissance Dynasty*, 1969

Marshall, P.J. (ed.). 'The Eighteenth Century' in *The Oxford History of the British Empire*, Oxford University Press, Oxford, 1998

Mathieson, William L. *British Slavery and its Abolition 1823–1838*, 1926

Mellor, G.R. *British Imperial Trusteeship 1783–1850*, 1951

Merivale, H. *Lectures on Colonization and Colonies*, Oxford, 1928

Mitchell and Deane. *Abstract of British Historical Studies*, Cambridge, 1962

Morley, J. *The Life of William Ewart Gladstone* (1903), 3 vols, 1912

Namier, L. and Brooke, J. *The History of Parliament: The House of Commons 1754–1790*, HMSO, 1964

Nieboer, H.J. *Slavery as an Industrial System*, The Hague, 1900

Onstott, K. *Drum*, Pan Books, 1962

Patterson, Orlando. *The Sociology of Slavery*, Harvard University Press, Cambridge, MA, 1967

——. *Slavery and Social Death*, Harvard University Press, Cambridge, MA, 1982

Pepe, G. *La politica dei Borgia*, Naples, 1945

Phillips, W.D. *Slavery from Roman Times to the Early Transatlantic Trade*, Manchester, 1985

Poole, William F. *Anti-Slavery Opinions before the Year 1800*, Cincinnati, OH, 1873

Pope-Hennessy, James. *The Sins of the Fathers*, Sphere, 1970

Postgate, J.N. *Early Mesopotamia – Society and Economy at the Dawn of History*, Routledge, 1992

Powell, T.G.E. *The Celts*, revised edn, Thames & Hudson, 1980

Ragatz, Lowell J. *The Fall of the Planter Class in the British Caribbean 1763–1833*, New York, 1928

Rawley, James A. *The Transatlantic Slave Trade*, Norton, New York, 1981

Reddock, R. 'Women and the Slave Plantation Economy in the Caribbean' in S.J. Kleinberg (ed.), *Retrieving Women's History*, Berg, 1988

Robinson, H.C. *Exposure of Misrepresentations Contained in the Preface to the Correspondence of William Wilberforce*, 1841

Schuyler, R.L. *The Fall of the Old Colonial System*, Oxford University Press, Oxford, 1945

Smith, A.E. *Colonists in Bondage: White Servitude and Convict Labour in America*, North Carolina, 1947

Stock, Leo F. (ed.). *Proceedings and Debates of the British Parliament respecting North America*, 5 vols, Washington, 1924–41, vol. IV, p. 531

Sypher, W. *Guinea's Captive Kings: British Anti-Slavery Literature of XVIII Century*, Chapel Hill, University of North Carolina Press, Williamsburg, NC, 1942

Tattersfield, Nigel. *The Forgotten Trade*, Jonathan Cape, 1991

Taylor, Thomas. *A Biographical Sketch of Thomas Clarkson, with occasional brief strictures on the misrepresentations of him contained in the Life of William Wilberforce*, Joseph Rickerby, 1839

Temperley, H. *British Antislavery 1833–1870*, 1972

——. 'The Ideology of Antislavery' in D. Eltis and J. Walvin (eds), *The Abolition of the Atlantic Slave Trade*, University of Wisconsin Press, WI, 1981

Thorne, R.G. *The History of Parliament: The House of Commons 1790–1820*, Secker & Warburg, 1986

Turner, Mary. *Slaves and Missionaries: the Disintegration of Jamaican Slave Society, 1787–1834*, Urbana, Ill., University of Illinois Press, IL, 1982

Wadsworth, A.P. and Mann, Julia de L. *The Cotton Trade and Industrial Lancashire 1600–1780*, Manchester University Press, 1931

Ward, J.R. *British West Indian Slavery 1750–1834*, Oxford University Press, Oxford, 1988

Watts, Michael R. *The Dissenters*, 3 vols, reprint, Oxford University Press, Oxford, 1986

Wilberforce, R.I. and S. *The Life of William Wilberforce*, 5 vols, 1886

Williams, Eric. *Capitalism and Slavery*, University of North Carolina Press, Williamsburg, NC, 1944

Williamson, J.A. *John Hawkins*, 1927

——. *Hawkins of Plymouth* (revised edn of *John Hawkins*), 1949

Wilson, A.N. *The Victorians*, Hutchinson, 2002

Wood, B. *Slavery in Colonial Georgia 1730–1775*, Athens, GA, 1984

Documents and Manuscripts

British Library, Add MS 21, 254.5.6, Proceedings of the (London) Committee for the Abolition of the Slave Trade, 1787–1819

British Library, Add MS 41, 267A, The Clarkson Papers, vol. VII, 1818–1826

British Library, Public Records, London, A Collection of the Public General Statutes passed in the Third and Fourth Year of the Reign of His Majesty King William IV, 1833

The National Archives, BT 1/5, Minute Books of the Privy Council Committee on Slavery, 1788–9

The National Archives, BT 6/9–11, Examination of witnesses before the Privy Council committee on the slave trade, 1788–9

The National Archives, CO 28, Military and civil correspondence to and from Barbados, 1816

The National Archives, CO 137, Jamaica Manumission Returns, 1 January 1817 to 31 December 1830, 1832

The National Archives, CO 137, Official civil correspondence to and from Kingston, Jamaica, 1792–1813

The National Archives, CO 137, Petition to the King from the Assembly of Jamaica, 1791

The National Archives, CO 137, A Return of every slave tried and convicted by civil courts during the late rebellion In Jamaica or in consequence thereof, 1833

The National Archives, CO 138, Military and civil correspondence to and from Kingston, Jamaica, 1811–13

The National Archives, PC 2, Orders in Council relating to the Slave Trade, 1808

The National Archives, PC 2, Register of the Privy Council, 1788–9

Rhodes House Library, Oxford, Brit. Emp., s. 18, Correspondence of committee secretaries – Committee on Slavery, 1828–33

Rhodes House Library, Oxford, Brit. Emp., s. 20, Minute Books of the British and Foreign Anti-Slavery Society, 1823–34

Rhodes House Library, Oxford, Brit. Emp., s. 444, 558–9, Correspondence in the Thomas Fowell Buxton collection, 1823–33

INDEX